SANGOMA

SANGOMA

My Odyssey into the Spirit World of Africa

JAMES HALL

A Jeremy P. Tarcher / Putnam Book
published by
G. P. Putnam's Sons
New York

TO JAY LEVEY AND KAREN GLASS

A Jeremy P. Tarcher/Putnam Book
Published by G. P. Putnam's Sons
Publishers Since 1838
200 Madison Avenue
New York, NY 10016

Jeremy P. Tarcher, Inc.
5858 Wilshire Blvd., Suite 200
Los Angeles, CA 90036

Library of Congress Cataloging-in-Publication Data

Hall, James.
    Sangoma : my odyssey into the spirit world of Africa / James Hall.
       p.   cm.
    "A Jeremy P. Tarcher/Putnam book."
    ISBN 0-87477-780-1 (hc : acid-free paper)
    1. Swazi (African people)—Rites and ceremonies.   2. Swazi (African
people)—Religion.   3. Shamanism—Swaziland.   4. Initiation rites—
Religious aspects—Swaziland.   5. Philosophy, Swazi.   I. Title.
DT2746.S95H35   1994   94-10138 CIP
299'.68398—dc20

Design by Mauna Eichner

Printed in the United States of America
1   2   3   4   5   6   7   8   9   10

This book is printed on acid-free paper.

Acknowledgments

I am indebted to my editor, Robin Cantor-Cooke, for the encouragement and guiding inspiration that brought forth this book. I must thank my brother Tom Hall for sending me his computer to do the writing, and John Dlamini for the use of his electricity to power it. To Mgondolo, Gogo Ndwandwe and the other sangomas who advised me what I might reveal in this book without compromising the secrets of our calling, I thank you all.

Contents

Glossary

baba	father
Bandzawe	African tribe whose lidlotis, through a sangoma, perform the Kufemba divination ritual
Benguni	African tribe whose lidlotis assist the sangoma
bhayiskhobho	movies
bhejane	rhinoceros
bingelela	sangoma's dance/song of greeting
imbita	medicine to internally cleanse the body
imvimba	payment of cows paid by a seducer of an unmarried girl to her parents to legitimize child
Indlu Yemaphupha	a house of dreams
Indumba	spirit house
inhloko	sangoma's insight or psychic ability
Inkhanyan	song sung by lidlotis to announce a litfwasa's readiness to complete kutfwasa
insangu	marijuana
intebetebe	footbridge
khetsa	choose
kubhunyasela	taking herbal medicines by burning and inhaling them

kufemba	"sniffing out" divination ritual performed by Bandzawe spirits through a sangoma
kukhokha	drawing out hidden objects using psychic powers
kuphotfulwa	kutfwasa graduation rites
kutfwasa	a process of secret rituals and studies a person possessed of lidlotis undergoes to become a sangoma
kutsandvo	herbal love potion
lalatela	ritual by which a three-month-old baby is presented to the ancestors
libala	illness affecting infants
lichishamlilo	medicinal plant
lidloti	ancestral spirit
ligwalagwala	bird whose bright red feathers are worn in hair by Swazi royalty and certain elders
likheshi	elevator
lingedla	long, carved fighting stick
lintongomane	peanut
lishoba	oxtail brush
litfwasa	sangoma-in-training (person undergoing kutfwasa)
lobola	dowry of cows
maganu	seasonal drink brewed from fruit of the umganu tree
mutsi	medicine
Mkhulumnchanti	God
ngcondvombili	a person of mixed parentage
nkhosi'ami!	my god!
nyankwabi	child who carries sangoma's medicine basket
sangoma	diviner healer empowered by ancestral spirits
sanwati	medicinal plant used to treat ulcers
sekusile	good morning
Sevuma	we agree
shayelwa	drum beating ritual whereby ancestral spirits are summoned
sibhaca	Swazi dance performed by men and boys

sidliso	bewitched food
sihlati lesimhlope	herbal emetic for bringing good fortune
sihlati lesimnyama	herbal emetic for bringing good fortune
sikhulu	chief
sipoko	ghost
siwebhu	ceremonial whip
siyabonga	we thank you
siyendle	sangoma's hairstyle
Siyenga	professional song sung by sangomas at conclusion of kuphotfulwa
spoliyane khotsa	headache remedy made from burnt, pulverized roots
thogoza	traditional greeting to a sangoma
tilwane	metaphorical "wild animals" said to be responsible for mental illness
timfiso	sangoma's necklaces
Timzmzu	African tribe whose lidlotis are found in bodies of water
tindlulamitsi	giraffes ("tree passers")
tjwala	Swazi home-brewed beer
togoloshi	spirit creatures said to be responsible for sexual dysfunction
umbuto	warrior; member of the king's regiments
umhlabelo	bone-fracture medicine
umlungu	white person
umnunzane	senior male member of a homestead
umsamo	sacred place inside the Indumba, furthest from the door
umtsakatsi	witch
umtuntu	sangoma's medicine basket
umutsi kuvikela	herbal medicine that protects user from harm and misfortune
yebo	yes

GLENDOWER: *I can call spirits from the vasty deep!*

HOTSPUR: *Why, so can I, and so can any man. But will they come when you do call for them?*

WILLIAM SHAKESPEARE
Henry IV, Part One

one

Swaziland

OWHIDE DRUMS BOOMED like cannon fire. Half-naked Swazi women beat them with sticks worn smooth from use. In the evening's heat we crowded the interior of a grass and mud hut, the home of the ancestral spirits. A single candle burned on the dirt floor before me. Its dancing light shone in the whites of the women's eyes and in sweat that ran like tear tracks from purple-black shoulders and shone like dew on the dark areolas of their breasts.

A slim teenage girl with lynxlike thighs, several powerfully built middle-aged women, some children silenced by the thunderous drums into respect for the ritual now unfolding, a single impassive young man and an old crone with her hair molded with clay into an inverted red bowl over her wizened face: these were the people who were leading me with their flying drumsticks and chanting voices through my initiation rite.

More than two years had passed since the first hint that I might have the makings of an African tribal healer. The subsequent investigations, discoveries, contemplation, and decision that brought me here had seemed momentous as they were occurring, but they all paled compared to what was happening now, now that the learning had actually begun. The past was being literally and noisily drummed out of me by these women beating upon carved wooden kettles with leather tops to which tufts of cow hair still clung. The drums surrounded me as I sat expectantly, the way the women had positioned me: straight-backed with legs extended forward on a thin reed mat, my hands on my knees with palms up like two radar dishes ready to receive signals. The people belonged to this place, the ancient-looking spirit house called the *Indumba*. They knew what to do. Two women, clad only in beaded necklaces and calf-length patterned cloths tied around their waists, stepped forward and covered me with a heavy white sheet. When they draped it over my head it was as if they were snuffing out a candle, or the life I had known up to now.

It was December 1988, and in other places a terrorist bomb was igniting the skies over Lockerbie, Scotland; Ronald Reagan was lighting his last Christmas tree on the White House lawn; and moviegoers were watching *Working Girl* and *The Accidental Tourist*. Here on the southern tip of the African continent, where the seasons were reversed, the summer solstice was approaching. I sweated under my sheet, feeling impossibly distant from everything that was happening elsewhere in the world but excited by what was transpiring in this mysterious lost place. The rite I was undergoing was strange and magical and wonderful, everything I had hoped for. I resembled a ghost beneath my white shroud, and, indeed, this ritual was intended to put me in touch with other ghosts: ancestral spirits, or *lidlotis* in the SiSwati language I had begun to learn.

I could see little more than the candle's thin filament, gauzy through the fabric that enshrouded my head. But the cloth did not muffle the drums. Their thunder assaulted me, and the vibrations they sent out rose through the balls of my feet, my thighs, and buttocks and lodged in the base of my spine. The people were shaking rattles now, bringing them close to my head and withdrawing them like buzzing insects. The chanting ceased when a woman raised her voice above the rest and led a song like an African hymn. In words I did not yet understand, the woman's deep contralto called out in pleading tones, which were echoed by a chorus of others. As she sang, the energy level within the hut rose. The people called upon the ancestral spirits they said were within me to come forth and address them.

There seemed little I could do to help things along. But I was not expected to do anything, just sit still and let the spiritual realm manifest itself through me. How this was to be done I had no idea. I wondered: even if my European ancestors by some unknown scheme of the afterlife had become spirits, how could they be expected to acknowledge drum and chanted signals sent out by Swazi natives? There were lots of questions to consider as I sat mummified in my shroud, battered by the powerful rhythmic sounds all around. Certainly the biggest question was how had a white man from conservative Winnetka, Illinois, a former Eagle Scout and a Catholic, become a candidate to be an African shaman?

I remembered everything that had brought me there as the drums thundered, the rattles shook shrilly, and the women raised their voices to beseech their spirits (*my* spirits?). My thoughts flowed through familiar waters and returned as they often did to the liquid night-time skies of Guinea in West Africa, where I first heard the word that would change my life:

Sangoma.

▲ ▲ ▲ ▲

For two months in 1986 I lived in Conakry, the capital of Guinea, as the guest of "Mama Africa," the singer Miriam Makeba. We sat in the rock garden of her small house as I conducted interviews for her "as told to" autobiography, which I was to write. It would be my first book of distinction, and one that I hoped would move me out of television writing and into literature. Instead, the project was to move me into a bizarre world I had not known existed until one night when I asked Miriam about her mother.

Miriam's face, capable of such emotion when she sang, became inscrutable, and her large brown eyes focused far away. "My mother was special. She could . . . see."

Something mysterious had come over Miriam, and I proceeded carefully. "How?"

"She was what we call a sangoma. She had powers. People came to her with problems, and she told them what they were. Then she cured them."

"She was a tribal healer?"

"My mother was a Xhosa, like Themba and Zola." She mentioned our mutual friends in California who had brought us together, with this book project the result. My life was like that: a chance meeting or a friendship led to the most unexpected places. "But she trained to be a healer in Swaziland. She had no choice but to become a sangoma. The lidlotis—the spirits—wanted her."

I did not believe or disbelieve the story of Christina Makeba as related in respectful tones by her famous daughter. It seemed remote and dreamlike, an African fable. Miriam's mother had been a modern, fashionable woman in 1950, but had known enough of the ancient ways to recognize the signs of spiritual possession when they struck her: an inexplicable swelling of her feet and other mysterious illnesses that baffled the city doctors. These were followed by strange visions and sudden prescient insights into family members and neighbors. A local healer confirmed what everyone suspected, that Christina Makeba was possessed by the lidlotis, and these spirits were calling her to become a sangoma. She left the repressive apartheid state of South Africa and journeyed to Swaziland, where she underwent the secret rituals of *kutfwasa* and became a sangoma. When she returned home she enlisted teenage Miriam as her assistant.

The ancestral spirits endowed Christina with supernatural healing abilities, psychic insights, and precognition. By casting down an assortment of goat bones and sea shells and reading the patterns they made, she was able to discern people's ailments. But the lidloti spirits were demanding. They desired that Christina dress in unusual garments, perhaps in a foreign skirt or a man's loincloth, and it was Miriam's job to fetch these things, along with the snuff her mother would take while in the throes of one of her spirit-induced trances.

"Could she really tell people's illnesses by looking at them?" I asked.

"Sometimes she did not even look at them, she just looked at the 'bones.'"

Miriam fell silent for a moment, and then said in a voice little more than a murmur, "You know, I was not going to tell you about my mother. White people have made criminals of our tribal healers. It is all superstition and madness to them."

"But you trusted me?"

She replied in the same soft voice, "I do not know if the Africans in Los Angeles could sense this in you, but I can. You can see, I think."

"What do you mean, 'see'? Like your mother?" I was curious, in an amused way.

"Do you remember when we were discussing my first husband you said the first time I made love with him I became pregnant?"

"Well, you were talking about it, and I asked."

Miriam shook her head. "You did not ask. You said. And you were right."

I did not remember the incident clearly. I knew that I occasionally filled in a blank in one of Miriam's stories when her mind wandered while reminiscing. Apparently, and without realizing it, I was doing this often, and with uncanny accuracy.

A series of inky jungle nights passed under jewel-bright stars or a beaconlike moon as we spoke in Miriam's garden, with dense foliage dark all around us. Wooden xylophones played by the Guineans filled the heavy air with a jittery, atonal tinkling. Such nights were conducive to reflection on the fantastic, and the possibility of some strange insight within me came up again. It seemed all the times in my life when I had made an offhanded prediction or presumptuous statement that turned out to be true returned to me. There was that time my brother called and I blurted out of the blue, "Larry! You're having a baby!" He was surprised, and annoyed: that was to have been *his* good news. Or the year before when I saw two cars waiting behind one another at a light and thought, They're going to crash. Then I watched with strange curiosity as the one in back, as if following a script, drove forward and rear-ended the other. And with Miriam, as our interviews continued, personal details of her life that I could not have known popped out of my mouth, seemingly without conscious thought. Aware of this trait now, I was embarrassed, and apologized.

Miriam smiled at me. "It's the sangoma in you."

"Well," I shrugged, "what am I to do about it?" Sangomas were black Africans steeped in tribal ways and ancient wisdoms. And I wasn't. Period.

Miriam's regal, unlined faced regarded me intently. Though in her late fifties, she seemed ageless. Her embroidered robe flowed over her like a blue stream. "You must seek out a sangoma, who will tell you the truth."

"And what would that be? That I, alone among the white race, am possessed by lidlotis and I should undergo kutfwasa and become a sangoma? What then?"

"That is up to you. But I think many whites must have lidlotis. They just don't know."

We wrapped up this interview and the others; I returned to Los Angeles, wrote the book, found a publisher, and by Christmas I was back home in Chicago. But Miriam's suggestion that there was some sort of spiritual mystery in my life was never far from my thoughts.

I knew of few things that possessed the reassuring permanence of the giant Christmas tree at Marshall Field's department store. Three stories high, adorned with oversized ornaments, it filled the atrium above the seventh-story restaurant. When my mother first brought my two younger brothers, my sister, and me to lunch beneath the big tree, we drank Shirley Temples. Now the drinks were brandy Alexanders, and we were two. One brother had a job elsewhere in the Chicago Loop, another was in Colorado, and my sister was raising her own family in New Orleans. That left myself and my mother. My father worked in the nearby suburb of Cicero. He and I did our drinking at Wrigley Field, where he held season tickets to watch the woeful Cubs give lessons in humility.

My parents and I were three strong-willed people; we rarely agreed on anything and fought regularly, sometimes bitterly, so we would have to step back periodically and remind ourselves what we meant to each other. We could never seem to get enough of one another's company. From my father I inherited Swedish blood that gave me a cool temperament and Scottish blood that endowed me with a practical nature, and from my mother, Italian blood that heated me up and a touch of French blood for a piquant trace of hauteur. My father had been born and raised in Southern California and wound up in Chicagoland. The reverse happened to me. I graduated from the Division of Cinema at the University of Southern California, and was accepted into the Screen Writers' Guild on the basis of profitable if forgettable TV work. My ambition was to write novels, and I wanted to relocate to Chicago to do that.

Beneath the Christmas tree at Field's that day, my mother dressed with simple elegance, her hair was light brown, and the eyes that met mine were intelligent and warm. To collect my thoughts I gazed up at the gargantuan tree and out across the impeccably attired patrons along the walnut-paneled walls, and the high, mullioned windows overlooking a snowy State Street. What would the holidays be without this little ritual? I could think of no more inappropriate place to raise the subject of my African discoveries than here. Perhaps for that reason, it seemed the ideal place.

"Something interesting happened to me in Guinea."

My mother gave me one of her attentive and businesslike looks that had impressed the voters of Winnetka, who had just elected her to a second term as mayor of the affluent North Shore suburb. It was Winnetka where I had grown up raking autumn leaves and shoveling snow, where I watched the sun rise over Lake Michigan and dated my first black girl, the only one in town: cheerful and energetic Mary James, now a Stanford-trained nuclear physicist. My mother found this agreeable during those liberal days of Woodstock and civil rights. Now that we were deep in the Reagan night of racial intolerance, I did not know how her enthusiasm fared, for I still dated African-American women. I was thirty-two and it was rare when I spoke to her about my personal life, but it seemed important I do so now.

I explained what little I knew about sangomas, and when I was done, my mother, who had listened intently but without reaction, asked, "How does Miriam know you are such a thing?"

"Well, I'm not anything, yet. But it's intriguing that perhaps I could be. How would Miriam know? Her mother was a sangoma. Miriam thinks she may have some of these spirits herself. Supposedly, sangomas can sense one another." I finished with a shrug. "Anyway, the only way to know for certain is to consult another healer."

"And you're going back to Africa to do that?"

"When the opportunity presents itself, I will. I *am* curious. Why me? The next time I'm over there, I'll arrange something."

My mother's gaze grew severe. "Why did you let them talk you into their religion? Why didn't you tell them about yours?"

I explained that a sangoma was not a priest but a healer; that Africans had other people who officiated at their religious rituals. I was satisfied with my Catholicism, as casually as I tended to take it. Like many American Catholics, I was a "smorgasbord Catholic" who picked and chose what I wished to apply to my private life. I did not do this thoughtlessly or arrogantly, but I was unable to reconcile the American belief in personal choice with the Church's demand for unquestioning obedience. I engaged in premarital sex, which meant that either I or my partner used birth control, which meant I was going to hell. Under the circumstances, going to confession when I knew repentance was beyond me seemed foolish, and going to mass seemed hypocritical. But I still went to mass, felt uplifted by it, and assumed a hopeful attitude that everything would somehow work out.

I reminded my mother that my first ambition as a child was to grow up to be a priest. There was something in my character from an early age that was willing to trade worldly pleasures for an ideal, a belief. Perhaps this temperament would suit me well for kutfwasa training if I came to believe this sangoma business was relevant to myself.

My mother and I left the restaurant, and we passed through the Gourmet Shop, a jumble of delicacies from all over the globe. My mother browsed as I, six feet, two inches and a head taller than she, loomed behind. She stopped, and a thoughtful, distant, and sad expression passed over her face. "Mother would have liked this place," she said.

"Don't worry," I smiled. "Where grandma is they have an even bigger and better Marshall Field's."

"I know . . ."

I had made my little joke, but I suddenly felt a strange discomfort, and a chill came over me. A moment passed before the sensation left. I looked about at the brightly lit store with its colorful displays, an unlikely spot for a haunting, and wondered what it was that had just passed through me.

I returned to Los Angeles after the holidays. The year that followed brought an increasingly bizarre series of electrical mishaps that were never explained. They began innocently enough as I drove late one night down a deserted Los Feliz Boulevard at the base of Griffith Park. The street was suddenly and noticeably darker. Glancing back, I saw that a street lamp had gone out as I drove beneath it. I drove on and did not give the incident another thought until a week later when the same thing happened.

This time the top was down on my most cherished possession: a streamlined white 1937 Cadillac convertible I had restored. I saw the street lamp burn out directly overhead as I passed beneath. At the traffic light I thought, "This must go on all the time. Funny, I never noticed."

But I was forced to notice on my final night in the only Los Angeles apartment I had ever grown attached to. The classic old building was being demolished for a high-rise, and a moving van was coming in the morning to fetch my things. I had the flu, the rain was dribbling down in cold mists, and driving down Westwood Boulevard the Cadillac's brakes went out. By downshifting and applying the hand brake I avoided disaster and made it to a service station. Cold, wet, and disgusted, my joints aching from the flu, I trudged back up the steep incline of an almost empty Westwood Boulevard. Glaringly bright white arc lamps shone down from high metal poles for no other reason, it seemed, than to high-light my misery. I drew abreast of the lamp closest to the service station and suddenly found myself in darkness. I glanced up into the drizzle and saw the blue afterglow fade inside the globe. Its twin across the street had also gone out.

I continued on, depressed at losing my apartment and feeling lonely and adrift in the city. The next set of street lamps blinked out in tandem as I came near. They joined their companions behind in casting the pavement into darkness, though all the store lights and the traffic signals at Santa Monica Boulevard were working. The street lamps ahead still shone, until, two by two, they went out as I came close to them. With each outage, I grew more depressed until, four long blocks up, I turned onto a side street. I looked back, and every street lamp behind me down to Santa Monica Boulevard was off. All the other lights burned indifferently, but the street lamps seemed to share my dark mood. It was as if I had extinguished them.

The cold weather continued when I moved into a Spanish Revival-style house near Griffith Park. Prior to writing sessions I liked to limber up mentally by placing a chair before the white stucco dining room wall and meditating for a few minutes. It seemed I was concentrating with particular intensity one night when something happened: my eyes were closed when I heard a sudden and noisy crackle of electricity, alarmingly close above my head. I cringed, my eyes popped open, and though I saw no unusual light—no sparks or flashes—the crackling electricity continued a moment longer above my head. It stopped, and I bolted out of my chair. The room smelled of ozone, as if lightning had struck there, and the pungent scent of something burning. I looked up at the art deco chandelier I had installed. The thing had shorted out, I reasoned, and had sent out bolts of electricity. And yet, it seemed undisturbed; its stained-glass panes glowed peacefully. I stepped up on a chair and bumped my head against the fixture. My hand shot up to my head and my fingers came back black with ash that must have fallen from the chandelier. Something *was* burning. Traces of smoke still lingered. I raced from room to room and then outside in an attempt to spot flames. I figured that in the cold, the sixty-year-old wiring had gone brittle, and broken. I imagined the space above the ceiling filled with smoke, and a smoldering fire that would at any moment burst forth, incinerating my possessions, if not myself.

The smell of smoke was still strong when I reentered the house. But everything looked normal. I shut down the electrical circuit serving the dining room, and wandered into the bathroom. My head felt funny. I looked fine in the mirror, my dark blue eyes floating a little dazed in my long face. I put a comb through my hair, and a rain of black ash and burned hair ends fell into the white porcelain sink. When I had inspected the chandelier, there had been no ash. Had it all fallen onto my head when I clumsily bumped the fixture?

The following morning an electrician came over and took down the lamp. Everything was in order. The ceiling wires were fine. There was no trace of fire, smoke, or ash above. I protested that something had happened, that I had been blitzed by a tremendous crackle of electricity and there was smoke in the room.

But the electrician was stumped. So was I.

A few days later my barber was trimming my hair when he stopped combing suddenly. I saw his puzzled expression in the mirror. "How did you do *that?*" he asked.

"Do what?"

He was staring at a spot high up on the back my head that I could not see in my bathroom mirror. "Burn your hair?"

"You're not going to give me another lecture about using a hair dryer . . ."

"No, this is a *burn*."

I felt my gut tense. "Describe it."

"Well, it extends forward about an inch from the crown, like a scar. And it's burned down to about a quarter of an inch. You've been washing your hair, but it's still black up there."

I said nothing, but thought rapidly. As a writer I had cultivated various sources when I needed information or tips. Returning home, I called up a firefighter I knew from the gym I went to, a no-nonsense African-American and a fast-tracker in the Los Angeles fire department.

"Ron," I asked, "what can you tell me about spontaneous combustion?"

"There are certain volatile chemicals we have to look out for. And you've heard about grain storage bins that ignite. But you usually need a spark."

"What about people?"

"*People?*"

"Sure," I said with a smile. "Did you ever read *Bleak House?* The villain explodes into an oily black ash."

My friend had no time for Dickensian melodrama. "People don't burn, unless they're doused with gasoline or caught in a conflagration. We're all water."

"What about hair?"

"Maybe. But you still need a spark."

But where, I wondered, had the spark come from? What exactly had happened during my brief but intense moment of meditation that had generated that noisy but apparently sourceless crackling of electricity? Was I lucky to be alive? Yet, all I could think of was how comical it must have looked, my running around with puffs of smoke coming from my head in a desperate search for the source of a fire whose source was myself.

After that, I kept a diary of all the times street lamps burned out. The dates and locales varied, but the manner never did. I would be driving by or walking along and a single street lamp among all those up and down a boulevard would suddenly extinguish the moment I passed it: in downtown Los Angeles, on the Sunset Strip, ascending a freeway ramp, traveling the winding canyons of Beverly Hills, cruising Palm Drive in Desert Hot Springs, or the wide boulevards of the San Fernando Valley or Orange County. Even the hydra-headed street lamp before the McGraw-Hill Building on Sixth Avenue in New York and the one a few blocks beyond at Radio City Music Hall winked out.

In all, I recorded thirty incidents in 1987, and an equal number in 1988. What impressed me most besides the frequency of occurrences was the number of times I was in an agitated state of mind when they happened, rushing somewhere or troubled by something. I thought of the experience just about everyone has shared of pushing a telephone's keypad while in a hurry or upset, only to have nothing happen, so you must try again, wasting time when you least want to. It's as if the machine was mocking our haste. I presumed the phenomenon was due to some electrical impulse we throw off at such times. I also found it strange that some street lamps were working well until, impulsively, I shot my head up and saw them go off. And why did they always die when I was passing beneath them? Why didn't they go off ahead or behind?

Though I discussed the ongoing mystery with no one, it was almost fun in a Twilight Zone kind of way to think that there might be something about me that was causing this. Or was it due to something quite outside myself, perhaps a communication meant to keep me on edge, alert, and receptive to the possibility that there was a mystery that justified an expensive and difficult journey to locate its source?

That journey eventually came. I returned to Africa early in 1988. In January, the Makeba book was published to favorable reviews. The following month my publisher sent me to Cape Town, South Africa, to research a book on church leaders then spearheading the anti-apartheid movement. On my way, I stopped at Harare, the capital of Zimbabwe, to meet Miriam. She was giving a concert for the government, and though I saw her every few months in the U.S., this was the first time we had been in Africa together since our series of interviews in Guinea. I found her in a suite high atop the brass-hued Sheraton Hotel on the edge of town. She looked as magnificent as ever with her hair done up beneath a turquoise and gold turban, her soulful eyes regarding me like a mother would a son as we sat facing each other on the sofa.

"Swaziland is right beside South Africa," Miriam said in a confidential tone. "I have a niece there."

"And she can take me to see a sangoma?"

"Yes. Leave everything to Yvonne." Miriam took my hand in hers and patted it for good luck. "This could change your life."

I phoned Yvonne Motsa from South Africa and arranged to fly to Swaziland to see her for a weekend. Whether or not the trip would change my life, I had no idea. But my desire to investigate had not diminished. Another street lamp blew out in front of the Heerengrudnt Hotel on Cape Town's main drag when I drove beneath it. I wondered if I were having an effect on street crime.

Aboard the Royal Swazi National Airways flight I read up on the kingdom I was about to enter. The tiny, pineapple-shaped country, slightly larger than Connecticut, was ruled by the world's youngest monarch, nineteen-year-old Mswati III. A population of less than a million mostly eked out small incomes on family farms. The British had colonized Swaziland and given half the tribal lands to South Africa, with the result that today half of the Swazi king's subjects were ipso facto slaves under the apartheid system. Swaziland was scenic, traditional and an island of tranquility in a stormy sea that was, on one side, South Africa and, on the other, civil-war-ravaged Mozambique.

I awoke the next day in one of the tourist hotels that were clustered beneath the vertical flank of a rocky mountain range overlooking a verdant valley. I had sent a note via messenger to Miriam's niece Yvonne when I arrived, and she sent word that she and her husband, Timothy, would come by in the morning and take me to see the sangoma. I waited a long time for them in the lobby, feeling unaccountably tense, and then decided to wait outside. For another hour I stood beneath the hotel's porte cochere and watched a flaming red bougainvillaea bush shed petals like drops of blood.

Finally, the Motsas arrived, cheerful and full of apology. They were a stout middle-aged couple, Timothy short and bald, and Yvonne taller, soft-spoken, and burdened by a worried, preoccupied air that never quite left her. I entered their small blue car with venetian blinds sloping down the rear window, and we headed out into the sun-drenched morning. The Motsas knew the place we were going to; both had been treated by healers there for ailments they did not divulge. The drive took us past the small, six-sided parliament building on what had once been pasture land. Cattle still grazed on the lawn and seemed to roam wherever they pleased, including the roadways. A billboard announced in English that this year would see both the king's twentieth birthday and the twentieth anniversary of Swaziland's independence from Great Britain. But my thoughts were with the sangoma visit. Only when we passed beneath a mountain's blue stone side did I become aware of a remarkably beautiful valley opposite us. No buildings or roads interrupted the expanse of high grass, only a dark, snaking river. In the sunlight, the grass was such a bright shade of green it appeared phosphorescent.

"The emerald kingdom!" I murmured. This velvet green valley edged by muscular mountains pleased something within me. Far below, cattle stood motionlessly as if in a tableau.

Beyond the new, whitewashed campus of the University of Swaziland, we entered the neighborhood that was our destination. Small mud huts with thatched grass roofs and cinderblock houses with corrugated metal roofs were all familiar to me from other parts of Africa. But Swaziland was less crowded and felt more pleasant and comfortable than any place I had known on the continent. The people were medium brown in complexion, casually dressed in both European and traditional Swazi clothes, and were good-looking, in my opinion. Tall eucalypti and the fanlike leaves of banana trees shaded a rutted red dirt road over which our car bucked like a mule. A turn brought us before a small cluster of huts, and Timothy stopped the car in a cloud of orange dust.

Some men who had taken shelter from the sun in a tree's shade drank something from a large tin can they passed between themselves. They shouted a greeting to us. Half-naked children raced around the rusting body of a 1965 Pontiac with a guava tree growing out of its roof. A woman wrapped in a boldly patterned cloth placed a bench for us to sit on against the cracked wall of a large square mud hut, and we waited ten minutes for the sangoma to prepare herself inside. Yvonne and Timothy advised me repeatedly not to worry, which made me apprehensive.

"Did you tell them anything about me?" I asked Yvonne.

"Oh, no. It's the sangoma's job to divine everything about you herself."

The woman who brought the bench beckoned from the entrance of the large square hut. I followed the Motsas's example and removed my shoes before entering the building they called the Indumba, or spirit house. I had to stoop to go inside. Weathered planks had been nailed across the top of the doorway so a person had to bow with respect even if he was ignorant or forgetful of the custom. The hut was dark and cool. Blankets were draped over a cord along one wall, covering the one window. We sat down on thin reed mats placed over the dirt floor. The interior of the thatched grass roof vanished into an unseen peak in the darkness. A pattern of sloping poles and layered reeds had been charred black from the smoke of innumerable fires. A fire smoldered now, filling the air with an incense that carried the aroma of fresh pine needles. The sensation of looking up toward the roof's invisible apex was like being inside a primitive and mysterious cathedral. Truly, it seemed, this could be a spirit house.

In the hut's center sat a round woman with a round face the color of milk chocolate. Her eyes had an Asian slant to them, her mouth was small but sensual, and her hair was finely braided like twine and greased with a shiny cinnamon-red substance. There was strength, not flabbiness, in her bulk, which seemed to also characterize the many other heavy Swazi women I had seen. With her small hands she delicately extracted a pinch of snuff from a container and inhaled it first up one then the other nostril, all the while looking at the Motsas and me in Buddha-like silence.

"This sangoma we call MaZu," Timothy whispered to me. "She is not a Swazi. She comes from Zululand. But she trained here at this homestead."

Yvonne positioned my legs forward in a V shape so each foot touched the side of a grass mat between the sangoma and me. MaZu opened a small purse and emptied its contents on the mat. Out came the famous "bones." They were from small animals: joint bones and pieces. Some were distinguished by strings of small beads or metal bands wrapped around them. Among the animal bones I spotted two worn wooden dominoes and an old coin. But for the clatter they made when MaZu stirred them, chanting an incantation, the hut was absolutely quiet. A shaft of white light sliced down from the entrance, casting the rest of the interior into gloom, but striking and illuminating the mat before me. My mind seemed open and receptive, and I felt drawn into the reverence the others showed toward the moment. Although it was in one sense only an African doctor's diagnostic session, the presence of the ancestral spirits that supposedly gave the sangoma her supernatural vision, the priestly robes draped over the bodies of MaZu and her young assistant, the incense, and the ritualized way we proceeded made it seem almost a holy event.

Yvonne asked me for some money, I withdrew some multicolored bank notes, and she took one and slipped it under the mat. MaZu was ready to begin. I wondered if she would discover the lidloti spirits Miriam said I had.

MaZu held a large seashell out before me, close to my face. Yvonne instructed me to spit on it, and I did. MaZu then bowed her head, murmuring an incantation, touched the four corners of the mat with the bones held in her cupped hands, and cast the pieces before her. They fanned outward, rattling, then lay still. Bracing herself against a wooden staff held in her left hand, MaZu shot her almond-shaped eyes back and forth between the bones and me and in an urgent, almost shouted, singsong voice, began to speak. What she was telling me seemed vitally important, though I did not understand a word. With each statement, she paused to snap her fingers. Yvonne and Timothy snapped their fingers in accompaniment, and answered *"Sevuma!"* ("We agree!") to each of her utterances. Yvonne nodded to me to do likewise, and a rhythm was made: the diviner proclaimed a finding and we replied like a chorus.

MaZu stopped. She closed her eyes and drew a long breath. She was perspiring. Yvonne and Timothy stared ahead. They had forgotten about me.

"Well?" I prompted in a whisper.

Yvonne whispered back, "She says she sees a bright serpent over your head."

"A real serpent? Or a metaphor?"

"No, a real serpent, wiggly, and bright like lightning."

I immediately thought of that evening when the electricity crackled over my head, burning my hair. But how could a stranger know of that when I hadn't told anyone?

"What does it mean?"

"It's not good," Timothy said. "It means that someone is bewitching you."

I wanted to know who, and why, but the sangoma launched into a second litany, and we were obliged to respond to her urgent words with snapping fingers and "Sevuma!" When she finished, Yvonne explained, "She says your grandmother is with you, which means she can protect you."

I wondered if some kind of psychic connection was made during this ritual, for I seemed to know the reference was not to my father's mother, who died when I was small, but to my mother's mother, to whom I had been close until her death seven years before. Yvonne was saying, "You are in good health, MaZu says. You are strong. But you are bothered by pains in your back and your stomach."

That was certainly true. I inherited back problems from my mother, who had once been hospitalized with them, and stomach problems from my father. At one time ulcers had put both my father and grandfather in the hospital. I found it remarkable that the sangoma should mention these ailments, which were the only ones I had besides a left ear deafened by a viral infection when I was a child.

"Oh," Yvonne whispered, "and she says you have a problem hearing."

"She said *that?*"

With a small cry, MaZu began a final burst of words. I concentrated intently, as if my fate were being decided by the unknown forces at work in that place. Yvonne and Timothy's responses grew louder as the recital continued, and their energy was as intense as the sangoma's.

"Did your family have a black servant when you were small like the whites do in South Africa?" Timothy asked.

"*Not* like in South Africa, but we had cleaning ladies who came in. Some were black . . ."

"There was one," Yvonne said. "The sangoma says she was in love with you. You were a little boy. She knew she could never have you. She put a curse on you—maybe she remembered things from Africa—so no one else could ever have you."

Before I could respond to this incredible bit of news, Timothy reported, "You have never been as successful as you should be because something has been holding you back."

"What is that?"

"Your lidlotis," said Yvonne. So, MaZu had found the ancestral spirits Miriam spoke of.

"I have lidlotis?"

"Oh, yes. She says you have many. Some are on your back, keeping you down until you do what they want."

"Who are they?" I was fascinated by each new revelation, but if I was to accept any of this I would need to know some facts.

"We cannot say," Yvonne replied. "But you will find out when you come back."

"Come back? Why?"

"To undergo kutfwasa, to become a sangoma."

The diviner and her assistant were staring at me expectantly, and Timothy was shaking his head in amazement, but I raised a cautioning hand. "Wait, wait. Slow down. I'm coming back for kutfwasa?"

"You didn't believe MaZu?" Yvonne asked. "Was she telling lies about your back and your stomach? About your frustrations and the bright serpent?"

"That's all uncanny, I admit, but it could be coincidence."

"So *many* coincidences? Did she sound like she was guessing?"

She had not. MaZu's revelations lacked the vagueness of most psychic readings. She got right to the point, named names, stated ailments. Of course, I had no reason to believe in the curse she spoke of, though it left me with an uneasy feeling.

"You should know," Timothy said, "that it is rare when the spirits choose a person to be a sangoma. It's an honor, and the people will respect you very much."

I felt flattered that I was considered a suitable person to become a shaman by these people who believed these customs to be sacred. The adventure in such an undertaking appealed to me. I was a writer, but the sedentary and bookish life I led often made me feel cut off from the world. "James" had been my baptismal name in honor of Saint James, who preached, "Be ye doers of the word, and not hearers only." Perhaps the days for me to passively record words were past and the opportunity to play an active role was at hand.

I thought of the secret world that would be opened to me, and the magic. I thought of the wealth of herbal medicines I would learn, the discoveries to be made there. The ancestral spirits were an intriguing mystery worth investigating. And the art of healing offered the type of selfless responsibility I felt lacking in my life. All these things seemed compelling reasons to return.

I asked, "How long does kutfwasa take?"

"That depends," Timothy offered. "At least a year . . ."

"A year!" I blurted.

"What is your hurry?"

Well, what *was* my hurry? I would be done with the South African book in a few months. I had several thousand dollars in various bank accounts, and royalties I could expect from the Makeba book. Residual checks from TV shows were still coming in. I could afford a sabbatical, and a writer's life was always a gamble anyway.

Yvonne told me that I would be expected to pay a small fee when I started kutfwasa, and two cows at its completion. I had been in Africa long enough to respect the symbolic value the people placed on cattle.

Though expensive, the cows' true worth would be as an homage to my instructors if I chose to undergo the training.

Would I? With a heady feeling and amazed at my nerve, I declared that I would return to Swaziland at the end of the year, and begin kutfwasa.

MaZu nodded her head serenely, understanding the tone of my resolve if not my words. She seemed unsurprised, and I felt she had expected my decision. Yvonne looked solemn. Timothy smiled, and shook his head in wonder at the outcome of the visit. I was in a kind of wonder myself when I left the spirit house that day. But it had been a sense of wonder as much as curiosity that had led me there.

On the ride back to the hotel, while I contemplated the enormity of the decision I had just made, Yvonne informed me, "MaZu said something else. She said you must not speak to white people about what you will do. They will fill you with confusion and make you afraid." Then she gave me her opinion. "The whites are all the time jealous. They will not want you to succeed here and prove the value of our ways. But do you know that you are not all white inside? You have African spirits. The sangoma said so. Those spirits will see you through."

That would certainly prove interesting, if true. "Tell me," I asked, "has any European, any white person, ever done this in Swaziland, undergone kutfwasa and become a sangoma?"

In reply, Timothy snorted with amused contempt, "Never, ever."

"But why not? If these ancestral spirits are real, then everybody has them because everyone has ancestors. How come there aren't any white sangomas? Why don't the spirits choose whites?"

"They do," Yvonne asserted. "But the whites deny them. And the frustrated lidlotis bring them bad luck: sicknesses, mental illness, all of it. Like you, whites chosen by the lidlotis could be healers, and the happy spirits would bring them good fortune. Instead, these poor whites don't know what their problem is, and they rush around to their worthless doctors and their psychiatrists who can't help them."

Timothy said, "They don't see because they don't want to see. How can you see with your eyes closed? How can you breathe when you are holding your nose? How can you hear with your ears stopped? But you, James, you can feel because you have an open heart. You are not like these whites."

"*These whites* . . ." I had heard this said to me often, in bitter tones against what Africans perceived as my race's smallness of heart, its ignorance and bigotry. "*These whites* . . . ," my African-American friends would complain to me in the privacy of their homes and night clubs. I noticed they never said in my presence "*you* whites," and I didn't think the omission was out of politeness. They seemed unaware that I, too, was white. I once pointed out this obvious fact to a woman friend, a TV writer who had the café au lait complexion Josephine Baker used to boast of, at a time when she too was railing against the injustices of "these whites." She looked at me with utter surprise. "But I don't think of you as white." When I pressed her, she considered, "With white people there's always this self-consciousness when they're around black people." She did not say "with *other* white people," as if again forgetting what I was. I asked her what she saw in me. "You're fair," she replied. I wondered what it meant, to be fair? To be unbiased, and to judge without prejudice? It was good that she thought that of me, and I took it as a compliment. Fairness seemed a precondition to humanity. And it seemed necessary for sorting out the real from the superstitious, the magical from the illusionary, all of which I expected to find in the Indumba, the spirit house MaZu said was now open to receive me.

▲ ▲ ▲ ▲

When I returned to the United States to finish the book on South Africa's anti-apartheid clergymen, I held onto my resolve and enthusiasm to undergo kutfwasa. And with the passing months, as Hollywood was shut down by a lengthy writers' strike and my eyes watered from walking the picket line in the L.A. smog, as George Bush emerged the winner from a depressing and cynical presidential race, and as the number one hit song, "Don't Worry, Be Happy," seemed an ironic commentary on life in those days, I looked forward to getting away. I often telephoned the Motsas in Swaziland to keep my upcoming enterprise from seeming too unreal to me. They worried that the harsh life I would encounter might prove too difficult, and they assured me that I'd never be far from a hospital. (They weren't suggesting I'd be facing physical peril, they were trying to be reassuring.) I told them that just as I enjoyed hiking the Sierra Nevada mountains and exploring the wilderness, the simple life I was about to live appealed to me. My only fear was that my skepticism, my stubborn Midwestern "show me" attitude, might get in the way of my understanding of the delicate spiritual realm I was about to enter. Yvonne said she trusted my sensitivity as much as her aunt Miriam did, and besides, she knew I had lidlotis and it was only a matter of time before I was convinced of this.

I had moved so often in Los Angeles that I had lost count. The banal details I attended to now as I prepared to leave the U.S. seemed like just one more move. My furniture went into a storage locker, my Cadillac went to a firm that rented out classic cars to the movies, my magazine subscriptions were routed to my parents' home, and my health insurance policy was canceled (Blue Cross didn't cover Africa). I arranged for my literary agent to wire money to the bank account I would open in Swaziland; I had less money than I had thought, but I didn't think I'd be needing much.

My friends were accustomed to my long absences and trips to Africa. I told a few of them about the purpose of my upcoming excursion, disregarding the advice of MaZu who had only known South African whites and not my open-minded friends. I was cheered by their support. Some of my writer acquaintances were rhapsodic. According to them, I was about to embark on "a once in a lifetime odyssey." I listened, amused, to hear that I was going to "Save from extinction ancient tribal wisdoms . . . go where no modern person has ventured . . . bridge the racial divide . . . find the cancer cure among African herbs . . . discover true love!" Of course, these predictions were made by screenwriters who saw life as only a series of high-concept possibilities. I particularly liked this one: *"Jaded urban American sophisticate finds spiritual renewal, romance, and the meaning of life as a jungle medicine man."*

My last stop was to say good-bye to my family in Chicago. My youngest brother, Tom, who just turned twenty-nine, was enthusiastic; my younger brother, Larry, who was thirty-one and more conservative by nature, was cautious but not condemning; and from my sister I received sunny and uncritical good wishes. My father promised to reserve judgment until the venture proved either a success or a disaster. I suspected he anticipated the latter because he emphasized his desire to help get me back on my feet when I returned. But my parents had grown more tolerant of my meandering writer's life after my TV successes and the appearance of the Makeba book on the Chicago best-seller list.

My mother, though, was apprehensive, and seemed to sense that the cheerful sheen I applied to the journey masked something more momentous and dangerous. I wondered if my mother, the daughter of a woman said to be psychic in her own way, could also "see" things or, for that matter, if there was something about female sensibilities that lent credence to the famous woman's intuition I had often witnessed in my life. (The Motsas told me there were many more female than male sangomas.)

My mother was on her way to a mayors' conference in Boston, and we spent our last moments together roaming the Paul Gaugin exhibit at the Art Institute of Chicago. In contrast to the gray December weather outside, the gallery walls glowed with pink Tahitian fantasies that anticipated the warm and exotic summer scenes I would soon be experiencing in Africa.

To break my mother's somber mood, I told her, "The diviner said that grandma is with me."

She nodded her head thoughtfully. "Yes. I always pray to mother so she will look out for all of you children."

"Do you think she would have approved?"

Quietly, my mother replied, "Well, she did have this ability to sense things, like one of your sangomas. What else did the diviner say?"

I spoke of the "curse" that was supposedly put on me by a jealous maid once employed by the family. My mother did not scoff, and with an almost sangoma-like swiftness and certitude she said, "That would have been Fannie Mae."

"I remember her! She was older. She lived with us."

"Yes, when I was in the hospital for my back surgery. You were about five. She liked you."

"And I must have liked her, because I still remember her. But if she liked me, why would she put a curse on me and wreck my life? So I'd never have a wife or kids?"

I could see my mother's mind working, considering if anything as far-fetched as a curse could have any bearing on my status as a childless bachelor. She said of our cleaning lady, "She was older, in her fifties then, and her grandparents had been brought over as slaves. The diviner said she knew voodoo or something from Africa?"

"Yes, if any of this is true."

My mother was not looking at me when she replied, "You never know."

I was surprised. "You believe this?"

"No. I just said you never know. You're going there to find out, aren't you?"

"That and many other things, I hope."

The eyes that were avoiding me, taking refuge in but not seeing the Gaugin paintings, were red and misting. I assured her, "It's only a year."

"Yes, but . . . It's far. I won't be able to talk to you." She pulled a tissue from her purse and dabbed her eyes. "It's the not knowing!"

Quickly, she turned and left me, headed for the ladies' room so she would not cry in public. I watched her go, feeling completely wretched. Despite the certainty I felt about what I had to do, a depression descended upon me like a gray weight. I turned toward the sculpted wooden entrance to Gaugin's home that someone had salvaged and mounted against the gallery wall. For a while, I stared at it numbly before the words chiseled onto a pillar came into focus: *"Soyez mystérieux."*

"'Be mysterious,'" I thought dimly. "How French." I was tired. My eyes sank shut as I stood there.

Mystery . . .

▲ ▲ ▲ ▲

The Art Institute had been only four days ago. Now I was in Swaziland, nine months after that first visit. But as I now sat beneath the white shroud in the Indumba spirit house, the drums pounding relentlessly and the women singing to call forth the lidlotis, memories of America were already acquiring the hazy patina of a previous life. In order to adjust to my new existence here, I would have to make a clean break from life and reality as I once knew them. I'd have to learn a new language and the mind-set of a culture in which time moved differently, ancestral spirits participated in the affairs of the living, and an untamed nature was often the master. But I felt up to the challenge, buoyed by the courage of someone almost wholly innocent of the difficulties he would encounter.

I did not know how long I sat beneath the sheet. I felt a tugging on the fabric, and hands pulled it off me. The room was hot, and air currents made me aware of the sweat on my body and the hair clinging to my forehead. I did not know if this evening's ritual was a failure because no spirit emerged, but the people in the hut didn't seem disappointed. The women beat the drums, sang and shook the rattles with the same vigor as before. The young man I noticed earlier had vanished. Some small children were asleep, tumbled against each other like bundles of ragged clothing with dirt-encrusted feet. I had been warned that African huts were full of bugs and rats, but this Indumba was clean and free of pests. The teenage girl, whose name was Doyenne, left her drum and squatted before me. The single candle on the floor silhouetted her trim, naked torso as she held out a short wooden spear and a fighting stick with a bulbous head. I nodded and leaned forward to take them, my legs and buttocks numb from sitting on the cardboard-thin grass mat. I was clad in a knee-length cloth tied over my shorts. I caught sight of the girl's mother, who was none other than MaZu, the woman who read the bones for me the last time I was there. When I saw MaZu again upon my arrival this morning, I learned through the few English words she knew that although MaZu worked as a sangoma and knew the medicines, she had not formally completed kutfwasa and would still be there to help guide me for a few months until her graduation.

MaZu gestured for me to stand up. She swung her arms and shoulders to suggest how I might improvise a dance of greeting. I felt drowsy from sitting under the shroud, and my bare feet on the firm dirt floor fell into a shuffling movement. I was relaxed, and swung the toy spear and fighting stick loosely, but it must have been with some spirit because the women watched with wide grins and began ululating, a high-pitched warbling that was their sign of approval. The candle was behind me, and my shadow was cast huge on the opposite wall. I saw a strange sight in that shadow: myself dancing in the African spirit house to madly pounding drums and the applause of these people from seemingly another age. I thought of the contrast: my skin pale alongside theirs, my straight brown hair different from their black braids and kinky hair texture, the angular features of my long face with its narrow mouth and straight nose alongside the broader, flatter features of these women and girls. The Swazis were short compared to Americans, especially myself. I had always thought I looked like I'd stepped out of a portrait by Modigliani or El Greco: tall and thin, with long arms and legs and an oval-shaped face.

In a moment, MaZu with her bowling ball physique rose and began to dance opposite me with a grace and verve that belied her bulk. There was another woman who was undergoing kutfwasa there; she also stood and danced. Her name was LaShonge and she appeared to be in her thirties. She had a square face, a wide, smiling mouth, eyes animated by a mischievous humor, large hands and feet, and short-cropped hair. There seemed a little of the tomboy in her manner. But while I sensed her nature might be both more reckless and sensitive than MaZu's, she had the same generous spirit, and her dance welcoming me to the Indumba seemed to be responding to the rhythm of her heart as much as to the rhythm of the drums.

The drums finally stopped, along with the clapping hands, rattles, and singing voices, and MaZu, LaShonge, and I fell grinning onto a mat. A child was sent up the road to a neighbor, who had a kerosine-powered refrigerator. She returned with two bottles of beer. MaZu took one, handed it to LaShonge, and said, "Look!"

Her agate-brown eyes gleaming, LaShonge placed the end of the bottle in her mouth and pried off the cap with her teeth. We passed the beer between ourselves, and my two fellow students encouraged me to drink. Through signs and rudimentary English, they explained that LaShonge had lidlotis and hoped to become a healer. Her family was poor, and they would welcome the income and prestige a sangoma would bring to their household.

MaZu and LaShonge covered themselves with red wraps and began to sing a cappella one of the lidloti songs I had heard performed while I was under the sheet. I remembered its melody, and stretching out on my side, propped up on one elbow and with sweet-tasting beer in my belly, I began to whistle along. The two women laughed with delight and slapped my legs. Fascinated, they rubbed their hands over the hairs of my forearms and calves, which contrasted with Swazi men's hairless limbs. I located my jeans and offered money for the beers, but they refused.

Many times I had been the only white person in an all-African environment. While living with Miriam for two months in Guinea, I saw only one other white face, a doctor's. In America, with my African-American girlfriends, I attended several weddings, barbecues, family dinners, and even a funeral in such black communities as Chicago's South Side and Baldwin Hills in L.A. For two years I was the only white on the creative staff of the NAACP Image Awards TV show, whose producer was a friend of mine, and consequently mine was the only face bobbing like a pink cork amid the crush of glamorous black celebrities backstage. I grew accustomed to this company, and was accepted with some initial curiosity but never hostility. I had no desire to "act black," mimicking speech, mannerism, and clothing that weren't mine. I believed that the happenstance of biology assigns us a skin color that is intrinsically no better or worse than any other, and we could choose to feel at home in our skins or be miserable. I appreciated differences. I found the delicate features of Asian women immensely attractive, and considered African people handsome.

I did not know why this latter attraction seized me as strongly as it did when I entered my thirties, but it was serving me well now. Swaziland was a black-ruled and populated country where I saw only a handful of white faces past the walls of the tourist hotels. The white people I found in the capital town of Mbabane, where I went shopping upon my arrival for a portable stove and other things I'd need. Soldiers, police, bureaucrats, and everyone else was black, so that within minutes of arriving in Swaziland I noticed something: there *were* no blacks. With no one to stand in contrast, skin color ceased to be a distinguishing feature and people stood out as individuals. In fact, it was the whites—tourists from Britain, Portuguese business owners, representatives of foreign governments—who all began to look the same: solemn, furtive people who drove around with their windows rolled up, slipped stealthily through the markets, or lay inanimate around the hotel pools. They seemed uncomfortable and out of place.

If I felt at ease, which I soon did, it was because of the welcome the Swazis gave me once they understood I had come to kutfwasa. I was someone new to their experience: not a boss, missionary, teacher, charity worker, or other white authority figure in a relationship that invariably cast Africans in the role of inferiors to be educated, enlightened, or governed, but as a white who was subordinating himself to them in order to learn, and someone who honored their sacred beliefs by taking them seriously.

This is how I was seen by the people of the homestead where I was to live and study. The place belonged to Prince Vovo, one of the estimated 120 children of the long-reigning and polygamous King Sobhuza II, founder of the modern Swazi state. His death six years earlier at the age of eighty-three had left his people feeling orphaned.

Prince Vovo was also the older brother by a different mother of the new king, Mswati III. (The royal laws of succession elevate the deceased king's last born male child to the throne so there might be a long reign and an invigorating transfusion of new blood into the kingdom.) Prince Vovo had three wives and three homes: one in this area called Kwaluseni, a hut in the royal village at Lobamba, and a large cattle ranch elsewhere. His wife at this homestead was Gogo Ndwandwe, a well-known and respected sangoma who was the mentor of all those who came to undergo kutfwasa there. It was she who had approved my coming. MaZu and LaShonge spoke of her as an extremely knowledgeable woman but a disciplinarian and hard taskmaster.

I said good-night to MaZu and LaShonge after that first ritual, and stepped out into a warm, cloudy night. From down the lane where a school was electrified, a light shone through a patch of trees, but there was no electricity at this homestead, and I picked my way around black silhouettes of objects on my way to the main house. Soon I saw it before me: a squat, unpainted cinderblock building where for the time being I had been given a room accessible only by passing through a dusty dark garage with a floor of powdery red dirt.

The bed springs squeaked like agitated mice when I lay down at the end of my first day. My things were still packed in bags on the cement floor. I blew out a candle that someone left burning for me, and listened in the darkness. The strangeness of my new surroundings made me alert. I did not know what I was listening for. A lidloti spirit was not a ghost and did not go haunting about. The SiSwati language had a different word for ghost, *sipoko,* probably derived from the English word *spook.* It would have been nice if I could have seen a ghost, and had such vivid and early evidence of the supernatural. But nothing came, and I fell asleep.

The drums had been my initiation that day. Their fierce sound and rhythm had seemed to embrace me bodily and were said to be the signal that reached the spirit world and called it back to the Indumba. Had they succeeded in doing so, and was I not aware? If there were spirits, had they responded to the summons?

I did not dream that night. Toward dawn the drums sounded again. I woke up, and had a vision.

two

Rite of the First Fruits

A N ELDERLY WHITE WOMAN *stood in profile before me. We seemed to be in the conservatory of a large, old house. It was almost a hundred years ago, judging from the woman's long black dress with black frills about the neck and wrists and the Victorian-era brown flannel trousers I could glimpse on my legs below as I sat. The woman stood against a high window of many panes that let through a gray light, and she was calmly watering a hanging fern from a brass pitcher. The woman, who I sensed was a relative of mine, had a firm, commanding presence. She turned toward me with a faint smile. Her words were pleasant and conversational, but their content was nightmarish. "One of your lidlotis was executed in prison." She meant when it was mortal, before becoming a spirit. When she added, "Three hundred and fifty years ago," I replied, "Sometime in the 1500s." "I'm surprised they didn't tell you," the woman said, and I knew she meant the people in the Indumba spirit house.*

And then she was gone, and I was in a small, spartan room where a dusky half-light and the sound of beating drums entered through the window. I was momentarily disoriented, not from finding myself in this room but from not finding myself where it seemed I had been a moment before: in a mansion's conservatory with the old woman. What I experienced there seemed far too vivid to have been a dream. I rarely remembered my dreams anyway. My first thought was equally confused: "A lidloti of mine was executed in prison?"

I would think about the dream/vision later, but now a woman's strange, dramatic cry rose above the drums—"*Yooooooi!*" I heard other women singing in urgent voices. I had been told by MaZu that the spirits were greeted before sunrise every morning. I checked my watch. It was 4:45 A.M. I was also advised yesterday when I went to town that I should buy some fabric to wear on these occasions. I now grabbed a cloth I had bought with a black and white peacock design. I tied it around my waist so it dangled to my ankles, and went outside through the dusty garage. The sky was overcast and still dim. I spotted MaZu dancing in place before the Indumba hut, her eyes closed and seemingly in a trance. Her steps were small and repetitious, interspersed with short hops. LaShonge danced beside her, also with eyes closed and, like MaZu, she held carved dancing sticks. The women seemed attuned to something deep within themselves.

MaZu's daughter, Doyenne, and the old woman with clay-plastered hair beat the drums and sang. The senior woman was named Gogo ("Grandma") Mabusa, and she was a sangoma. She wore the sangoma's beaded necklaces, which rattled against her bony chest and thin wrists while she beat a drum. MaZu turned suddenly with LaShonge follow-ing, and with eyes closed, in the throes of what seemed a deep spiritual possession, knelt before the small and frail-looking but respected elder, Gogo Mabusa; and addressed her in a loud, strained voice punctuated by choking grunts. She was so worked up she began to foam at the mouth. I looked on with concern, and wondered if I, too, would be expected to act this way one day.

MaZu ran inside the Indumba and dropped down shivering onto the dirt floor. I followed her in with other people of the homestead who car-ried the drums which they then set up and continued beating. MaZu, chanting and wailing, quaked as she knelt, and LaShonge's efforts to cover her with a sheet were frustrated as MaZu repeatedly shook it off. Then MaZu changed: her quaking became a nervous quivering, she drew her arms in under her body as she knelt and began to hum like a bumblebee. This time LaShonge succeeded in covering her, and clutch-ing the sheet, MaZu began to sway and dance in her kneeling position.

The drums stopped, and Gogo Mabusa crouched beside MaZu and greeted either her, or the spirit that had taken hold of her. MaZu an-swered with inarticulate humming sounds. Gogo Mabusa responded by ritualistically clapping her hands. The drums picked up once more, MaZu's trembling and humming diminished, and she grew still. There was a joyful tone to the singing of the onlookers, for children and the women had come in to observe and add their voices to the chorus. When MaZu opened her eyes, she saw me and smiled shyly. I used one of the handful of phrases I had picked up from a SiSwati grammar book: "*Sekusile,*" or Good-morning, though literally, "It has already risen," re-ferring to the sun.

"Hello, James." She signaled for me to wipe the sweat from her back with a cloth. I obliged. LaShonge fetched a tin of brown liquid from the corner of the room, removed the cover, and carried it outside. With a nod of her head, she indicated that I should follow.

That morning would be a crash course in the daily rituals I would be expected to practice. The spirits were to be greeted with dancing prior to every sunrise and sunset, and twice daily we kutfwasa students had to take a variety of medicines. Sangomas made and administered many medicines, called *mutsi,* from the herbs of the forest, but the ones we acolytes were to use were only for kutfwasa, for they were intended to make us more receptive to the spirits and the spirits more responsive to us. Because I was eager to learn, I set only two preconditions to my use of these medicines: they couldn't be either hallucinogenic or addictive. Gogo Ndwandwe, the head sangoma who was in charge of us, assured Yvonne Motsa that they were not, and Yvonne had passed on the word to me.

Directly outside the Indumba, I was introduced to the lidloti tree, a three-foot leafless tree stripped of bark and planted on a carefully shaped mound of earth. LaShonge placed the tin of liquid before it and knelt down, with MaZu on her right in the senior position and I in the junior position on her left. We bent low to the ground, and I was instructed how to cup my cupped hands together as a sangoma does when he or she petitions the lidlotis or greets another sangoma. As I brought my cupped hands down vertically against each other, they made a loud, authoritative noise, almost like a paper bag popping.

With a stick, MaZu began to stir the medicine vigorously until it grew a frothy head as thick as meringue. Still kneeling, we each ate the foam in turn. It tasted like malt and earth. I hadn't tasted anything like it since eating dirt as a child. The women were bare-chested and I had only a cloth about my waist. I followed their example and dabbed myself with the medicinal foam, touching my head, shoulders, chest, arms, and knees with this herbal concoction meant to help me communicate with the ancestors.

A medicine with a similar purpose awaited at a small fire which was burning before a square mud-cooking hut. This was on one side of a small courtyard separating the Indumba and the prince's cinderblock house. The courtyard's fourth side was occupied by an elaborate round superstructure of bent branches awaiting a grass covering. I was told upon my arrival that this was to be the prince's hut, where the homestead's lidlotis would be addressed. The lidlotis were said to not only give sangomas their powers but to look after their living descendants. The homestead's senior male, the *umnunzane,* who was Prince Vovo here, spoke to the spirits conversationally within the hut. He did not literally pray to them, since lidlotis were not deities but rather spirits of deceased relatives. Beneath the great grass dome, he requested that the ancestors (who were closer to God [Mkhulumnchanti] than he) intercede on behalf of his family. I thought the half-completed hut, with its perfect form of interlaced branches, one of the most beautiful things I had yet seen in Africa.

Atop the burning embers of the courtyard fire, LaShonge dropped some yellow root shavings onto an inverted pot lid. They soon began to smoke, giving off a robust odor like sweet tobacco. MaZu leaned forward and inhaled the smoke through a two-foot-long bamboo pole. She explained, "Lidlotis like." LaShonge inhaled next, then passed the pipe to me. The herb's harsh smoke made my throat burn and my eyes water. We passed the pipe back and forth until the medicine was a smoldering black ash atop the hot pot lid. With a smooth stone, LaShonge crushed the black pieces to powder, dashed a cupful of water over them in an explosion of hissing, and plunged her fingers into the boiling liquid. She quickly withdrew them, blackened with ash, and licked them clean. MaZu did the same, gesturing for me to follow. I consumed the remainder of the medicine with them this way, licking it off my fingers, the ash tasting like ash and nothing more.

All these medicines were taken ritualistically, with clapping of cupped hands in the sangoma style that I had been taught. Twice a day we were to consume the foam medicine, dabbing ourselves with it also, and smoke and drink the ash of the second medicine. But there was more for me to take this morning, while a rising yellow sun burned away the overcast and our surroundings began to show their true green colors.

MaZu led me into the mud and stick cooking shed and sat me down on an empty oil tin before a small kerosine stove. She untied the knot on my cloth skirt. I pulled it off and now wore only my briefs. MaZu lit the kerosine stove and placed a tin of boiling water over its hissing blue flame. Into the water she dropped a handful of powder, and over me she draped a coarse blanket. Her hands forced my head down so my face was less than two feet above the boiling liquid. She dropped the blanket over the other side of the stove, then covered me with a second blanket and sealed the area by my feet so no air could enter. I saw that this medicine was to be taken through my pores. I sat hunched within the cocoon of this simple steambath, sweating instantly. It felt good, as if poisons were flowing out of me while the hearty fragrance of boiling herbs, like cinnamon tea, were passing through my skin to fortify my body.

After fifteen minutes of steaming, the blankets came off. MaZu shut down the stove, poured the tin of hot medicine into a plastic tub, and indicated my cloth. I wrapped myself and followed her outside. Steam rose off my body in the early morning air, but no one paid attention to me. People undergoing kutfwasa and patients who came here for treatment all took their medicines this way.

Six-foot bamboo poles gray from age enclosed a concrete square that was the homestead's bathing spot. The people cooked in various huts, but all came here to wash. MaZu placed the tub of medicine inside, cooled it with water drawn from a rain barrel, and rubbed her body to pantomime that I must now bathe with it. She then sealed the entrance with a tall piece of corrugated metal. I stripped off my cloth skirt and briefs, then splashed myself with the ruddy water in which small granules of pulverized roots swam like small animals. This, too, felt good. It was the first hot bath I had had in these first two days in Swaziland.

When I removed the sheet-metal door, MaZu was gone. In her place was the young man I had seen in the spirit house the night before. He was short, in his early twenties, trim, and well-built, with broad cheek bones, sparkling brown eyes, and a genial, placid expression. He smiled at me and said, "Hi, I'm Sam."

"Hello, Sam. You speak English."

"Yes, I went to school. That is why MaZu asked me to show you this." He held up a bucket filled with another red liquid.

"Another medicine? How do I take this one?"

"You drink it all up. Then you vomit."

I blinked at him stupidly before saying, "Vomit? How?"

Sam looked at me with the same pleasant, unflappable expression. "You know. Your stomach turns inside out."

"Yes, yes, but what if I can't? I mean, what if I don't want to?"

"The medicine will make you want to," he told me.

Dutifully, I followed him into a small field that separated the bathing stall from a dirt road bordering the homestead. Rows of maize plants grew two feet above the reddish brown soil. I still wore only my running shoes and the black and white cloth wrapped around my waist. Sam stopped, seeming content with a spot between some maize plants, and set down the bucket. Inside was a plastic cup. "Good-bye."

There were perhaps four liters of liquid in the bucket. "All of it?" I asked.

"All of it," he smiled in a friendly way. Then with a springy, nimble step that suggested he was an athlete of some sort, he returned to the homestead.

I was determined to do this because I had committed myself to kutfwasa. I stood with legs spread apart, took a deep breath, and dipped the cup into the bucket. I raised the medicine to my lips, and drank. It had a powerfully pungent and salty taste but did not make me nauseous. In fact, it was mild for an emetic, and I wondered how it was supposed to make me vomit. I drained the first cup and dipped down for a refill. Not a hundred feet away people passed along a dirt road beneath languidly dropping telephone lines. Some of them noticed the tall, bearded white man with the cloth wrapped around him standing in the field drinking. One man stopped and stared at this novelty. I was seized by an American impulse to holler, "Mind your own business!" But I did not, he went away, and my stomach began to bloat from cup after cup of the salty medicine. When I felt pressure in my gut, I leaned over. Nothing. Half the bucket remained. I drank more. Another half cup, and the pressure overwhelmed me. My insides convulsed, and as I bent forward the red medicine shot out of my mouth in a cascade that struck the ground and splattered my white running shoes. I vomited a second time.

I doggedly drank until the bucket was empty. I vomited most of it back up. It was tiring. My eyes were burning and my nose was running. My throat felt raw. But I also felt something more: I felt cleansed, physically purged. And I felt mentally purged, triumphant, as if I had passed a test by overcoming an inhibition I carried from a society that saw vomiting as a sign of illness. Here it was the opposite: a way of taking medicine and cleansing oneself.

I returned with the empty bucket to find Sam in the Indumba, the spirit house that would be the center of my kutfwasa universe. MaZu wanted to do a reading of the bones to see how I was situated, spirit-wise, now that I was in training. LaShonge assisted her, and Sam translated. The session was more informal than the first one. Of my alleged lidlotis, MaZu determined there were many, and they were ready to emerge.

I asked Sam if they would appear during a ritual like the previous day's, when I was placed under the sheets amid beating drums, rattles, and singing. He confirmed that they'd come eventually, for I was obliged to undergo this rite nightly. Then he asked, "Did you see something last night in bed, like you were dreaming only it was like you were there?"

Surprised, I asked, "Yes. Why?"

"MaZu says one of your lidlotis visited you last night and made you see."

"That's remarkable," I said.

After I described what I saw, MaZu advised me to consult Gogo Ndwandwe, our head sangoma, who would tell me the vision's meaning. But for now I was to work in the Indumba, she said. Sam excused himself to go to his job at Swazi Milling, where he processed maize meal, the country's staple food. This was cooked as a soft breakfast porridge laced with brown sugar or as a hard lunch and dinner porridge with a meat or fish sauce and, on the side, one of the spinachlike edible weeds that abounded in Swaziland.

MaZu placed each of the animal bones, seashells, dominoes, and coins that comprised her set of divination bones on the mat between us. She swept her hand over them, said something to me in her native tongue, then sat back expectantly, waiting for me to do something. The people of her neighboring Zulu tribe spoke a language similar to SiSwati. Know one and you know both. My problem: I knew neither. While I sat blank-faced, LaShonge tried to be helpful by repeating, *"Khetsa! Khetsa!"* I opened the SiSwati-English dictionary I carried around with me, and found the word: "Choose."

I smiled, reached forward and took a large, polished sea shell. MaZu gave an exclamation of amazed delight, and several adolescent girls who had come in to see what I was up to cheered happily. Sam lived elsewhere, and I was told that Prince Vovo was rarely here at this the smallest of his homesteads. I seemed to be the only male who now lived at this place. But it was the idea of a white kutfwasa student that fascinated the women. Every time they saw me, they welcomed me with smiles and gestures of greeting as if determined to make me feel at home. They were succeeding; I was feeling less awkward and more at ease.

MaZu placed the shell I had chosen before me, and again waved her hand over the pile of bones, commanding me to choose. I spotted a polished stone and took it. MaZu and LaShonge exclaimed in wonder, and the girls squealed with delight. I had no idea why.

When I was instructed to choose again, I pointed to a hump-backed animal bone. But MaZu shook her head no. I shrugged, and indicated a similar bone wrapped in beads.

"Yebo!" ("Yes!") The girls cheered and applauded. What in the world was going on? MaZu looked at the others and, nodding her head, touched her temple with her forefinger. So, she thought I was intelligent. On what evidence?

Then I seemed to know. I leaned forward, touched MaZu's forehead, and then pointed to the bones. "Are you *thinking* about the bones?"

She understood and nodded. So that was it: she would think of a bone, one of the thirty or so in the pile, and I was to select it. And somehow I was doing it. This was a test of psychic ability.

We proceeded. Sometimes I guessed the correct bone right away. Other times it took several tries. The pile diminished, gradually making its way over to my side. When I had them all, MaZu raked them all back toward her, stirred them, then ordered me to choose once more.

I seemed to perform even better the second time, but I was concentrating a great deal and it was tiring. That day the homestead heard the news that the white man chose well. I wondered what the odds were against correctly selecting a particular bone. Was such a test actually an indication of psychic ability?

For breakfast I had fried some eggs on a tabletop stove I had installed in my room; now for lunch the elder sangoma Gogo Mabusa cooked up hard porridge and spinach, and LaShonge roasted ears of fresh maize over the coals. It was starchy, filling food, tastily spiced with a pepper and onion sauce.

After eating, I went to the main house to speak to our teacher, Gogo Ndwandwe, whom I had only met for a moment on my first day there. Heavy wooden furniture overcrowded a small, gloomy sitting room dark from curtains drawn across windows fitted with iron grilles. Blurry photographs of long-dead kings hung on dingy walls. A door leading to the bedroom opened, and Gogo Ndwandwe padded in on small bare feet and sat down on a sofa. She was a tall, bone-thin woman with light brown skin, sharp, angular features and narrow pointy breasts beneath her thin wrap. Married to Prince Vovo for eighteen years she was his third and most recent wife. He had one child by her, a seventeen-year-old son named Dumdum who was tall and gangly like his mother. In the Prince's frequent absences, Gogo Ndwandwe ran the homestead.

I stood, respectfully I thought, when she entered. But her first words were, "You must kneel when you speak to me. I am your *baba.*" She used the word for "father," which was how a sangoma teacher was customarily addressed by kutfwasa students.

I knelt down on the threadbare carpet, brought my cupped hands together twice in the sangoma's hand clap, and replied, "Yebo, *baba.*" This was the strangest thing I had yet done, saying "Yes, my father" to a person I hardly knew and a woman.

But Gogo Ndwandwe smiled with pleasure. "Oh, my! Now, tell me all you've been doing?"

I recounted for her the taking of medicines, the smoking and vomiting, the drum-beating ritual at the Indumba spirit house and the dancing. She nodded her head approvingly. I explained my vision of the elderly woman the previous night, and mentioned that I had been impressed when MaZu's bones acknowledged the vision.

"Yes, the lidlotis, they speak to us that way, by showing us things and sometimes themselves! That old woman you saw, when she said your ancestor was in prison, this meant he or she was trapped and unable to do kutfwasa. So, that person died."

"You mean if a person selected by the ancestors does not undergo kutfwasa, he'll die?"

"Oh, yes!" Gogo Ndwandwe asserted. I did not reply, fearful that my skepticism might be interpreted as disrespect. But this woman was too astute to let my expression pass, and she said, "You don't believe it? But there are many ways to die. If you live your life without children, then in that sense you die because what was you does not continue. Like you, you don't have children."

"But who's to say I wouldn't have children eventually even if I didn't do kutfwasa?"

Gogo Ndwandwe, with her animated eyes and bony hands twitching with the excitement of her words, replied, "Now that you are here, we will see that you will!"

I nodded my head politely and said, "I'm afraid you will find that I am a person with many questions."

"You must ask! How will you learn?"

She proceeded to lay down the rules that I as a kutfwasa student must live by. I had to faithfully observe the twice-daily taking of the medicines, for these would strengthen and purge me until I was ready to receive the lidlotis. To avoid returning to my previous "unclean" state, I would have to avoid spiritual contamination from other people. She told me individuals are carriers of bad spirits they pick up through contact with other people, much the way they spread a virus. In kutfwasa I would be required to live a spiritually germ-free existence. For this reason I was told by my teacher that I could never shake hands with people or come into physical contact with anyone other than the patients I was treating. Contamination by an evil spirit could bring mental depression or physical illnesses to a sangoma.

"When you say I mustn't touch people, you mean . . ." My voice trailed, and Gogo Ndwandwe nodded her head solemnly. "You must not have a girlfriend," she said.

Yvonne Motsa had hinted that I'd have to be celibate for the duration of kutfwasa. I was sexually active and healthy, and I didn't know if I could do it. But I didn't know that I couldn't do it. It would be strange, I thought, to be moved by the sight of an attractive woman but not be able to do anything about it. What would happen when the pressure of bottled-up sexual energies grew too great?

Nietzsche said, "Whenever the religious neurosis has hitherto appeared on earth, we find it tied to three dangerous dietary prescriptions: solitude, fasting, and sexual abstinence." Solitude? No, I would not do kutfwasa in solitude. Certain animal organs disliked by the lidlotis, including kidneys, liver, and brains, were forbidden, but there would be no fasting. But celibacy—which I was to embrace not out of religious fervor or to show my fealty to the spirits by renouncing the pleasures of the flesh but instead as a preventive measure against spiritual contagion—

this would be a challenge. If celibacy, like any other part of kutfwasa, proved too difficult, then this venture would end. But I had come too far now to quit without trying.

"Well, it's only for a year," I said to Gogo Ndwandwe with forced good humor. She looked at me with surprise, and said, "But you must count on being here two years. You cannot rush the lidlotis."

I was so taken aback I stared at her, speechless. Gogo Ndwandwe was a friendly and likeable woman. By the end of our first interview she was referring to me not as her student but as her "son." But I reacted to the thought of putting my life on hold for such a length of time with a mild panic. I appreciated this woman's confidence in my ability to do kutfwasa, her generosity in allowing me to stay there, and her unflagging conviction that I had lidlotis. But two years was no longer a sabbatical. It was the exchange of one life for another, with impoverished and possibly dangerous conditions replacing all that was familiar and comfortable in the life I had known. Suddenly this adventure seemed a bit too long, a bit too hard, and a bit more than I had bargained for. My eyes dropped, my voice deepened, and I must have looked an abject figure kneeling there on the faded, worn carpet when I promised, "I'll try."

Gogo Ndwandwe's expression was serious as she clapped her cupped hands together twice and said, *"Thogoza!"*—the sangoma's greeting and exclamation of agreement to the pronouncement of another sangoma. By addressing me as a sangoma, was she that confident of my success, or was she trying to build my confidence?

I was a little dazed when I left my new mentor, but depression never quite set in. Though poor in material goods, my surroundings were novel and naturally beautiful. and it was pleasurable just looking at the waxy yellow mangoes ripening on the trees, and the billowing white clouds sweeping a sapphire sky. The trees were in their summer glory. Green, uninhabited hills pressed in from the north, and to the east rose the impressive blue stone Mt. Mdzimba, where Swazi kings were buried in caves along a flank that sliced down like a knife blade.

While taking in the panorama, I was hailed by Sam, back from his job at Swazi Milling. His blue worker's overalls were lightly dusted with flour. He lived nearby, he told me, but he liked to visit Prince Vovo's homestead because he was a Dlamini, of the same royal clan as the king, and through the complicated ties that bound Swazis together, he was considered the nephew of Prince Vovo. The prince had just arrived at the homestead, Sam said, and he offered to take me to greet him.

Prince Vovo was presently enjoying some fiery Swazi beer with the neighborhood men. I spotted the group seated on benches behind a mud hut where the beer was brewed. Over a fire, a woman was stirring a barrel of the milky brown liquid with a wooden oar.

On our way to meet the prince, I told Sam how struck I was by the absence of men at the homestead. Sam shrugged, and explained in his unhurried, deep voice, "the boyfriends, they went away." I had read that the traditional polygamous Swazi homestead, where multiple wives produced the sons needed to tend the cattle and work the fields, had all but vanished with industrial development and a changing economy. But it seemed the polygamous mentality lived on not only in elders like Prince Vovo, who could afford his three wives, one mistress, and thirty-six children, but also in poor young men like Sam, who at twenty-four had two children out of wedlock, no way to support them, and a casual attitude toward their fates. The woman stirring the beer, a shrewd-looking, dour-faced person who never removed the black woolen cap she wore, had two toddlers whose father, a prison guard, rarely visited. A divorced schoolteacher living in a cinderblock structure next to the main house had a new baby girl by a croupier at a tourist casino. Both MaZu and another homestead resident were unwed mothers, and the elderly sangoma Gogo Mabusa was raising two little girls for her unwed nieces. Even Gogo Ndwandwe had given birth to three daughters before marrying Prince Vovo.

I assumed traumatic cultural changes were causing such dislocations, but Sam and everyone else seemed to accept them with nonchalance. But if they did, it was because of an important truth I would come to learn: the stigma of illegitimacy did not exist as it did in white societies because here all children were considered members of a family, the Swazi nation/family which nurtured and imbued them with a sense that everyone belonged on the basis of their blood. The Swazis were a proud people who looked out for one another to a degree I had never seen before.

If the Swazis had a calm, unworried, and confident manner seemingly at odds with the smallness of their nation and the poverty of their circumstances, it was the result of their solidarity. I was to learn many characteristics of Swazi life from my host, Prince Vovo, whom I now found in the center of a half-dozen men passing around a tin of homebrew and arguing the merits of a legal case. The prince was called upon to judge many tribal matters. He had a large, bulbous head atop a thin, narrow-shouldered body. The flesh of his high forehead, where gray hair was receding like surf returning to the sea, was furrowed in thought above lively brown eyes. The prince wore traditional Swazi male attire, impala loinskins tied over a boldly patterned cloth descending to his calves. A second cloth was tied toga-style over one shoulder, and on his feet were sandals dyed red by the Swazi soil. I occasionally saw Swazi men in native attire, walking with the long, proud strides of warriors and carrying carved fighting sticks raised in their right hands. Most men, however, wore loose-fitting shirts and trousers, like the neighborhood men now drinking with the prince.

"Welcome, welcome to my home, young man!" The prince spoke English with a genial tone that matched his gentle, courtly manner. "Whatever I can do, you must please tell me."

I stood awkwardly in the appraising sight of the men and apologized, "I'd like to shake hands with all of you, but I've just been told . . ."

"Oh, do not despair!" assured the prince. "These are your friends here. They understand! Do you drink *tjwala,* our beer?" He called out for a woman to bring me a cup of my own, explaining, "You are not to share utensils with other people, because you are *litfwasa.*" He used the word for a person undergoing kutfwasa. I tasted the beer. It had the eye-watering fire of pure alcohol, and a smoky taste. I sipped sparingly as the prince told me about himself. He was fifty-two years old, educated at missionary schools, and considered himself one of the last of a dying breed of old-fashioned tribal leaders who disdained politics and thought problems should be resolved through palaver. He was under the impression that I was from England, so I told him that no, I was from Chicago, in America, and to prove it I went to my room and returned with a bottle of Jack Daniels which I presented to him as a gift. Another glass was called for, the prince poured some whisky, and this was passed around as a toast to my success there.

"I also know about herbal medicines," Prince Vovo told me, "though my wife, your baba, she is the expert! I know all the animals in the bush, and where the good guava fruit is, and which rivers flow throughout the year." He waved a crooked finger at me. "And I will dress you like a proper Swazi man, not these blue jeans!"

The other men laughed heartily, perhaps at the notion of my dressing as a "proper Swazi man," which was more than they were doing. Prince Vovo then advised me to apply at the immigration office in the capital town of Mbabane for a two-year temporary residency permit, which would be granted on his say-so. I thanked him for his help, but with this reminder of the length of my stay, my mood dropped as if down a chute.

Perhaps what was bothering me most was that the success of this enterprise, with all the time and resources I might put into it, would in the end be determined by supernatural forces that I was not sure even existed. How would I get through to these spirits, and they to me?

That night, Gogo Ndwandwe showed me one way.

"Bring your red cloth!" she instructed, when I saw her in the court-yard. I went to fetch it, then returned to follow her out into the starlit maize field. We arrived at a short, gnarled log rising from the ground, and Gogo Ndwandwe and I knelt before it. "It is time I introduce you to my lidlotis so they will know about you."

Following her example, I covered myself with the red cloth, bringing it up over my head until I was hidden. Gogo Ndwandwe clapped her hands, and murmuring in SiSwati, called upon her spirits. I peeked up at the knotty pole rising against distant storm clouds that were lit within by flashes of yellow lightning. When Gogo Ndwandwe was finished, she told me to address my own lidlotis.

"Do I pray to them?"

"No, you speak to them like people, just like they are here."

A Catholic lives in a universe inhabited by spirits: angels and saints and even ancestral spirits, like my grandmother, to whom my mother prayed to protect my brothers, my sister, and me. How different, really, was this? I softly clapped my hands twice and, crouching beneath my red shawl, tentatively addressed the unknown entities out there in the Afri-can night. "Hello."

My tone was respectful, and as I spoke my self-consciousness gradu-ally went away. "Good evening. My name is James Hall. I come from America, though I think you probably know all this. I'm not sure if you're out there somewhere, or inside me like they say. But I'd like to get to know you. Who are you? Where do you come from? Why did you choose me to do this?"

With two soft hand claps to end it, I rose up out of my covering to find Gogo Ndwandwe smiling at me. "That was very nice. That's all the lidlotis ask, that you show them respect."

She sent me to the Indumba, where for the second time I underwent the nightly ritual of sitting beneath the sheet while the drums pounded and the women sang. Only this time, having been fortified by so many medicines said to act like spiritual magnets, I noticed something. Pat-terns began to appear before my eyes, whether they were open and star-ing at the candle flame's diffused image through the fabric around my head, or closed. Brown lines and sharp angles leapt and met to the drums' fast rhythm. I wondered if this was how it began.

After I emerged from under the sheet, MaZu traded places with me. She sat covered until her body began to quake. Then she seemed to convulse and threw off the sheet. The women raised their voices in jubilation. MaZu knelt facing us, her body quivering and her face contorted with a concentration that seemed almost painful. Sam was there, seated next to me, and he explained laconically, "A lidloti has arrived."

With eyes closed, MaZu spoke SiZulu to us in a strained deep voice. "It is a man," Sam whispered. "This is no longer MaZu."

"He must be a Zulu," I suggested.

Sam shook his head as the spirit that had come to possess MaZu spoke at length. "No, he is an Indian. He is saying he is from Natal, where MaZu comes from."

I was surprised by this. "Then she has ancestors from India?"

"No. A lidloti can be anybody, even someone you aren't related to. This one, he says he owned a chemist's shop where the Zulus came to buy. He knew their language, and they taught him African medicines. Now he wants to live in the Indumba, and help MaZu be a good sangoma. This is a nice lidloti, I think."

Interesting, I thought: an Indian proprietor of a bush pharmacy returns from the dead and attaches himself to a Zulu woman. I wondered what surprises might await me if and when the geometric patterns I saw coalesced into spirits.

That night I had another strangely vivid dream. I awakened startled, so real had it seemed. I slept, saw it all again, and woke up realizing I was meant to remember it. What I saw was myself, asleep in that room, drifting off the bed as if pulled by invisible hands. Then I floated like a feather down to the floor. The same mysterious force pulled me slowly away, and would have taken me outside if the wall hadn't stopped me.

It was Gogo Ndwandwe who interpreted this dream. We were on an excursion to a forest a mile from the homestead to dig medicinal roots. Sam and I carried spades and machetes over our shoulders, and MaZu and LaShonge held the canvas sacks we would fill. Gogo Ndwandwe led the way, a commanding personality full of energy that day. "Your dream, it was the lidlotis telling you you must not sleep on a bed. That is why they took you off. All people doing kutfwasa must sleep on the floor, to show they are humble and strong. I'm glad they told you. I was afraid; I didn't want you to think you are a slave." She told me I should purchase a foam rubber mattress called a sponge that was popular and portable since you could roll it up and take it from hut to hut.

Gogo Ndwandwe continued, "And then in your dream you were almost pulled out of the room? Truly, the lidlotis don't want you there. You must get a hut of your own."

I was glad to hear that. My room off the garage was a gloomy cell, hot and stifling when the sun beat down on the tin roof. Small holes in the roofing sheets admitted dust-speckled rays like strings of used dental floss. Rain entered these same holes. Red dust from the garage covered everything, and cockroaches abounded. I was impressed at the speed and confidence with which Gogo Ndwandwe interpreted my dream. I agreed to abandon the bed, hoping I could also soon leave the room.

"The Most High hath created medicines out of the earth, and a wise man will not abhor them," says Ecclesiasticus. We set to work, digging with pick and shovel. From beneath the shade of her wide-brimmed straw hat, Gogo Ndwandwe pointed to various plants, and we dug them up. With an axe I split apart a thick root and hauled it out over my head like Samson.

"Oh!" Gogo Ndwandwe exclaimed, "you are strong! I think you are not like these other whites we see in Swaziland."

"You mean they don't work like this?"

"Never! They have garden boys."

"Well, from now on, you can consider me *your* garden boy. Once I get to know these plants, whenever you need something, you can send me out into the woods."

"Oh, that would make my lidlotis very happy!"

To aid my memory, I jotted plant descriptions into a small notebook and made hasty botanical sketches.

"Oh, you are clever!" Gogo Ndwandwe praised. She explained that few sangomas were educated, or could read and write. I found this disturbing and asked how they preserved the wealth of knowledge they possessed. "They remember and pass the knowledge on. Even me, I can write, but I am lazy to keep my journal of medicines. It's all up here." She tapped her head.

During the course of the day I learned various plants and roots and their complicated SiSwati names: *Lichishamlilo, Imbita Bantfwana, Sanwati*. Except for some leaves that would be boiled, all the roots we dug were to be dried and processed back at the homestead. They would become medicines to treat ulcers, constipation, sore throat, headaches and dizziness, and children's stomach ailments. There seemed a vast wealth of medicinal herbs within the small, dense woods and sun-dappled clearing where we worked. The air was fresh and clean, and my body craved the exercise. I had been a daily gym-goer, and now that I had to endure celibacy I suspected I'd need a lot of physical release.

I found some release twice a day in our dancing. While MaZu seemed clearly in some type of spiritual possession as she danced, and

LaShonge was edging closer to that state, I was still myself, though less self-conscious as the days passed. The three of us danced in place, side by side before the Indumba, the drums behind us, swaying our bodies with the dancing sticks for balance, raising our knees and then launching into quick tiptoe steps interspersed with small hops.

Before sunset we ate and smoked and anointed ourselves with the secret spiritual medicines. In the evenings I sat in the Indumba beneath the sheet, listening to the drums until my buttocks were numb and my lower back ached. But I never became impatient or bored. The energy of the drums stirred me. I felt my body shaking at times, as if some force in sympathy with the drums' power was seeking release.

All those spiritual medicines that were accumulating within me, the steaming and vomiting I did every few days to cleanse myself, the communications with the spirits at the lidloti pole and the pounding drums night after night, were they beginning to work? Beneath the sheet, I was noticing a change. I began to feel extremely passive, not sleepy but withdrawn, and then my body would feel like a shell and my consciousness a separate entity floating within. As my mind seemed to shrink inside my head, my sight and hearing dimmed. My muscles felt light and flaccid, and I seemed to cease breathing. My awareness of my physical self continued to diminish, and was replaced by striking images that were not perceived through my eyes. It was my mind, shrunken and independent within my body, that saw a parade of startling pictures, all set against inky blackness:

> A pair of woman's hands. A child's face, smiling right at me. The upper corner of a brick building. The trim lower back of a young black woman as she stretched, leaning away from me . . .

And then a vision that did not go away but repeated itself as the nights progressed:

> A zebra. Two. Soon a small herd of eight. They ran, surrounded by darkness, but did not advance toward me. I thought I must be traveling alongside their long, bobbing heads, their flying manes. Black and white zebra stripes. The rhythm of their pounding hoofs was the rhythm of the Indumba drums. They ran on and on.

What did they mean, these zebras? I came to expect them when I slipped beneath the sheet. At night, lying on the floor atop my new foam rubber mattress with the Southern Cross glistening in the sky neatly framed in the window above, I saw them in my dreams.

I saw myself, running shirtless beside them through the green veld, the sunlight bright all around. A river was ahead. I outraced the herd! I dove into the blue flow and splashed about. The zebras ran in all around me, splashing, my friends.

▲ ▲ ▲ ▲

I had been in Swaziland three weeks, it was late December, and the Incwala, or Rite of the First Fruits, was underway at the royal village. Warriors began to appear at the homestead clad in leopard-skin skirts and carrying cowhide shields. Traveling from their homes, the warriors stopped by Prince Vovo's homestead for some home-brewed beer. Some of the men explained to me that the king would be calling upon the nation's lidlotis to bless the Swazi people and bring good crops and peace in the year ahead. They urged me to accompany them. Other than some trips to town I had made to withdraw money from the bank and to buy food, I had not left the homestead since I began kutfwasa, and with Gogo Ndwandwe's permission I tagged along.

The impressive ceremony was held in a large cattle enclosure built of tree branches. Thousands of warriors weighed down by heavy cow-tail shawls and women in full skirts, orange wraps, and black beehive hairdos danced slowly in place, in great lines, gravely singing a dirgelike invocation to the ancestors. It was my first chance to see young King Mswati, who was taller than most of his subjects and magnificent in a headdress of black, red, and white feathers. His entrance was greeted with a high, sustained whistling from the warrior regiments, and he carried himself with precocious confidence.

The slow, ponderous dancing continued for hours to deep songs that mimicked the sounds of nature. Listening to the hard beauty of the men's voices, I seemed to hear the ages passing: the slow revolution of the earth on its axis, the arc of the moon across the sky, the weathering of mountains. In their whistles could be heard the wind and the rain. In the trill of the women's voices I could hear the birds, the animals, the fecundity of nature. In the slow, sure redundancy of the dance steps I could feel the passage of the seasons, the endless progression of time.

This harvest-time petitioning of the tribal ancestors seemed propitious, for I was on the verge of harvesting the first fruits of my kutfwasa. The visions were continuing during the nightly drum-beating, or *shayelwa* rite. And I was detecting subtle changes within myself. What had begun as a tolerance on my part, a willingness to consider phenomena I once considered impossible, had evolved into a feeling of almost physical openness, as if seeds within me, long frozen in winter earth, were sprouting, pressing toward some kind of light. There seemed to be evolving a transparency in my body and mind. More and more was entering with less and less resistance.

Everything I had been doing since my arrival was intended to reach another realm of existence and bring its inhabitants back to their point of origin: the mortal world. This was still a fantastic concept to me. But in letters to family and friends I mentioned that a breakthrough was coming. And so it seemed during the waning days of 1988.

Gogo Ndwandwe had been predicting it. MaZu and her bones had foreseen it. At night more and more people were crowding the Indumba in order to witness it. And when it struck, I could not deny that it happened. The lungs were mine, but not the will that used them, and though the strange howl that erupted from beneath the sheet came from my throat, it was not mine. Those who heard it swore to this fact.

three

Sibolomhlope

I FEARED I was being hypnotized by the drums. By how much, I wondered, was I being swayed by the expectations of the people in the spirit house and my own hope that my alleged ancestral spirits might emerge? I told myself I wanted this enterprise to succeed, but not on the basis of fakery and dubious evidence. But that was a conscious decision, and I had no control over subconscious desires and impulses that could well have been the source of the howls and noises emerging from me while I sat beneath the sheets in the Indumba, *unless* . . .

Gogo Ndwandwe reported, "I sent a man to the Indumba to check on you. He said he thought you were drunk. You were shouting and shaking. But when you came out of the sheet, you were normal, and he could see you were not drunk. That's just the way it is with lidlotis; they take you and then leave you alone. One is trying to come out of you now. It's like giving birth."

My instructor said she was pleased that the nightly drum-beating ritual was showing results. MaZu and LaShonge were also happy. That the spirits emerged with shouts, howls, and strident voices was normal to them, and I shouldn't feel embarrassed. My concern was with loss of control. I didn't like it: the bizarre behavior, the convulsions that shook me, the hoarse cries. The idea of disappearing within myself to be replaced by someone else seemed classic schizophrenia. I had no idea how the lidlotis were supposed to emerge, and now that everyone said it was happening, I felt apprehensive.

And yet, at the same time, I was intrigued. I had never suffered from any psychological problems, and it did not feel like I was now. The things that were happening to my body seemed to come from a source other than myself. It was mysterious, which made me feel a wonder greater than my concern. The Africans took comfort in magic; it was a power intrinsically neutral, neither good nor evil, but something to utilize. The shayelwa drum-beating ritual was intended to bring out the lidlotis and transfer their power to the sangoma for the purpose of healing. Even if it seemed that I was being manipulated by a supernatural force—though I was not yet ready to admit this possibility—I felt the best way to keep my head was to take the sangoma's businesslike attitude and see this as a necessary and welcome start to a job that had to be done. I would use magic, not fear it.

So I was of two minds, wary and open, and many emotions when I again sat down on the grass mat in the spirit house, extended my legs, and let the women cover me with the long white cloth. It was New Year's Eve 1988. Sam, who enjoyed visiting the Indumba, was present, and he held a small tape recorder I had given him. The device, which had never been seen in the Indumba, was considered somewhat sacrilegious by MaZu and LaShonge. (Cameras were also thought intrusive.) I was concerned that the bond of trust that was growing between the Swazis and me would be broken if I were perceived as only an inquisitive scholar doing research. Some Westernized Swazis I met refused to believe I was undergoing kutfwasa, and laughingly accused me of being an undercover anthropologist. But Gogo Ndwandwe permitted my little cassette recorder when I told her I needed to know all I could about my lidlotis in order to accept them. And in her Indumba, her word was the law.

The drums boomed, and beneath the sheet I soon felt the sedated feeling, a withdrawal from the noise of rattles and voices. Next came a kaleidoscope of visions: geometric shapes, the dancing zebras, things I didn't remember but which triggered physical reactions. I could not follow very well what was happening, for my sight seemed to shrink to a faint spot of tunnel vision surrounded by darkness. Only later, after I was able to talk to others who were there, add my own recollections, and most important, listen to the tape, could I fully understand what had happened. For several nights Sam had sat with his knees up and his impassive face staring, waiting for the moment when the lidloti would arrive and he could start the cassette recorder.

This New Year's Eve, fifteen minutes after I slipped under the sheet, he pressed the button.

My body shook until it convulsed, though from where I seemed to be deep within myself I felt nothing. My arms had a will of their own, and they lashed out, groping with the sheet covering me. The women pulled it off. My body rose, and I seemed to feel two excitements simultaneously: my own, and one belonging to somebody else acting through me, the being who now roared mightily with life-affirming joy and kicked up his—my—legs in a merry jig. The people in the Indumba said they had never seen a dance like this before. They clapped along with enthusiasm, happy that at last this spirit had arrived. My body was like a marionette pulled by the strings of another's will as it jumped left, right, and then dropped with a pleased sigh emerging from my throat to the floor, to kneel before the assembly. From inside myself I was as curious as everybody else: what was this thing? And I clearly heard, along with the other people, his first words:

"Aye, there be spirits here tonight!"

But I was to hear nothing more. What consciousness I had held onto up to this point faded away. But Sam had done his job; the tape whirled inside its cassette. Sam would tell me that he put down the machine and knelt respectfully beside the body that seemed no longer connected to me but had become a spirit incarnate. Now Sam asked, "Who are you?"

A voice that was my own and yet not my own, for it possessed an unhurried, gentle, otherworldly tone, replied with a touch of Scottish brogue, "John. I am of the MacDonald clan."

"Where do you come from?" Sam asked.

The voice picked up by the recorder was indistinct, muffled as if the speaker was facing another direction. But a reply was made, "Scotland . . . I was a soldier."

Impressed, Sam repeated, "You were a soldier!"

"Killed me a man," the broguish voice said in a tone that sounded like sadness. "I was a farmer . . ." He stopped with a small sob, as if overwhelmed by loss. Sam listened respectfully as the spirit mentioned a family he had loved. In reply to Sam's question, "What can James do for you?" the tape recorded the faint word, "Tartan."

The people of the Indumba listened in silence, and no words came from my mouth for a minute. Sam looked on attentively as the lidloti's emotions brought tears to my blank, unseeing eyes. Finally, it said, "Tell James to get along now and get himself a family."

He began to hum a tune, and then said distinctly but with growing softness, sounding nostalgic and pained, "My farm. My cows. A candle in the window on a frosty mornin'. A taste of spirits to cut the winter chill. My daughters. My sons! All of 'em gone, now . . ."

No words came from my mouth after that. My body had sunk forward on its knees until my face was close to the dirt floor. The women covered me with the white cloth. The silence ended when the drums were again beaten and the people sang the farewell song. As if breaking a spell, the sounds pulled me back from wherever I had been, and I regained consciousness feeling as if my heart were bursting. So many emotions swarmed through me; wonder, loss, and nostalgia. But they seem borrowed, not my own, as if I had entered the head of someone else and felt everything he was feeling.

Smiling faces greeted me when I looked up from where I knelt. The women stopped beating the drums and clapped their cupped hands repeatedly in the sangoma style. MaZu was speaking the incantation to close the rite. I felt hot, my head was full, seemingly twice its weight, and my eyelids were heavy.

"Your lidloti spoke to us," Sam reported. He was his same laconic self, and it felt good to see his composure in the confusion I felt. What these people were telling me, had it actually happened? Had a stranger been in my place? The red light atop the recorder was still lit. I turned off the machine, thanked the people, and went out into the night to listen to the tape.

The stars were out. From that latitude, the Milky Way was directly overhead, bright and dense. I did not return to my miserable little room but walked along the dirt drive and stopped beside a tree. I leaned against it and looked up, feeling subdued and still saddened from the emotion of that thing, whatever its source might have been, that had taken possession of my body. But my mind had remained my own, thinking its thoughts ever more dimly until I blacked out. I switched on the recorder and listened to the tape.

When I finished, a skeptical voice spoke in my mind like a prosecutor summing up his case: "The moment you've been waiting for just proved nothing. You were, of course, only reacting to the stimulus of the drums. It was an hysterical reaction. It was also a willed reaction, because you've invested a lot in this venture. You were hopeful of results, and therefore you created results. 'John MacDonald' was your creation, invented to satisfy the expectations of the people here as well as your own. But it *was* a nice piece of work. Spooky."

It was a solidly rational, intellectual argument, and inarguable. I didn't try to rebut it on an intellectual basis. It was true that I had hoped for results, and I admitted it. But illegitimate results could only mislead and harm me. It was also true that I had no evidence that my subconscious had not simply invented this "spirit." But my instincts told me something else: that John MacDonald lived, and was real. My father's mother's name had been MacDonald, I was named James MacDonald Hall, and I felt a sense of kinship to this spirit. MaZu might not have been related to the Indian shopkeeper who visited us earlier, but I wondered if I were a descendant of this lidloti, if a lidloti it was.

The spirit had asked for a tartan cloth. Gogo Ndwandwe told me lidlotis commonly requested a piece of fabric so we might symbolically clothe them and show our concern for their welfare in the afterlife. Other lidlotis requested beads, symbolic adornments. But what impressed me most was the sadness the return to mortal life had triggered in this man. He must have lived many years ago, for he spoke of his family and land as long gone. Where was he now? Still with me? Back where he came from? Both there and here? If these spiritual entities existed, I would have to radically alter my Sunday school view of the afterlife—all those gold-rimmed clouds, all those rosy-cheeked cherubs with diaphanous wings!—that I had never taken seriously anyway. What if it were true that the dead came back to intervene in the lives of the living?

Reality as I knew it, a cool and hard thing, a thing I could touch, seemed suddenly suspect, its hardness little more than obstinacy and denial against the inexplicable. Something unknown was before me now, and I felt hollow and defenseless in the face of it.

The night suddenly erupted into sound. From all parts of the neighborhood, people banged on pots and pans, shouting "Happy! Happy! Happy New Year!" A staccato burst of firecrackers, a rifle firing; the noise was utterly strange because not a single person could be seen in the darkness or through the shroud of black trees and bushes.

It was a new year. 1989. For the first time I realized how cut off I was. There was no TV at this homestead, I hadn't a radio, and in Swaziland's two tabloid-sized newspapers, only a few paragraphs clipped from wire services covered international news. I felt isolated.

Then an ironic-sounding voice reprimanded me, "*Ye, wena!* ("Hey, you!") It is just possible that an hour ago you were taken over by an ancestral spirit. Time will tell if that's true, but if it is, *that's* your news. Happy New Year."

▲ ▲ ▲ ▲

Gogo Ndwandwe was delighted by the appearance of my supposed lidloti, which she declared would be "the first of many!" Each, she said, would add to my psychic power until I was able cast down the bones and divine the hidden ailments of strangers. How many lidlotis could I anticipate? MaZu claimed to be possessed by fifteen ancestral spirits. Gogo Ndwandwe didn't know how many she had, but guessed thirty.

To aid our receptiveness to new lidlotis, Gogo Ndwandwe decided to administer a new medicine to MaZu, LaShonge, and me one morning a few days after John MacDonald's appearance. This tall, thin woman with her beak nose, through which a sinus condition relieved itself in harsh snorts, flew around the homestead, all nervous energy, cackling out orders, waving her bony arms, pushing people here and chasing them away from where she didn't want them. Without warning she would let out a piercing, high-pitched whistle like a boiling tea kettle that could be heard everywhere. She said it was her lidlotis' signal that someone was arriving at the homestead, though in the flux of people constantly coming and going I never knew who in particular the whistling was for. I saw too that Gogo Ndwandwe had a quick and vicious temper, and would shriek bitterly at people who incurred her displeasure. I once saw her reduce LaShonge to tears when she found her secretly drinking home-brewed beer. But our teacher was in a good mood this morning as she prepared to administer a medicine called *likhambi* to us on a sunlit patch of courtyard before the spirit house. The stuff was intended to purify and sharpen our minds.

"Come, my darlings!" she cooed. "LaShonge first!"

I suspected something unusual was about to occur when LaShonge lay down on a grass mat with her eyes squeezed tightly shut, her face screwed up in a grimace, and her body stretched out so stiffly she appeared to be modeling for her own coffin. I thought that taking medicine by vomiting was as strange as it could get. But I was wrong.

Gogo Ndwandwe stood over LaShonge, unscrewed the cap of a small brown bottle, and poured out a bright green medicine into two tablespoons held by MaZu. "This is going to bite her!" she informed me.

She set down the bottle, took the spoons from MaZu, and emptied them simultaneously up LaShonge's nostrils. LaShonge blanched, sat up quickly, and ran away, the Kelly green medicine running down her ample bosom.

MaZu was next. She showed even less tolerance for whatever it was that Gogo Ndwandwe poured up her nose. She kicked her feet high in protest, let out a cry of pain, and also ran away.

My turn. I removed my T-shirt, lay down, and tilted my head back. I primed myself with the thought, "I can do this." I looked up in time to see spoons dripping green ooze coming at me like some horror device in an old 3-D movie.

I felt the medicine flow down into my sinuses. A raw, minty taste filled my mouth. I closed my eyes tight against the burning. It was like acid, and I felt a rush of pain. "Enough!" exclaimed Gogo Ndwandwe. I bolted upright and gagged. The stuff poured out my nose and mouth. I couldn't speak and scarcely saw through teary eyes. Instinctively, just like LaShonge and MaZu, I got up and ran, feeling this was the only way to keep my head from exploding. It felt like battery acid had been poured into my brain, and my sinuses burned hotly when I burst into my room and dropped down on the mat. For an hour I sat helplessly, blowing my nose, wiping my eyes, and trying to spit out an aftertaste of, seemingly, pine resin mixed with ammonia.

Had it worked, and was I spiritually "sharpened"? That night beneath the white sheet I began to see a new set of visions that excited me: vast, empty stretches of plains beneath a gun-metal gray sky of winter. A herd of deer moved through the brown grass on the horizon. I took this panorama to be from America, though I didn't know where such an uninhabited place could still be found, or a deer herd so large.

The following night, more of the same, and then *fitfully arriving*

images burst into view and faded into the blackness they came from. A
man of ruddy complexion wore an animal skin about his loins and fur
wrapped around his calves. He looked strong. His face was unclear to me.
He performed a ceremonial dance.

The loud drums had once more beaten my mind deep into myself,
and I had no more self-consciousness viewing these images than a person
does watching an involving movie. But a part of my mind wondered
whose views these were. I sensed a lidloti was seeing these things, looking back upon his life, and I was being treated to his vision. *The man*
danced before conical huts. Or were they tents? Dark, half-naked children
stood about. But they were not Swazi children. Seated women with black
braided hair beat upon drums painted white with triangular blue and red
designs. The man's face was still unclear, but he was like them. He
was . . . a Native American.

The next day, I told Gogo Ndwandwe of my vision. She was interested. "Sometimes, it is like you are watching the television?" she asked.
"It's that way with me. Things come at you, like the *bhayiskhobho*." The
SiSwati word for the movies was bhayiskhobho, which must have come
from the English word "bioscope," a turn of the century motion picture
process.

After I explained what I had seen, Gogo Ndwandwe sounded disappointed, "This new lidloti, he dances to drums but is not an African. He
is not a sangoma, I think."

"But in his time and place, he was. He would have called himself a
medicine man."

"Then that's good. He must come out soon and greet us!"

It was comforting to hear the absolute conviction of Gogo
Ndwandwe and others that it was lidlotis who were responsible for my
visions and not my deluded mind. Even if the spirits did not exist, I was
beginning to feel the nightly visions must have come from somewhere
outside myself. They were too vivid and immediate, and my own powers
of imagination had never been equal to them. But if a new lidloti was
arriving, he could not have been related to me by blood. Perhaps there
was another bond, for a sangoma was much like a Native American
medicine man. Both healed with the roots of the earth, both harnessed
supernatural forces and worked through ritual.

The next day, Gogo Ndwandwe called her three students together,
which she did when she, our baba, wished to give us news or critique our
kutfwasa performances. She sat on the concrete apron before the Indumba as we knelt in the dirt courtyard directly before her, our heads
low so it was impossible to look up into the face of the head sangoma.

This was in keeping with Swazi custom that the young did not look directly into the eyes of their elders. I did not find such diffidence servile but refreshing in a way, especially in contrast with America, where egalitarianism was used as an excuse for bad manners. Living here, I was also reminded what foul-mouthed people Americans are. I had not heard an English-speaking Swazi use a single one of the obscenities with which Americans routinely assault one another. The SiSwati language had no equivalents for these words. I couldn't help but find this symptomatic of some kind of societal mental health.

"It is time James started to dress like a litfwasa," Gogo Ndwandwe said, using the name for a kutfwasa student. Up to now I still tied a black and white cloth around my waist for the rituals and wore shorts or jeans at other times. Gogo Ndwandwe listed the necklaces of beads and animals horns we needed to make; each would contain a special medicine to attract lidlotis.

She was interrupted by a horrible cry from behind us, and we all jumped at the sound. A woman was on the ground, thrashing wildly and screaming. She had come for treatment for a mental disturbance Gogo Ndwandwe called "tilwane" (wild animals). Animals seemed to possess her now as she shouted and groped, rolling in the dirt. In an instant, our teacher was on her feet, snapping her bony fingers and shouting instructions. LaShonge fetched a tub of water, and MaZu a jar of brown powder that Gogo Ndwandwe grabbed and emptied into the water. She spotted Sam and ordered him and me to restrain the deranged woman.

We reached her at the same moment as some women from the homestead. They removed her blouse and skirt as we held her down, and Gogo Ndwandwe poured medicine over her from head to foot. She shouted over the woman's cries for us to rub it in. "More! Harder!" The woman's howls had an animal intensity, and she fought us all the way. I was at her feet, and twice she kicked me in the face when I plunged my hands into the tub of medicine to rub over her legs and ankles. I did so urgently, concerned that the woman would harm herself. Sam smeared medicine across her shoulders, and the women rubbed it over her head and torso. My fingers began to itch sharply, and I wondered if a mosquito had bitten me. We continued to rub medicine over the woman, and she began to tire. She no longer kicked and clawed, and I could pause to scratch my hands. The itching was persistent now.

"Stop!" Gogo Ndwandwe ordered. Sam bolted away. I stood up and looked at the whimpering patient. In little time, the medicine had calmed her down. Then I looked at my hands. They were bright pink. Something was wrong.

I hurried after Sam to the homestead's single water tap attached to a pipe that rose from the field. The rush of air exacerbated the itching in my hands, and a thousand invisible ants seemed to be biting them. Sam rubbed his hands beneath the water's flow, and I joined him. MaZu spotted us, "No!" She was right. The water merely spread the medicine down my wrists and forearms. I was in trouble, now. My skin was bright red. Tearing at it with my fingers, I ran to my room. I burst through the door in pain and commanded myself, "Think! What have I got? What have I *got?*"

I emptied out the contents of my shaving kit and squirted on antiseptic. No relief. I felt like I wanted to tear off my burning skin with my teeth. Ah, Solarcaine! I emptied half the tube with a single squirt, and rubbed in the ointment. It seemed to help. MaZu appeared at the window with another ointment. I rubbed it on quickly, and it also seemed to help. The pain left. After a few minutes, the sensation diminished to sparkling pins and needles. I went outside, angry, to confront Gogo Ndwandwe. She smiled at me. "It was itching, no?"

I demanded to know why she hadn't warned me. She countered, "There was no time! You saw the way she was!" Nor would she have permitted me to wear gloves if there had been time. A sangoma must always lay his or her bare hands on the patient, she insisted; a sangoma's hands have curative power. "Look at your fingers!" I did and found my hands back to normal. Gogo Ndwandwe explained the medicine was not dangerous, but was a mixture of caustic roots that caused a fiery but temporary skin irritation so shocking to hysterical patients it calmed them down. I spotted the woman lying on a mat beside the Indumba, asleep. The medicine had worn off, even without ointment.

Other patients were there, beside the Indumba. For the duration of their treatments, they lived with us. Male or female, old or young, they stayed for a night, a week, a month. They slept wherever they could, sometimes sharing my room. Along with the sangomas, the students, and the other permanent residents, they became a part of the homestead. Sick people in this culture did not sit alone with their ailments and the sterile companionship of a television set in an institution. The patients here could, if they wished, be alone. They could drink home-brewed beer with the neighborhood men behind the mud huts if they liked. But they were integrated into the life of the homestead, and I was impressed at how eagerly they did chores with what strength they had. A woman being treated for migraines swept the courtyard using twigs bound with string, a man suffering from depression chopped wood, an older woman taking a cure for a kidney ailment helped weed the maize field. One elderly woman could only sit on a mat in the shade of a guava tree, but she was never alone. Other women used her as an excuse to assemble and gossip. In the sangoma's world, the ill were not permitted to be cut off from life but were brought to the doctor's house, where they contributed to the ongoing life around them. I liked it.

By this time, one month into my kutfwasa, I was also doing the homestead's chores. Early morning was the time to weed the field with long-handled hoes. Beneath the broiling afternoon sun, Sam and I set to work with his cousins on a new pit latrine, digging a rectangular hole five feet across and ten feet deep in the crimson soil. Gogo Ndwandwe gave me the task of chopping up roots with a machete and setting them out to dry as a first step to making medicines.

And at night, the shayelwa drums set into motion visions beneath the white sheet. These images triggered a quivering in my body and bursts of incoherent sound from my throat like those that accompanied the appearance of what the people called my first lidloti. Anticipating the arrival of a second spirit, Sam was on hand to turn on the tape recorder. Though I still had doubts, my skepticism was not so obstinate that I refused to see something potentially miraculous in the visions of the empty Midwestern prairies as they might have looked a century and a half ago. A sense of wonder had brought me this far, and had reaped as its reward a Scottish farmer. Now my consciousness, shrunken and dulled but still present, witnessed the convulsions of my legs and torso. My body truly seemed independent of my mind. I felt no physical sensation at all, and I could scarcely see. But unlike the last time when I had blacked out, I continued to witness and remember, feeling all the while tremendous awe. If a schizophrenic loses himself to become another personality, then I was not one because I remained aware inside myself. Sam pressed the button on the recorder, the people raised their singing voices in celebration, and someone who was not myself threw off the white sheet and stood up with a "whoop."

The women beating the drums and shaking the rattles ululated with pleasure as the lidloti stood tall and commanding before them. Not a person there saw James Hall. As far as they were concerned, I had left; I had been replaced. My body was still there, but it had changed, made prouder and seemingly stronger by the being that now energized it. A girl bowed down and offered the dancing sticks. The spirit took them and knelt before the drums. The women stopped beating. The lidloti used the sticks to beat a slow, stately rhythm. The women picked it up, the spirit stood and began to dance to it, bending far forward and bringing his knees up to meet his chest.

Inside myself it was as if I was in a movie theater watching one of those scenes where the camera pretends to be a character's point of view: we see what he sees. It was like that now, seeing through sight once removed, though much dimmer than a movie or even one of my visions. But I also seemed to feel another's emotions. I saw Sam coming toward me, and I felt an unaccountable anger. Hands rose before me, my own, but not powered by me. They picked Sam up and tossed him backward. He fell onto the dirt floor by the drums, and in the confusion I dully saw frightened girls flee outside.

Gogo Ndwandwe, who would later tell me the girls ran to her room and told her of the disturbance in the Indumba, entered wrapped in a blanket and found the spirit kneeling, crouched over, and trembling. Sam sat impassively nearby, as if nothing had happened, and the head sangoma spoke sharply to him, "I tell all of you, you must kneel and never stand when you address a lidloti! No wonder it was cross!"

Was that the source of the anger that had passed through me? I was aware of Gogo Ndwandwe kneeling beside my body now, clapping her cupped hands twice to greet the lidloti. She was not addressing me when I heard her ask in English, "Please, tell us who you are."

The spirit replied in English. "I am . . . White Feather."

"White Feather!" Gogo Ndwandwe repeated. "Where do you come from?"

After a moment's pause, he said somberly, "They took our land. They stole our land."

"You are a black man?" she asked.

The voice replying was deep and strong, "I danced the sacred dance. I felt the power within me. I cured the people, and no man dared speak ill of my power."

"You know medicine?" Gogo Ndwandwe inquired hopefully.

Some moments passed, and the spirit's voice grew indistinct. What the people heard was touched by an ineffable sadness. "I did dig the roots from the earth. I did know the power of the river and the forest . . . If I could have saved my people . . . Who is this who speaks of God, and serves the devil?"

I felt a terrible turmoil within this man who was also within me. I was close to blacking out. I again seemed to feel what he was feeling: an amazement at the gulf of time that had come to separate him from his past, and pain from the loss of all he had known while on earth.

"Gone!" he cried. "All is gone!"

Tears fell from his eyes—from my eyes. He slumped forward. "All . . . is gone!"

Pityingly, Gogo Ndwandwe pleaded, "Please do not cry, White Feather. We know the whites, what they do."

She ordered LaShonge to bring the medicine tin and stir it to a froth. "This is your spirit food. You may eat."

The lidloti leaned forward toward the tin on the ground and bit into the thick foam.

I was not aware of drinking, of any sight at all. The sadness of this spirit was so huge it pushed aside all other awareness.

The medicine seemed to restore him, for he raised my unseeing eyes. "This house is wrong. My house must be a circle."

As if rejecting the place, he began to crawl forward. The crying left him too weak to stand. The people hastily made way for him.

I felt a sensation of earth beneath my hands, a glimpse of the concrete step passing before me.

Gogo Ndwandwe, Sam, and the others followed the lidloti outside to see that no harm came to him or me. When he stopped, a few feet into the courtyard, LaShonge placed the tin of foamy medicine before him. Again he drank. Sam knelt down beside him and said with concern, "Please, Mr. White Feather, you must release James."

The spirit sank down to the ground, and sighed heavily. MaZu covered him with a sheet. Minutes passed, and he knelt with his cheek to the earth, sighing, drifting away . . .

Never before in my life had I felt so emotionally drained as I did when my full consciousness returned and I looked around at the sad expressions of the people surrounding me. They had all been moved by the lidloti's grief. Tears were in Gogo Ndwandwe's eyes. My own face was wet, and I felt as if I had been crying for hours. Sam somberly reported that a new spirit had come, and I told him I knew, that I remembered a great deal. He told me what had happened from his perspective, how he had forgotten to pay the proper respect to the lidloti and was tossed around like a doll.

Gogo Ndwandwe pulled the blanket she wore tightly around herself, less against the night's chill than as protection against the eerie emotion she seemed to feel. "Oh, he was sad, that one! I was crying, I tell you! His people were massacred by the whites, and all their land was taken."

I wanted to listen to the tape to get a complete picture of all that occurred, but now I was exhausted. I did not get up, did not move, and scarcely found the voice to ask our baba how she knew whites had done that to the spirit?

"I *know!* It is the same with every sangoma when it comes to spirits, and it will be the same with you. There are things we know without being told." She was speaking of *inhloko,* the sangoma's insight or psychic ability. As if using this now, she guessed my thoughts, and said, "You know it was a spirit who just came to you now. You *know.* Your head may want to play the mule, but deep inside, you know."

I wanted to believe but was too overwhelmed to attempt such a leap. A tremendous sadness still weighed me down. "Oh, Sam, my friend," I said, seeing him beside me in the faint candlelight coming from the Indumba. He stared at me with concern. I loved him then for that concern. "I'm tired. I think I want to sleep right here."

"Fetch his blanket!" ordered Gogo Ndwandwe. "It's the lidloti talking, saying it wants to sleep there in front of the Indumba."

Sam departed for my room. MaZu and LaShonge knelt a short distance away, looking at our instructor and at me. Gogo Ndwandwe said with affection in her voice, "Good night, Sibolomhlope."

I looked up at her, wondering what this new word was.

"A sangoma takes the name of his most powerful lidloti, and White Feather is a powerful spirit. He was a medicine man, as you will be. In SiSwati, White Feather is 'Sibolomhlope.' Say it."

I did. Gogo Ndwandwe had MaZu and LaShonge repeat it. She told them from that moment forward I would be known and addressed by this name.

They left me, and Sam returned with the blanket. I thanked him and lay down. I was too tired to feel discomfort from the hard, compacted earth. Perhaps in the morning I would tell myself something different, but at least for now I did believe that I had been visited by a spirit from beyond the grave. He had spoken to us, he had plans for me. As I lay looking up, the sky against which the stars were set looked pale, more gray than black. It seemed as if space stood revealed as an opaque curtain that obscured an unknown realm that was full of light, brilliant. But at that moment I could see the unknown shining faintly through.

▲ ▲ ▲ ▲

In the morning, doubts did return. Sleep, daylight, the passage of time all added new perspective to the incredible occurrence of the previous night. *Was* it incredible? Socrates believed in reincarnation: "The soul, being immortal, and being born again many times, and having seen all things that exist, has knowledge of them all." Education to him was no more than remembering: "For all enquiry and all learning is but recollection." But I was learning that lidlotis were not reincarnated souls but separate individuals who attached themselves to a sangoma so he or she might learn through the spirit's recollection about medicines and curative techniques. In my religion, St. Augustine also believed the human mind possessed *a priori* knowledge, the "seminal reason" of the immortal soul: "For I can run through all the organs of sense, which are the body's gateway to the mind, but I cannot find any by which some facts could have entered." He might have been describing my puzzlement following a lidloti appearance.

So which was it? Was White Feather, whose name I now bore, real or merely my subconscious's imaginative response to the stimulus of the drums? Gogo Ndwandwe was right: what I felt, which was that he was real, was different from what I thought, which was that he was illusionary. It was a difficult time for me. If I was acting out some neurotic need in the Indumba, then I wanted to flee that place, get as far away as I could as fast as I could, because never in my life had I exhibited such behavior and it was frightening to think I might be insane. Why should I come here to crack up when I was perfectly normal back in the U.S.?

Everyone at this homestead insisted that all people undergoing kutfwasa shouted and saw things, and my only delusion was my inability to understand that the spirits emerging from me were real. But I needed more than their confidence. What proof did I have that lidlotis existed?

As if to address the question, and noting my depression the morning following White Feather's appearance, Gogo Ndwandwe signaled to me from where she sat beneath a spindly guava tree in the courtyard, a tree that had been bent over nearly parallel to the ground from the weight of chickens that roosted in it at night. She pointed to a pile of medicinal herbs drying in the sun. "Bring me that root, Lusiba," she said, using the diminutive of my new name, Sibolomhlope. I took a stringy red root that seemed to be prominent in the pile and returned to her with it.

Gogo Ndwandwe smiled at me knowingly. "I was thinking of this root, but I did not tell you. There were many roots in the pile. How did you know?"

I felt my face flush. "I didn't know."

"Yes," she insisted. "You did. You ask for proof that the lidlotis are real. Here is your proof." She brandished the root in the air before me. "They allow you to see! It is not important what they do or say when they come out from under the shayelwa sheet. Your lidloti last night, he tired me! I want them to come out, greet us, and go away. When the time comes that you can look at the bones and see that the total stranger who comes to you has an ulcer or his wife is cheating on him, *then* you will know the lidlotis are with you."

"When will that be?" I asked.

"It has already started! MaZu is still having you choose among her bones, and she says you are clever to pick out the right ones."

I shook my head, "You know, when I came here I thought I came alone. But I didn't. All the people back home are with me, I keep thinking about them, and I feel a need to justify to them this thing I'm doing."

"*Hawu!* You live your life through other people? What does Sibolomhlope want?"

"Me?" I grinned at the thought. "I want a spirit to come out and give me his Social Security number and who won the '37 World Series, and speak Russian, play the trombone, do trigonometry and all the things I can't do. Then I'd believe."

Gogo Ndwandwe waved her hand impatiently. "Ah, the mental doctors would just find an excuse for that too! You can't find your lidlotis that way. You never will. I am telling you: the proof of the lidlotis is in the bones!"

That afternoon, her words seemed prophetic. Each day before sunset when we danced I was noticing a change. I was becoming less self-conscious and I was withdrawing more into the passive state I knew from sitting under the sheet, while my body continued to function seemingly on its own. During the afternoon dance sessions, the people of the homestead hid things, and we kutfwasa students tested our ability to see by ritualistically drawing out these things *(kukhokha)*. This was practice for the time we would be drawing out the hidden ailments of patients by studying the bones.

At first I simply squatted where we were dancing when MaZu and LaShonge went off to retrieve hidden objects. But the day after White Feather's emergence, when the homestead was talking of the powerful new spirit, a school teacher named Mamsie, a short and quick-tempered woman who lived with her small children there, called me over. "Lusiba!"

I went to her and knelt down. Immediately, other people gathered around. She declared, "I am hiding something!"

I answered her in SiSwati, the language in which the test was performed, and with my limited but growing vocabulary I followed the ritualized formula: I told Mamsie she was hiding something from the realm of men. Mamsie gave the ritualized reply, "*Sevuma!*" (We agree!") I told her the thing was made of metal, that it was money. What made me think this? It seemed a logical possibility: I had often seen coins hidden for the others.

"Sevuma!" Mamsie, joined by the onlookers, happily agreed to each statement of mine. I then told her it was a twenty-cent coin. I said this with the odd sensation that I was not guessing but somehow seemed to know the coin was a twenty-cent piece.

"Sevuma! Sevuma!"

Where was she hiding it? They would want to know. I told her that it was close by. "Sevuma! Sevuma!" That it was on her person. "Sevuma! Sevuma!" And then I took a wild plunge. I smiled and told her she was sitting on it.

"Sevuma! Sevuma!" Mamsie leapt to her feet, the half-dozen spectators exclaimed with delight, and the women ululated. "Take it!" Mamsie shouted. There on the bench was a twenty-cent piece. I took it and returned to the drums, which the girls were beating while singing the song that celebrated a student's success: *"Hamba, khokhe, mgoma, unemanga . . .!"* Ritual required that I drop the discovered object before the drums and thank the lidlotis. I did so with the words I had memorized. It was fun.

After MaZu, LaShonge, and I had finished dancing, Mamsie came up to me. "So, you can see now!"

I smiled at her. "I was guessing." I could not take credit for a psychic power I could not admit possessing. How had I known the location of the coin? I couldn't say.

"You were 'guessing'!" Mamsie repeated ironically. "Ah, your lidlotis must be strong if they can work even through your hard head!"

Gogo Ndwandwe was less pleased by my performance than I would have thought. "You must not smile, Lusiba! People will think that you're playing!" I promised to observe the dignity of a sangoma's rituals in the future.

So back and forth I went, like a ship listing from port to starboard, reluctant to believe, unable to disbelieve. And when the drums brought a new set of visions later in the week, I could only wonder, what now?

The nightly running zebras gave way to what seemed old newsreel footage brought to life. Streetcars and boxy automobiles from the 1920s appeared before granite facades of some city's downtown. The men wore straw hats, and the women flappers' dresses.

Now it was the forties. An airport. People ascended a ramp to a silver-skinned D-6. Quick images: an office, a black rotary telephone, an old manual typewriter. Ceiling fans whirled. A dictaphone with wax cylinders . . .

Nothing further came, and the next day I had little time to think about it: my studies had progressed and I was helping with the patients' treatments. Now Gogo Ndwandwe handed me a red rubber bulb-shaped syringe and some medicinal powders to mix, and asked me to administer an enema. I was grimly determined to complete the assignment, made more difficult because the patient was mentally disturbed. Fanukwente was a dark, rail-thin young man who never spoke. His clothes were filthy: Chaplinesque baggy pants, a frayed ribbed sweater, and a too-large woolen cap beneath which coal-black eyes stared out angrily, full of paranoia. Only by offering him some newspapers he liked to shred into piles at his feet could I convince Fanukwente to go to the bathing stall. Once we got there, he lay down on his stomach and lowered his trousers. But he would not cooperate further and clenched his buttocks tightly against the syringe. All the other sangomas had failed to treat Fanukwente, and I wondered why Gogo Ndwandwe thought I could succeed.

When I told her of my failure, she sighed, "Oh, he is stubborn, that one! I thought he'd go with you because you're his friend. You give him food and newspapers. Go, work on your inhloko with MaZu."

I spent an hour sharpening my insight by choosing from MaZu's bones, then wrote a letter of thanks to my brother Tom. I had asked him to locate a tartan of the MacDonald clan without telling him of the alleged ancestral spirit who wanted it. My brother, a geologist for an oil company, was a bit of an adventurer himself, and liked the mystery that shrouded my stay here. He quickly located the fabric at a Chicago store that specialized in Scotch tartans. Gogo Ndwandwe instructed me to go to the lidloti pole at night and present the offering to John MacDonald for his approval.

I wrote to family and friends regularly, letters full of scenic descriptions but no details of kutfwasa. I did not know if I'd be violating taboos by mentioning our rituals to outsiders, and I did not know how such things would be received by those I had left behind. What my friends learned instead was that banana trees in Swaziland grew small but tasty fruit, it was hot here but not insufferable, the kids took to me and grabbed my fingers whenever I appeared so I walked along with three youngsters hanging on one hand and two on the other, I was in very good health and happy, and what I missed most as an erstwhile news junkie was the American media.

My friends wrote back with news that the Ayatollah Khomeini had ordered a hit on Salman Rushdie, the *Exxon Valdez* had dumped history's largest oil slick on Alaska, and Barbara Bush had kicked the President out of bed so she could sleep with the ailing White House dog. They wondered why I missed the news media.

Within days of the new visions of city and office life in the 1920s, 1930s and 1940s, a new lidloti appeared. "A rich Englishman," MaZu reported, although to the people of the homestead anyone who spoke English was British. I was surprised at how little I remembered, no words and very little sensation. The spirit coughed a lot, MaZu said, and when I came to in a kneeling position before the drums, I had the sore throat to prove it.

As usual, Sam had been present. Sam liked the Indumba, for he had grown up around sangomas in a country homestead where Gogo Ndwandwe had gone to do her kutfwasa twenty years earlier.

But my friend had failed to press the record button on the tape machine, and I found a blank cassette. I felt a panic: had I lost this spirit completely? White Feather had come back a second time to dance. Gogo Ndwandwe told us we could always address an ancestral spirit at the lidloti pole and make requests. I would ask this new one to return.

Sam surprised me by saying, "Your lidloti said his name: Call Me Harry."

"He told you to call him Harry?"

Sam spoke slowly, as if each word was gravely important. "No, I asked him his name. He said, 'Call Me Harry.' That is his name, Call Me Harry."

"I see." Sam held out a piece of torn paper on which some words, almost illegible, were scribbled.

"He wrote this."

"What?" I quickly took the paper. "The spirit *wrote* this?"

Sam nodded. "Yes. He asked for paper and a pen."

I read it once, twice. Sam saw my expression, and he asked with concern, "What is it, Mr. Sibolomhlope?"

I shook my head, and read aloud. "'*The King and Queen will eat thereof, and Noblemen besides.*'"

Sam looked worried. "It sounds old."

"It is," I replied. For I knew this verse. "It's from America, the 1920s."

I slowly lowered the paper and looked far away, trying to decipher the puzzle. "This is ad copy," I told Sam. "For Jell-O."

four

Advertisements from the Spirit World

N THE BOTTOM of the paper he left behind, the new lidloti had written his name in quotation marks—"Harry"—as if it were an assumed name. I surmised what I could from what little Sam told me and what I remembered of the visions that preceded his appearance: "Harry" was a middle-aged American who worked in a city, most likely New York or Chicago, where the major advertising agencies were headquartered in his day, although he might have worked in the advertising department of a company like General Foods, the manufacturer of Jell-O. His professional life seemed to span the decades of the twenties through the forties, and like all Americans he was fascinated by the technology of his time: automobiles, skyscrapers, airplanes.

For more I'd have to wait for the spirit's return, or, as my inner skeptic would say, more make-believe. I was beginning to resent that sarcastic inner voice, necessary though it was to keep me grounded in reality. My challenge was to find if there was more to reality than the skeptic knew.

To facilitate the arrival of my lidlotis and keep them with me always, Gogo Ndwandwe fetched a special medicine she kept locked in her room and poured some of the powder into small cloth sacks less than an inch in diameter. I was to wear these always, literally for the rest of my life if I became a sangoma. MaZu taught me how to sew a latticework of string over each sack and cover these with a colorful line pattern of tiny white, red, and black ceramic beads. We centered the decorated sacks along strings of larger red and white beads to make necklaces. MaZu had a vision in which she saw me wear a long string of white beads draped over one shoulder in the sangoma style, and we made one of these with beads I bought at a general store in the neighborhood. Finally, my waist was encircled by two strings of black glass beads as small as caviar eggs. They were so light and tiny I soon forgot I was wearing them.

My hair proved a problem. No white person had undergone kutfwasa before, and it was discovered that my straight brown hair could not be braided into the sangoma's *siyendle* hairstyle, which clung to the head like an inverted bowl and shone from a mixture of red ocher and animal fat. After much discussion among Gogo Ndwandwe and my fellow students, it was agreed that I would wear a string wig on ceremonial occasions like old Gogo Mabusa, the elderly sangoma who after years of wearing the siyendle gave it up because she was tired of ocher stains on her clothing. Gogo Ndwandwe's cheerful and bright-eyed adult daughter Ncane, who would visit from time to time, set to work knitting a wig for me. She was larger than her thin mother and spoke English with the same lovely lilt that made the language so musical coming from a Swazi mouth. Gogo Ndwandwe's cackling, nasal voice was a noisy exception.

Finally, my jeans and shorts were replaced by two calf-length pieces of patterned cloth tied one on top of the other around my waist on the right side, exposing my right leg when I walked. A hunter in the countryside sewed brown fur loinskins for me from an impala buck. I tied these over the cloths, and I was now attired like a traditional Swazi male with a sangoma's accessories. When I presented myself to the people of the homestead they were pleased, and said I looked surprisingly credible for a non-Swazi. "The other whites who try to wear our things look like they are just playing," noted Sam solemnly. I thought perhaps this was because those others were doing it as a lark. But I was dressing this way because I was required to so as a kutfwasa student. For me it wasn't an affectation but part of my work.

I quickly grew used to the comfortable and light outfit, which was welcome in the warm weather. I was in good shape and did not mind having so much of my body exposed. Because MaZu, LaShonge, and I always danced barefoot, I found it convenient to go around the homestead without shoes. I wore sandals, however, when I ventured for the first time in my sangoma attire to the town of Manzini, fifteen minutes away by bus. The people were surprised, but they loved it. They pointed, shouted, and waved at me in the streets, in shops, from passing cars. A group of male laborers in blue overalls packed tightly together on the flat bed of a truck nearly fell out from laughing so hard. But it was appreciative laughter, not mocking, and feeling as self-conscious as I did this first time out, I could tell the difference. Men and women interrupted their conversations, smiled broadly, and greeted me, for Gogo Ndwandwe had seen to it that I was dressed not only properly but with considerable style. A black leather warrior's belt encircled my waist, and from it dangled a leather-capped, polished bull horn filled with snuff for symbolic offerings to the lidlotis. My right hand held a long fighting stick with a head carved like a claw, called a *lingedla*. Some strangers stopped before me, bowed low, and respectfully said the sangoma greeting, "Thogoza!" It felt like a triumph to be addressed this way, because they were accepting my kutfwasa and wishing me luck.

Gogo Ndwandwe, meanwhile, was assembling my own set of divination bones from extra pieces of her collection. She told me to present each piece to the lidlotis at the pole at night before I used them. Visiting sangomas tossed some of their own bones my way, which was customary to help a student build his set. This was done also by the first male sangoma I had seen, a handsome and impressively built man with a proud, regal profile and brown eyes like polished marble. He gave me his name in a gruff, businesslike voice, but as he spoke he looked straight through me, less interested in me it seemed than in assessing the spirits he saw within me.

My set of bones came together, each piece having its own meaning. Some represented living individuals and their relationship to a prospective patient: parent, child, grandparent, employer, clergyman, government official. Others represented spirits. Some bones indicated parts of the body where sickness might reside. A coin stood for the patient's financial condition. A lion's toe bone represented the presence of a lidloti and the rare possibility that the patient was a candidate for kutfwasa. To symbolize a homestead, I needed a hard, square scale from a crocodile's hide. I got it from one of the itinerant traders who arrived from Mozambique to sell starfish and other sea life used in medicines.

"The proof of the lidlotis is in the bones," Gogo Ndwandwe had told me. Every day I sat in on MaZu's divination sessions in which she read the bones and watched the visiting sangomas do the same. Without exception I was impressed, for as my knowledge of the SiSwati language grew I was able to follow the sessions more carefully, and I observed the sangomas telling strangers whom they had never seen before not only their ailments but secrets from their personal lives. MaZu told a woman, accurately, that she suffered from difficulties in her lower back. This woman's bones also showed that she was being troubled by a rival at work. Elderly Gogo Mabusa told a man in detail of his impotency before prescribing a cure. Gogo Ndwandwe described for a young man an auto accident he had been in but had survived. MaZu told a woman she felt weak from dizzy spells, had nightmares, and, as an aside, she should be advised that the girl doing her housecleaning was stealing soap from the pantry! The patients were always impressed and pleased by these reports. I was amazed, and felt the presence of a mysterious power that defied any conventional explanation I could give.

But by now my life was anything but conventional, and new explanations seemed increasingly more plausible, especially as evidence of psychic power in the Indumba accrued day after day. I suspected that acceptance would ultimately come to me when I, too, was able to tap into this power. There were indications already. Someone would hide something for me as Mamsie had hidden the coin, and I'd find it somehow. Prince Vovo had a girl hide a banknote. Half in a trance from the drums that beat when we danced, I located it on the dirt floor of one of the huts. This pleased the prince greatly; he praised me to the skies and said his decision to allow me to undergo kutfwasa at his homestead was vindicated.

And so, my defenses began to weaken, and as the drums pounded me into semi-consciousness while I sat beneath the sheet each night, my visions arrived with ever greater impact:

A memory, but one not my own: rocky hills where rows of olive trees grew. Puffs of white clouds in a sky of deep, Mediterranean blue. A stony villa that seemed Italian. I felt strongly the presence of someone I used to know, someone I loved very much.

My body trembled beneath the sheet, and Sam knew what to do. This time he pressed the record button accurately on the machine. Within myself, I was full of wonder, for at that moment I again knew the warmth I felt as a child when I was enveloped in the ample arms of my Italian-American grandmother. If my face muscles had not been flaccid and no longer controlled by my will, I would have grinned. For I felt her spirit arriving, the woman who left Italy at the turn of the century, passed through Ellis Island, and settled in Republic, Pennsylvania; my mother's mother: grandma.

She didn't use my body to jump, shout, sing or dance. She simply pulled down the sheet, folded her arms, and patiently waited for the drums to fall silent. Until they did, she calmly nodded her head.

The people saw at once that a woman had come to them. A visiting English-speaking male sangoma knelt beside her. "Please, good lady, tell us who you are." The spirit had nothing to say beyond a quietly uttered statement, "Tell Jimmy that his grandma is with him. I only want that he should be good."

She had no reason to stay. Not for her to tell her life's story, or to linger in that strange place. She lowered her head and quietly left.

The drums picked up once more, and I emerged in the throes of the most wonderful nostalgic feeling. Had it really been my grandmother? Sam, smiling, confirmed that it had. He told me what happened from his vantage point and gave me the cassette player to listen to.

I went outside, where the stars were bright overhead. There was no telephone at the homestead, I could not call home, and I had felt the distance keenly. My senses could not accept that when it was day here it was the middle of the night there and vice versa, and that here the hot, green summer was illuminated by terrific lightning storms and dazzling moons while back home winter was in its frigid, dreary depths. But now it felt as if I had just made a connection with home, that my mother's prayers for my grandmother's guidance in my life had been fulfilled, and that MaZu had been right when she read the bones on my first trip here and said my grandmother was with me.

I had loved my grandmother. With her husband she had opened a movie theater, the Princess, back in 1915, converted it to sound in 1927, gave away dishes to her Depression-era customers during the thirties, and during the forties offered my mother her first job selling tickets in the faux marble booth in front beneath the neon marquee. Whether what had just occurred had been a lidloti's visit or a cruel illusion, I felt happy with the memories it brought. At the lidloti pole I addressed my grandmother, thanked her for being with me, and passed on the love of her living relatives.

▲ ▲ ▲ ▲

The next day Gogo Ndwandwe sat in the cab of a pickup truck alongside the driver, an herbalist, and MaZu, LaShonge, two young men from the neighborhood, and I climbed into the flat bed in back for a long trip to dig medicinal plants. It was my first trip into the undeveloped country-side, a timeless African veld of high grass, flat-topped umbrella trees, and mud huts squatting beneath a blue dome of sky.

Our first stop was at the homestead of the area's chief. All land in Swaziland was considered "king's land," to be distributed by local chiefs in the king's name to families for setting up their homesteads, where the soil was tilled and cattle raised. Most of the land in town, as well as a few farms left over from the British occupation, was privately owned. Because we sought to dig roots on king's land, we needed the chief's permission.

We arrived at a collection of newly thatched grass huts widely separated by courtyards of compacted earth, where the people who greeted us wore traditional Swazi attire. The boys were naked but for small strips of animal hide dangling front and rear from waist strings, and toddlers wore nothing but strings of beads around their middles. When MaZu, LaShonge, and I sat down against a hut's mud wall, it was obvious from the apprehensive way the youngest children looked at me that they had never seen a white person before. Along with my loinskins and traditional clothes, I wore a safari shirt, and from a pocket I withdrew a handful of wrapped candies. I held these out, and an older boy with a large head and two missing front teeth was bold enough to come forward and take them. He returned to his companions, and the children continued to stare wide-eyed at me as they sucked on their sweets, holding onto the cellophane wrappers as if to something precious. Finally the one who had taken the candy approached me and reached out his hand to feel my hair. I let him, and this emboldened the others to come over and touch me. I laughed beneath the swarm of small, curious hands feeling my hair, face, and arms, and my smile encouraged them to relax and chatter merrily away.

They ran off to show their mothers their candy treasures. On the other side of the courtyard I could glimpse the chief seated before a reed screen with a group of men who might have been his counselors. Gogo Ndwandwe had gone to petition him there. A woman of the homestead came to thank me for the children's candy, and she presented us with a round black earthenware pot filled to its circular opening on top with a milky yellow liquid. *"Maganu!"* LaShonge exclaimed with joy. While we waited for our teacher's return, we passed the pot between us and sampled the seasonal drink made from fermented fruit found only in this low, dry area.

Gogo Ndwandwe came back and told us the chief had given his permission for our dig. She then said to me, "He wants to see you."

"Me?" I asked in surprise. Gogo Ndwandwe did not know what the chief wanted with me, and I was a little nervous when I stood and walked over to where the chief and his council were having their palaver.

I had never met a Swazi chief before, and, determined to make a good impression, I carried myself with what I hoped was somber dignity. It did not help that the potently alcoholic maganu drink had given me a buzz. The men, seated on the ground in a semicircle around their chief, regarded me gravely as I approached and squatted down before them.

I nodded my head and greeted them, *"Sanibonani, madoda."* They greeted me with a single low voice that sounded like an earth tremor. The chief was a large man, tall and strong in appearance, with proud, unblinking eyes. The men appeared middle-aged or older. Some wore beards, beaded necklaces, and togalike cloths over their upper bodies. Others were bare chested, exposing raised black scars from ancient wounds. Their fighting sticks lay in the dirt at their sides. As they scrutinized me, this white stranger in their traditional clothing, I felt that time stood still in this place.

The chief broke the silence, and addressed me slowly in English, "You stay at the Kwaluseni place of Prince Vovo?"

"Yes, *sikhulu,*" I replied respectfully, using the SiSwati word for chief.

"And you are from America?" I said that I was. He did not ask my name but seemed to want information of some sort.

"Then you can tell me something?"

"I will do my best, sikhulu."

I waited a little apprehensively while he gave me a hard look and rubbed his prominent chin, as if he were searching for some sign of weakness in me. The other men's gazes were just as severe.

"Is it true that this Michael Jackson has never slept with a woman?"

I must have blinked several times before finding the presence of mind to reply. I said that I did not know Michael Jackson personally, but it was commonly thought that he had never had sex with a woman. The chief listened attentively and then spoke harshly to the man next to him. This was overheard by the others, and they all spoke at once in a tone that mixed disbelief, outrage, and scorn. I felt compelled to add that we all liked Jackson's music, but this did not interest the chief and his council, only the idea of a thirty-one-year-old black man who was still a virgin. I heard the word *"Togoloshi"* mentioned, as well as the names of other evil spirits considered responsible for sexual dysfunction.

I was dismissed by the chief and returned to find our group back in the pickup truck. We drove along grassy trails and through shallow, rocky streams, stopping when we located a plant to dig. The work was hard, but I was fit from living a physical life in which even the simplest task was a chore. At Prince Vovo's homestead, bathing and washing clothes required carrying water in a ten-gallon plastic container from the outdoor tap to the bathing area. Until the mud and wood latrine was finished, going to the bathroom meant a round trip of a quarter mile to a neighbor's latrine. I knew this hike: I often had a runny stomach from the local water when I was unable to boil it.

As we dug that day, I was bothered by a scratch on my foot that had become infected from the germs that proliferated in the hot, humid weather. I limped along, but we had a tireless new worker to help us: Sam's good-natured younger brother, twenty-year-old Jabulani. Like Sam, Jabulani was short and strong, with a stockier, more muscular build that came from amateur boxing. He worked with his T-shirt rolled up to his chest, as if his hard, square abdominal muscles were solar cells collecting sunshine to energize his bright smile. Swazis were garrulous among themselves and reticent with strangers, but once they felt comfortable with you, they could bestow a warm and dazzling smile unequaled anywhere else, a smile like a benediction.

Jabulani was slightly cross-eyed, and when he looked at me he bobbed and weaved his head as if he were sparring, looking for an opening. He spoke English the way I spoke SiSwati, slowly, considering each word before it came out. The moment we became friends was when we were resting after dragging a large root out of the earth and he answered a question I had been wondering about since my arrival in Swaziland.

"Jabulani, why do Swazi men have large slits in their earlobes?"

He smiled broadly and said, "You want to know about that? It is a good story! You see, we had this king, King Sobhuza, and he was very old. He spoke deep Swazi, like only the elders remember. But he used those words. He went on the radio. All the people heard. He said the Swazis must listen to each other. He said we must 'open our ears.' Only he used a word that has two meanings, and the one most people know means to *cut* open your ears. Hey, that very night the people start to cut their ears! They want to be good Swazis. They want to make their king happy. The sangomas are making lots of money because they can cut and they've got medicines. The next day, I am with my friends. Our parents say, 'Go over that hill. There is someone who will give you all the peanuts you can eat!' So we go over that hill. There were people who are cutting the kids' ears. And the kids are sent out the other way so they don't tell the other kids. They cut my ears, too. But there wasn't any peanuts. Only blood!"

Jabulani laughed, and then said he had many questions for me. But he had no chance to ask for when we returned to work, the wound on my foot burst open in an eyesore of blood and pus, and I had to retire. My hand was also bleeding from cuts that I had received while slashing through some thistles with a machete. But the cruelest pain awaited me that evening. Someone left a cinderblock in the dark, filthy garage I passed through to get to my room. I picked it up, and as I lugged it outside my foot in its sandal struck another unseen cinderblock, splitting open the nail of the large toe. When I made it to the room and lit the kerosine lamp to examine my bloody, mangled toe, pain throbbed out, timed to every heartbeat. As I cleaned and wrapped the toe, I was glad it wasn't broken.

But by this point I had more otherworldly concerns than these accidents, such as if and when the "Harry" lidloti would reappear. Sam asked when he'd be back. "I liked Call Me Harry!" I could not will a spirit to return, and settled for petitioning the lidlotis when MaZu, LaShonge, and I addressed them at night while kneeling beneath our red sheets at the lidloti pole in the field.

Nearly a month had passed since Harry's appearance when, in late February, Sam saw the signs of an imminent lidloti arrival during an evening shayelwa session in the Indumba. My body shook as if electrified by the pounding drums while I sat beneath the white sheet. Sam turned on the recorder to document what would turn out to be my most unusual spiritual encounter yet. I would play the tape many times, for while I remembered some of the things that happened, it was as if I were dreaming, listening from inside myself, viewing little and dependent upon others' accounts. Also, the spirits kept my eyes mostly closed and seemed themselves unable to see. Sam's enthusiasm over Harry proved understandable; this lidloti could charm anyone.

Violent coughing erupted from my throat, and my body tossed off the sheet as if it was suffocating within it. The coughing fit passed, and the drums fell silent.

"Sam? Is that you, boy?"

Sam recognized the voice with its gruff but genial American accent. His expression lit up, and he answered with a smile, "Hello, Call Me Harry!"

The lidloti chuckled. Another coughing fit seized him, and when it passed, he asked, "Are you still smoking, Sam?"

"No."

"Don't lie to me. And you just stop it. That's how I died. Lung cancer. I was a three-pack-a-day man. I might still be alive today, an old fossil in my nineties but at least seeing my grandchildren in person instead of long-distance. Which reminds me, where is this Prince Vovo?"

"The prince?" *Sam said, surprised.* "He is not here."

"Better call him." *Sam gave an order to a child, who ran out. The people of the Indumba waited respectfully in silence as they did whenever a spirit emerged, but those who understood English wondered what the lidloti could want with the prince. As usual, Vovo was enjoying a tin of home-brewed beer outside.*

"Let me warn you away from the cigarettes. I was hooked, and not just because I was plugging the client's product. I was one of the boys who pulled LS/MFT out of the alphabet. That's 'Lucky Strike Means Fine Tobacco' to you, Sam. I preferred Camels, unfiltered . . ."

There was humor in the voice even when it was grave, a typically American note of optimism. Sam announced, "The prince is here."

Sam would later say he watched the interview that followed closely so he could report everything to me. Able to move without seeing, the lidloti possessing my body turned toward where Prince Vovo sat wearing a pleasant, vague smile.

"How do you do, Your Highness?"

Vovo nodded his head cordially. "How do you do? I see you are not James."

"And he's not me, prince. You don't mind if I call you prince, do you?"

"No-o," Vovo drawled. "When did you pass away, my friend?"

"During the fifties, when I was in my late fifties. You might say I killed myself."

"No!"

"From smoking. And I died with blood on my hands, just the same as the blood I had in my lungs, because I was plugging those things for three decades. That's why I hooked up with James, if you want to know, to make amends when he becomes a healer, if he does. I still keep an eye on the place where I used to work, saw James pass through years ago, saw what he'd become. He can help you, prince."

"Help me?" Vovo said, confused.

"Oh, yes. You're in the same fix as I was. Only you've got a different poison. Shall we take a look?"

I was aware of my body in motion. I was conscious of my arms rising and encircling the prince, but felt no physical sensation.

Vovo, who had been drinking, was slow to react when the spirit approached on its knees, went behind him and took hold of his torso. The prince stammered in polite confusion, "It-it-it's all right."

"Well, your liver is peeling away like an onion. Kidney's going. Bile is building up, prince, which can lead to gout, and will. I won't presume to touch the royal head, but I can tell you the brain cells are falling away like snowflakes. They can't be replaced, you know."

The lidloti returned to the room's center. Sam noted that Vovo's expression was still vague, but he continued to smile. The spirit sighed, "That's a nasty check-up, Your Highness. What can we do about it?"

"Why, we can do nothing." Piously, the prince added, "It is all in God's hands."

"He helps those who help themselves. Believe me."

"Oh, I do. I do!"

"James would like to help you help yourself, prince. You see, he likes you."

"And I love him!"

"He's met a number of your brothers who pass this way. There are more princes in this country than vice-presidents in an American advertising agency! But you're different."

"Yes," Vovo nodded.

"There is a regalness to you. Of all your brothers, you are the most poetic. You have the most philosophical frame of mind."

"You are truly a spirit if you can see these things, for this was what my father, the late king, prized most in me."

"*Looking at you, James often feels he's in the presence of your father.*"

"*Oh, you can indeed see, thogoza!*" The prince clapped his hands together twice in homage to the spirit's sagacity.

"*But James is just like everyone else who loves you. He's frustrated by what you're doing to yourself. Your wives, your children, your associates, they're all worried.*"

"*Yes,*" Vovo sighed. "*Yes.*"

"*I do hope you see this, prince. Despite the disappointments it holds for us, life is a precious thing. That may sound like corn, but basic truths are simple. We get into trouble when we try to complicate them. Life is so precious even we dead ones cherish it. Guess that's why we keep hanging around! Please, consider what I'm saying.*"

"*Oh, I shall! I shall!*"

With a chuckle, Harry finished, "*Good. Let's run it up the flagpole and see who salutes.*"

"*Pa-ardon me?*"

"*Let's shoot it into space and see if it orbits!*"

"*Beg yours?*"

"*You know, give it a try!*"

"*Oh, yes, certainly!*"

"*Been nice talking to you, prince. I'm going, now.*"

"*Good-bye, thogoza. God bless.*"

The lidloti lowered his head where he knelt. Like a deflating balloon, my body sunk down until my face was close to the ground. My senses reawakened, my consciousness enlarged from the walnut-sized space it seemed to have occupied within my head, and I came back.

Seeing that I had returned, blinking dazedly in the candle-light, the people greeted me with the ritualistic hand clap.

"Call Me Harry was here!" Sam smiled.

"I know. My throat's sore from his cough." The prince had departed into the night. I thanked MaZu, LaShonge, and the others for their efforts at bringing out the lidloti and I went outside feeling drained. I shook my head, smiling at a thought: ancestral spirits should be Vikings or Pharaohs, but an American advertising executive?

Prince Vovo had returned immediately to his drinking companions. He waved me over, beaming. When I arrived, he turned serious. "Your lidloti came. He spoke to me. It was not you speaking. He told me many things about myself, things nobody else knows. Tomorrow, I will be seeing the Queen Mother, and I will report this remarkable occurrence to her."

I was tired but could not attempt sleep until I played back the tape. When I did I was still unable to sleep, for the prince had said nothing to me about the conversation between himself and the spirit on the subject of his drinking. Swaziland had a reputation for being a hard-drinking country, and I did not wish to use American standards of sobriety to judge another culture. But it was clear to me, to his wife Gogo Ndwandwe, and everyone else who cared about the prince that his drinking was affecting his health. He ate little, and while staying here at the smallest of his three homesteads, he sat beside the brewing shack meeting with men and discussing matters over an omnipresent tin of milky brown beer. He'd do this from sun-up, when his eyes were egg-yolk yellow threaded with crimson veins, to late at night, when they were dark amber. The prince was never less than cordial to me, a warm and genial man I had come to like and depend on for his good humor. Whether Harry existed or not, if I could help the prince, I wanted to.

Gogo Ndwandwe was not encouraging. There was a cure for drinking, she said, and she had tried to get her husband to consider it. But he never felt the need. "He doesn't think he has a problem, Lusiba!" she said to me in frustration.

When I saw the prince the next day, I raised the subject gingerly. No, Vovo said, he didn't recall the lidloti mentioning any illness he might have. He admitted that perhaps he did indulge in the tjwala brew too much at times. It would have been unthinkable for me to use the word alcoholic, but the prince did so himself by denying that he was one. I listened sadly to an old refrain when he declared, "I can stop anytime. I have, many times!"

I was confused by what was expected of me. Had a lidloti given me an assignment to cure Prince Vovo? If so, I was failing without the patient's cooperation. Or, as it seemed on the tape, was it the prince's responsibility to seek treatment as the spirit had urged? Either way, I didn't know what to make of it, and I even wondered if this was some sort of test.

▲ ▲ ▲ ▲

I learned to beat the drums, a difficult task when we spent an hour to coax a lidloti from MaZu, LaShonge, or a visiting sangoma. But I was able to observe the transformation of these people I knew into seemingly different individuals, much as I must have looked when my body was said to be controlled by a spirit. One night big LaShonge, with her broad face, short hair, and rapid speech, turned into a lisping young man who announced he was of the Xhosa tribe though he spoke SiSwati. At the end of the ritual when LaShonge became her old self, she was amazed to have the spirit of a foreign tribesman within her. It was as exotic tó her as a Native American lidloti seemed to me. I envied LaShonge her conviction; she had no doubts about the authenticity of her lidlotis. I envied her knowledge of Swazi language and customs. I had a triple task: to become fluent in SiSwati, immerse myself in African tribal life, and go through the spiritual rebirth of kutfwasa. The harshness of the living conditions didn't help, but at least I still had a little money. In America, royalty checks continued to arrive, and a friend who was handling my financial affairs was able to send a few hundred dollars a month.

I continued to seek evidence of lidlotis in the divination rituals. As I sat watching, Gogo Ndwandwe's sensitive bones informed a woman that she had a pregnant daughter. The surprised woman went home to investigate and returned to say the lidlotis were telling the truth. MaZu told another woman her husband was cheating on her. This also proved correct. After another session, when old Gogo Mabusa mentioned in passing to a man that his ex-wife was hassling him and then went on to divine the reason he had come to see her (hemorrhoids), I followed the man out of the spirit house and asked him if he believed what he had just been told by the sangoma. He spoke English, and replied with some surprise, "Of course. She knew all about me. She said I was divorced. How could she know that if she never met me before?"

"Exactly," I said, feeling my usual bafflement. "Don't you think it could be a trick of some sort?"

"You tell me. Does she have a confederate?"

I shook my head in dismay. If only she had, I could yell "Fraud!" and stop torturing myself by trying to find a logical explanation for the sangomas' uncanny skills. But there hadn't been anyone to slip a note to Gogo Mabusa since she was illiterate; nor had anyone whispered in her ear. I had been with her in the Indumba from the moment the man had arrived to see her.

Then one afternoon, MaZu called me in and said her patient, a young woman, wanted my opinion about her ancestors. MaZu told me to cast down her set of bones and see if I could find which spirits were with the woman. It was a tense moment for me. Before I came to Africa I would have found a divination ritual bizarre and my participation ridiculous. But there I was, assigning to bones the names of members of the woman's family. I gathered them up in my cupped hands and recited an incantation to the spirits with MaZu accompanying me. I exhaled deeply, and threw the bones down on the mat. They fanned out, rattling, and lay still. I looked at the configurations, and the proximity of the bones representing family members to the bone I had assigned to the young woman and at one bone in particular that seemed to stand out.

"Your aunt. Your dead aunt. Her spirit is with you."

MaZu smiled at me and nodded her head. This was just what she had found.

What did it mean? What did the ongoing visions beneath the sheet mean? A week later I lost consciousness during the nightly ritual, and awoke to be told that a new lidloti had arrived that night and spoken a language nobody in the Indumba had understood. My loyal friend Sam had remembered to turn on the tape machine. I left the Indumba with the cassette in my hand and found a place to sit beneath the moon and listen.

I heard what sounded like Latin. And then: *"Tengo miedo."* It was Spanish. The spirit had said, "I am afraid," and at that moment I seemed to feel its emotion. I wondered what inspired its fear. In my naivete, I would have imagined a spirit would have already passed through its most fearful moment, the moment of its mortal death. I thought of the unhappy others: John MacDonald, White Feather, Harry. Even my grandmother had been subdued when she came to us. Regrets, unfinished business, a view of how the world had changed or obliterated what a spirit held dear, all these could make a return to the mortal realm painful.

And now this new lidloti was struggling. I knew Spanish and was able to translate the tape. Pausing to take long breaths, the spirit spoke for three minutes in a tremulous voice. Jotting with a pencil in the moonlight I wrote down his statement:

"I give you my name, which is Juan. I was a soldier. Now I farm the land. I have a wife. I have two sons and five daughters. We live near the pueblo. I hope to go to heaven. I cannot read or write. But I have my strength and my hands. I am sad. I have always felt some of this sadness in my heart. I do not know why. My family is good. The land is good when it is not dry. My children who lived are strong. They were all baptized at the church. I am not a coward, but I am afraid to look into the face of my God. Now it is light where I am. But there are shadows in this light. We are not without darkness, still. But we are closer to the light. I tell you this so you will know. You will find your song, and you will sing this song until you die."

The palm trees swayed in the night breeze and their black fronds covered and then revealed a spectacle of stars overhead. I watched the stars while considering what this new spirit had told me. I had always believed that the soul continued after death, but what this afterlife was nobody knew. Now this lidloti spoke of a luminous place that was removed from the half-dark, half-light of earthly existence and was closer to a divine realm of omnipotent light. But some shadows still clung to the lidlotis' world, and I wondered if one of the shadows that shaded their existence was a concern about the mortal lives they had left behind. And could one outlet for this concern be assistance to healers who eased the burden of the living?

I was emotionally drained as usual following an encounter with a spirit, and, depressed, I returned to my dreary room to lie down, close my eyes, and drift off not into sleep but into the bright colors of a vision:

I recognized the profile of a long, flat-topped mountain, terracotta in color. I had seen it often while living in Los Angeles: Mt. Cahuenga, where huge, unevenly spaced letters usually proclaimed "HOLLYWOOD." But there was no sign now, and at its base scrub fields appeared in place of freeways and buildings. I saw the familiar profile of the Verdugo Hills with snow-capped Mt. Baldy in the distance, but no urban centers in the foreground, just dry, pastel land. Vertical cliffs appeared about an ocean. I knew them well but did not see the Santa Monica Pier or the Pacific Coast Highway below them, only sparkling blue water and miles of flat, coastal marshes. I assumed these were Juan's recollections, and I was again looking back through time.

I awoke to a taste of dusty dryness in my mouth, and the sensation of heat from a harsh sun. I recalled unclear glimpses of an adobe structure and people about who were silent and still, as if seen in a tableau. Everything had been yellow and brown and very bright. Could I have passed this homestead in later years and picked up the spirit who continued to reside there?

"The pueblo," I murmured, the place he said he was from. My tired lips, chapped from the sun that day, moved again, "El Pueblo la Reina de los Angeles de Porcuncio." The town of the Queen of the Angels of the river Porcuncio, I thought, as I lost consciousness. The settlement he had been a part of, which would grow . . .

▲ ▲ ▲ ▲

In the morning my depression did not go away, and I knew its source: the time had come to commit. It was the end of February, three months into my kutfwasa, and I could no longer deny what I was feeling. When the pivotal moment had happened I could not say, but at some point the scales had tipped in favor of belief. I saw this now. I had vowed not to accept lidlotis without proof. Had Harry and now Juan simply been too real to consider imaginary? Had the daily accumulation of evidence showing the sangomas' psychic power, all the divination rituals I had witnessed in the Indumba, convinced me? I still had doubts, and I suspected I always would, but these doubts had diminished until they were secondary.

I felt weary and fearful, because I would have to break with my past and embrace an uncertain future. If I were to publicly accept lidlotis, then I would have to have the courage of my convictions. Could I find such courage in the face of skepticism and mockery, when people accused me of "going native," when people who had never been inside the Indumba declared its power superstition, and when they dusted off their conventional "psychological" explanations for all that occurs there?

Sangomas spoke among themselves about matters of the Indumba, but to outsiders they spoke only in general terms. I could see the wisdom of this, because I did not see how I could explain that there must have been within myself a germ of the sangoma's insight even before I began kutfwasa. Perhaps it had been there all my life. No amount of curiosity alone could have enabled me to endure the harshness of this new life and the difficulties that surely still awaited me. It was that unknown quality within all sangomas that I now recognized in myself. I hadn't been brainwashed into this discovery; the people here had left me alone to draw my own conclusions. And now I had, and I had to bear the consequences. And that responsibility seemed overwhelming.

As the day progressed, a depression such as I had never known gripped me. I sat in the shadow of a mud hut, my knees up and my back against the coarse wall. High white columns of cloud rose above the close green hills. One magnificent tower of cumulus seemed to rise up for miles. It appeared solid, as if sculpted from white marble. I stared at this giant, motionless column, impressed by its beauty. And then something happened. Perhaps the vertical shaft of cloud had risen too high. Slowly it began to melt. Its lofty top became a misty cap, and streams of vapor like tear tracks descended its sides.

Watching this happen, I felt a sadness swell within me. The melting cloud seemed myself. How beautiful it was, but how illusionary was its solid, powerful appearance. I felt as if I were watching the edifice of my life dissolve. My place in the world that had seemed so assured and my faith in the supremacy of my rational, technological culture—they were melting. And I, perhaps I had reached too high, into a supernatural realm

I was not prepared to enter. Westerners, my people, had rejected that realm long ago to pursue material interests and live in a world of science. It was hubris to try to reclaim it, and now the crash seemed upon me.

I felt that if I let them, tears would burst from my eyes. I was nothing but water inside. My instincts urged: go to the river.

The melting column was lost among other clouds that soon covered the sky. Without telling anyone where I was going, for I didn't trust myself to speak, I quickly left the homestead.

It was late afternoon, and a misty rain began to fall. I headed for a small river a mile away. The clouds thickened, and it grew dark quickly. I passed through a field of high grass that wet my loincloths, and when they got soggy I rolled them up to my hips. But I kept going, choking on emotion, with one thought in mind: to speak to *them*, to have it out with *them*.

I descended through a tangle of trees and vines and slid down the muddy riverbank to the water. Recent rains had swollen the stream to twice its size, and I entered a brown flow that rose to my hips and headed downstream toward a clearing where I could kneel down. The flooding left no shore; dense forest rose on either side, blocking the gray light. Branches burdened with wet leaves dropped into the water and brushed my face. Fist-sized stones were slippery underfoot, and fine raindrops pocked the stream as I waded forward, frightened by the fierceness of the depression that held me.

Ahead was a flat area nearly level with the water. Two large trees stood at each end with stony ground between them and a twenty-foot rise of thick vegetation behind. No living soul was within a half-mile of this place. But, I thought ruefully, it was not living souls I wanted to talk to.

I untied one of my long loincloths from my waist and pulled it over myself as I knelt low over the stony earth. I breathed with difficulty in my struggle to contain my emotions. I felt like I was having a nervous breakdown and was angered as well as frightened. When I clapped my cupped hands to summon the lidlotis, one word filled my head, and I shouted it out to the waters flowing before me: *"Why?"*

It seemed unbelievable to me: What was I doing here, in these African woods, by this little river, in the middle of nowhere? I plunged my hands into the earth beneath the stones, and they came back gritty and muddy. The rain was falling steadily now; my cloth clung wetly over me. It was growing cold, and I shivered. Aloud, I exclaimed, "And I'm kneeling in dirt! Talking to . . ."

Talking to whom? If I said their names out loud there would be no going back. I thought of the family and friends I had left behind, and hot tears began to flow down my cheeks. The commitment I was about to make would be a betrayal of them. Their attitude, and to a degree my attitude when I first arrived, was: Have your adventure, learn rare herbal cures and lost wisdoms, *but just don't believe any of it!* I had failed to keep the bargain. I had come to this river to be alone because I could no longer deny the powers that existed out there for me. And so I admitted, "Goddammit, I'm talking to *you!*

I was angry. I was angry at the price I was paying in time, money, and emotion: I hadn't cried during my entire adult life, and I felt ashamed. I was angry at the seeming indifference of these ancestral spirits to me. They were compassionate enough to help sangomas cure people; why hadn't they considered how difficult or inappropriate or absurd it was for a white American to undergo kutfwasa? Why didn't they ever show me their faces, and why didn't they condescend to address me or even acknowledge me when they emerged in the Indumba? Was I just a body to move and speak with?

I struck my fist hard on the ground. The sky was a murky twilight gray about a tangle of black branches. Rain fell loudly against the stream, stones, and leaves. Tears ran from my eyes and snot from my nose. I was cold and in such sick despair I lowered my head into my muddy hands.

"You got me into this," I said, steadying my voice. "All I ask is that you get me out of it alive."

I mourned the loss of my innocence, of the time when the unknown held no fear for me because, ostrich-like, I refused to believe the unknown existed. I seemed to know that what lay ahead for me now would be hard, very hard. I would be alone, and I would have to dig deeper into myself than I ever had before. Because I was committed now. No more equivocating or crying, I resolved, I was going to do it. I was going to see kutfwasa through.

And if these crazy spirits felt like finishing what they had started, I would become a sangoma.

five

Post-Mortal/Pre-Heaven

THE COMMITMENT I made at the river, when I acknowledged my fitful acceptance of the lidlotis, was the turning point of my kutfwasa. I was resolved to move ahead as quickly as I could. This was also Gogo Ndwandwe's plan. She had watched with alarm when I left the homestead in the rain that day. "You looked like you were going to go hang yourself, Lusiba!" she told me. She had sent out Sam, his brother Jabulani, and others to look for me, and when they came back to report I had vanished, she consulted her bones and saw I was somewhere along the river. "I was afraid the water spirits would take you. I prayed that your lidlotis would protect you. And they did! You could have drowned, Lusiba! You could have gotten sick. But you have strong lidlotis, they are happy you believe in them, and they want you to work, work, work!"

Our teacher was often upset with MaZu, who was known to break the celibacy rule. She had boyfriends and would sneak away to see them. MaZu was often sick as a result: "the lidlotis' punishment" Gogo Ndwandwe insisted. LaShonge, whose good humor and helpfulness made my stay easier, seemed incapable of enduring the harsh kutfwasa life without getting drunk at least once a week. Gogo Ndwandwe shouted at her in front of the entire homestead, "How can you read the bones if you can't even see them!" But still LaShonge sneaked away to the neighbors' beer shacks. As for me, I was known to be moody, a sure sign, Gogo Ndwandwe said, that I hadn't enough to do.

To reestablish discipline, our teacher told us we had to observe a neglected daily ritual no one had ever mentioned to me. Every morning, an hour and a half before sunrise, when the sky was still dark, MaZu, LaShonge, and I were to go to the river to address our spirits, wash in the water, and vomit with medicine. "It is obvious you have river spirits, Lusiba," she told me. "You knew to go there to talk to your lidlotis."

The next day MaZu, LaShonge, and I, accompanied by two young female kutfwasa students visiting the homestead to process medicines with us, woke in the pitch blackness of an overcast night and set out with our heads covered with white cloths. If anyone had been about at that hour they would have seen a spectral-looking procession singing softly and walking single file down a twisting dirt lane that led to the small stony river. A misty rain fell as we knelt along the water, clapped our hands in unison, and addressed the spirits with a murmured incantation. We disrobed and entered the stream to bathe ourselves in its water. Then we drank from the buckets we carried from the homestead and regurgitated the medicines they held.

It was so dark we saw only each other's silhouettes. The presence of four naked female bodies might have excited me if I hadn't concentrated fully on the ritual. I had gotten used to the sight of naked breasts in the Indumba. MaZu's were as large as udders, her daughter Doyenne's were firm and round like oranges, but the women's lack of self-consciousness robbed these body parts of sexuality. In my culture, women exposed their breasts as a sexual invitation. Here it was done for comfort, with no erogenous association. I still looked at the female sangomas who visited us, but it was interesting how much appeal was lost when disguise and mystery were absent.

We returned to the homestead just as a midnight-blue coloring in the eastern sky told of the dawn's imminence. Our voices cut through the stillness with a lovely, eerie song that lamented the loneliness of leaving home, family, and friends to do kutfwasa. Back at the Indumba, our spirits emerged, and we in their spell danced to greet the new day. No single lidloti with a recognizable personality possessed us at the dance time. Rather we entered a trance that was not passive but energetic, featuring howls and shouts, an insistent, groaning speaking voice, and an obliviousness to what was going on elsewhere. Day by day I was assuming more of these characteristics when I danced, no longer truly myself as my body swayed in place and my knees kicked up in unison with the other dancers. My mind again seemed deep within my body, looking out but seeing little. The lidlotis kept my eyes closed or reduced to slits.

One day in March, I was reminded of the price I could expect to pay as I was transformed through kutfwasa: I received a letter from my father. I had sent home pictures of myself in Swazi attire to test the reaction. It was swift. "If you come back to Winnetka like that," my father wrote, "I'll draw all the blinds and lock you in your room!" His use of the exclamation point at the end was intended to show his humor, but I clearly read his irritation and perhaps dismay. There was no reason why a conservative Midwestern Republican corporate man should feel any other way at the prospect of his eldest son becoming an African tribal healer, and I blamed myself for not speaking to him more about it before I left. But at that time I myself hadn't really believed it would happen. Now I saw I would have not only an internal conflict about what I was doing but also conflict with my family. It saddened me: if only I could share with them the magic of my discoveries!

▲ ▲ ▲ ▲

Some days, Gogo Ndwandwe, MaZu, LaShonge, and I worked from morning to night making medicines. Visiting sangomas would lend their knowledge, and even patients would help with the manual tasks. It was hard, dirty work. The roots and barks we dug were dried in the sun and kept in large canvas sacks piled in a mud shack Gogo Ndwandwe unlocked each morning. I lugged out the sacks and emptied out pieces of roots as small as peanuts and as large as footballs. Our teacher knew each piece by sight or taste. She plunged into the jumble, tossing out items for us to catch.

Seated on grass mats in the shade of low trees, we used machetes to cut the pieces into small bits we then fed into the round black mouth of an iron mortar. We crushed the roots into granules using heavy iron pestles up to three feet in length. Then we emptied the mortars into wood and wire sifters and shook these to extract even smaller granules. These were placed on the smooth flat top of a boulder and ground into powder with round stones. The whole operation, particularly the endless pounding of pestles into the mortar, gave the wrists, arms, shoulders, and back a good workout. Other roots were roasted on pieces of iron over the fire until we had charcoal that we'd pulverize with stones into a sooty black powder. While burning, the roots filled the air with hearty herbal aromas.

The work was done at a leisurely pace. The long afternoons passed with the women gossiping or giving me SiSwati language lessons. We collected all the roots into canvas sacks at day's end, returned them to the medicine shack, and at night in the Indumba we received the fruits of our labor. The various powders were mixed together into finished medicines, and these were distributed to those who worked to prepare them. We knelt in a circle with Gogo Ndwandwe beside a candle set on the floor. With a spoon, she ladled out the medicines to each of us until her large pile had vanished into our smaller ones. We used jars and cans as containers. By the end of kutfwasa each student would have a collection of medicines that would be the basis for his or her own sangoma practice.

I saw that there were two distinct types of medicines. The first I called "biological medicines": herbal remedies for physical ailments such as *spoliyane khotsa*, a powder licked off the palm as a headache remedy. The second I called "lidloti medicines." Other people might call them magic. Herbs were used to make these, too, but instead of curing conventional ailments like infertility, snake bite, and broken bones, they were concerned with an equally important part of a sangoma's practice: improving a patient's fortune and love life and protecting the patient from harm. The power of these medicines did not come from their herbal ingredients. Rather the herbs they contained were codes meant to communicate with the spiritual forces who did the work. The medicines were administered by a sangoma, who was in touch with the spirits, and sometimes this was done ritualistically. Thus summoned, the lidlotis stayed with the patient for as long as the medicines remained in his or her body, and it was they who provided protection from such perils as lightning strikes and accidents on the job. And most important, it was the lidlotis who manipulated in the patient's favor what everyone seemed to want: good luck.

The concept of luck is part of every society's popular mythology, and those who claim the ability to control it are much sought after. I never believed in luck, good or bad, but I was aware that people seemed to possess at times either a positive or negative "aura" or "karma" that either attracted or repelled. I also saw the role that coincidence played in people's lives. (What an unlikely chain of events had brought me to kutfwasa!) Science relegated coincidence to the probability tables or else the wilderness of chaos theory. I was interested to see if, fantastic as it sounded, I could find truth in the people's belief here that there was an herbal way to manipulate coincidence, and thus luck and fortune.

Two lidloti medicines said to do this when taken together by steaming, vomiting, and bathing were the light-colored *sihlati lesimhlope* and the ruddy *sihlati lesimnyama*. Patients were washed inside and out with these herbs so that cleansed they would "shine." The patient's positive attributes would be exposed and would become apparent to prospective employers, lovers and spouses, consequently improving that person's fortune. And spiritually cleansed, rather like a sangoma, the person was acceptable to the lidlotis. The spirits would manage the element of chance in the person's life. He or she would step off the curb at one point and not another, thereby avoiding a car. A random distraction that would have otherwise caused the person to forget his wallet or purse on a counter would be delayed. Happenings from the trivial to the life-threatening which could affect a person's physical and emotional well-being were influenced by the beneficial intervention of spiritual "guardian angels."

All this meant that there was no coincidence, and that things did not just happen. The universe was not quite the random place that I thought it was before. I thought about this as we worked all day on these magical medicines and my arms grew wiry from crushing roots with heavy metal pestles.

My first opportunity to test my luck medicines was with Sam's brother Jabulani, the twenty-year-old amateur boxer with the wide smile who had accompanied us the previous month on a medicine dig. Since then he had been searching in vain for a job. At the impoverished homestead where he grew up as one of nine children and where his education ended at seventh grade when money for school fees ran out, there was no work and not enough cropland to support everyone. Quiet and polite to the point of self-effacement, Jabulani grew depressed on days when he could not find money for food. He let me help him once or twice, but then, proud, he avoided me because he feared his refusal of more aid would offend me. At night, he slept on the kitchen floor. By chopping wood, he earned tips.

"Sometimes, it is easier to die," he said when I discovered him listless from hunger. It was such a sad cry from this normally sunny young man that I forced money into his rocklike hand and ordered him to be at my door first thing the next morning.

The luck treatment began at dawn, when I steamed Jabulani in the cooking shed with medicines from my own brand-new dispensary. I gave him another medicine to wash with, and a bucket of medicine-laced water to vomit. He was my first patient, and he promised to pay Gogo Ndwandwe for my services out of the salary he expected to get from the job everyone said would result from this treatment. As long as I was studying under Gogo Ndwandwe, all money I earned practicing medicine would go to her.

Jabulani was a good patient. He scoured himself with the medicine bath until his cocoa complexion shone, and he vomited with the other concoction until his eyes were red. Within a week, he found a position as a security guard. It was a low-paying job for which he had to rise at half-past four in the morning and then walk three miles to work. Still, it was a job—no job in Swaziland where unemployment ran at forty percent could be dismissed—and Jabulani was relieved and grateful.

Gogo Ndwandwe was happy. "You treated your friend, and now he has found work!" To her it was clearly a case of cause and effect. I was not yet ready to agree, but I was happy with the outcome, especially for Jabulani's sake. In my medicine journal I listed the episode under the "Positive Results" column of the anecdotal evidence I was amassing. I didn't expect a scientist to be swayed by such empirical proof, but if in time it was overwhelming, I might be.

▲   ▲   ▲   ▲

I continued to get up in the dark to perform the morning river ritual, but I soon found I was doing this alone. MaZu and LaShonge never cared to rise long before dawn to do this, which is why it was not performed during my first three months of kutfwasa. They now made excuses, and

Gogo Ndwandwe did not care to nag adults who should have known their responsibilities.

But in making the trip by myself, I found some moments of quiet and solitude that were difficult to come by in the busy, noisy homestead. As I walked the mile down to the river, distant mountains illuminated by moonlight hovered over the horizon as if airborne. Clear starlight illuminated everything, and when the moon was full it shone like a stage light. The long valley of squat mud huts and maize fields descended toward a narrow, shallow stream. I felt its nearness when the air grew sharply cooler.

In the sky, shooting stars dropped, punctuating my nights like exclamation points. There was a grassy mound of earth beside the stream. I knelt atop it, pulled the white sheet over my head, and greeted the lidlotis. In respectful but conversational tones, I told them what I wished from the new day and asked for their guidance and protection.

In a bucket I carried medicine I had boiled in my room. When I entered the stream, I wore calf-length rubber boots, and because the heaviest summer rains had ended, the crystal-clear, gently flowing water did not rise above them. I avoided low branches bristling with needles that could take out an eye. Fireflies sparkled playfully, threading silver trajectories all around me.

I brought a red plastic mug with me. I dipped it into the medicine, took a deep breath, and began filling my stomach with rapid gulps. I drank until I felt bloated, drank some more, and bent over to release the first spontaneous outpouring. I then prodded the back of my mouth with my finger until my body reacted. Another column of medicine shot out, and more followed until only spittle emerged. When I finished, I was glad the chore was over, felt refreshed and clean inside, and looked forward to the day ahead.

The air was crisp and delicious at that hour. One day, instead of returning to the homestead right away, I walked up the opposite river bank. I was curious because a rise had always blocked my view of the valley beyond. For my curiosity I was rewarded with my first waking vision, when no drums beat, when I was not semiconscious in a trance, and when I was not asleep. What I saw filled me with a sense of nostalgia as strong as a heartache.

Smooth, rounded contours of hills were black silhouettes against the deep gray sky to the east where dawn would break. A field stretched out ahead, and in the center of this blue and black landscape an amber candle flame glowed in a window of a far-off house. The light spoke of warmth, of welcome, of comfort and family. The candle, the window, and the hut were not illusions; they were there before me in that valley. But the Swazi hut seemed to have a second existence that stood revealed to me. I realized that this was Johnny MacDonald's house. The Swazi homestead had become the Scottish farm of my first lidloti. It was his emotions, which I seemed to feel, that made it so. I strongly felt the presence of his spirit within me. He was seeing through my eyes. I felt his sensations, and his thoughts entered my head like a whispered recollection, *"So many times I came home, guided by that candle in the window."*

I felt him moved by the sight, and I sensed him remembering how he returned from war to see this taper's glow between the farmhouse curtains. He rode all night, so eager was he to return home. Finally, he saw the candle beckoning. His children, the sleepiness in their eyes vanishing the instant they saw him. His wife, her blue eyes sparkling. How he made love to her that morning!

I would return to that spot often after I finished the cleansing ritual at the river. It was peaceful there; time stood still. I was pleasing my lidloti.

There would be more spirits to please, others who answered the drums' call and returned to us in the Indumba from the netherworld they inhabited, a realm I had begun to think of as "Post-Mortal/Pre-Heaven."

Most nights nothing would result from the drum-beating ritual intended to bring out the lidlotis. And then a new set of visions would appear suddenly, and I felt anew a wonder and appreciation for these spirits.

I saw the profile of a man's face. A Japanese man. Handsome, he appeared to be in his twenties, had a trim black beard and long black hair. I sensed he was not of this century. He dressed traditionally, though I only saw the upper part of an embroidered shirt, bright white. His head pivoted toward me, but before his gaze met mine, he vanished. I had never seen a lidloti's face and I wondered if his would be my first. But, no, I felt the presence of a woman, a beautiful woman.

On the other side of my sheet, Jabulani watched the ritual and started the tape recorder when he saw, by the graceful motions of my body, that a woman's spirit now possessed it. The women beating the drums liked female spirits, and they sang happily to greet her. The lidloti slowly stood, using my hands to wrap the long white sheet modestly about my body. But the people no longer saw me, only this unknown woman who began to sway rhythmically, who unfolded her arms and delicately waved her hands as if they were fans. She knelt down and made herself small before them, her hands clasped tight against her belly and her face close to the ground. Gogo Ndwandwe was present; she greeted her and asked who she was.

The voice that replied was soft, little more than a whisper, sweet and high. She spoke English with a Japanese inflection. "My name is Winter Blossom."

"Winter Blossom!" Gogo Ndwandwe repeated with a welcoming tone of voice. She liked this woman's name and her modest manner.

"My parents brought me to the ancestral shrine when I was born," she whispered. "They laid me on the snow in my blanket so the ancestors could see me. My face was very pink against the snow. My father said I looked like a cherry blossom—a blossom in the wintertime."

"Where do you come from?"

"I come from Japan."

"Oh, you are a Japanese lady! How did you find James?"

"It was at the place they have all the paintings from home," she revealed. "So many pretty screens. James came to see. My father had a screen. It was lovely: trees and birds. When I was a little girl, I sat for hours and looked at it, I loved it so. They brought it to that place. A part of me is with that picture still."

As if floating within the darkness of my body I heard the words coming from my throat, but I was mostly aware of the timidness and fear of this spirit. She replied to Gogo Ndwandwe's question about her knowledge of English, saying missionaries had taught her. But she seemed to have a confession to make, a dreadful secret, and along with the people in the Indumba I listened to her when she said, "I had a lover, the father of my baby. He had a beard, like James. He went off to war, and when they said he died I could not believe it, and I lost my mind. I went off to search for him. It was winter. My baby was tied to my back. The cold, it made me so I could not see because of my tears. The stones cut my feet. My baby cried and cried because it was hungry. I had no food. My breasts were dry."

There was no other sound in the spirit house but her plaintive voice. People who could not understand her words were moved by her sadness. Gogo Ndwandwe said, "Please, if it makes you cry, you must not tell us these things."

"But my baby was dying," the spirit continued. "Her face was not pink against the snow like mine was when I was small; it was white. I held

her. She was hard like stone. We were below the purple mountain. She was
dead, and I knew I must follow. The blade was cold in my hand. I plunged
it deep into my stomach. The snow was red."

The spirit wept, "All during that journey in the mountains I was sing-
ing a song:

> *There was a time I had a lover*
> *He held me in his gentle hand*
> *And if I search these hills and valleys*
> *I know God will bring him again."*

Gogo Ndwandwe sighed sympathetically, "Oh, that song is too sad!"
"May I go now?"
"Yes, you may go."
Like a wisp of vapor, the spirit of Winter Blossom vanished. My full
awareness returned, and with it complete control of my body. I wiped the
tears from my face and looked into the sad expression of my teacher.

"Oh, Sibolomhlope!" Gogo Ndwandwe exclaimed. "Your lidlotis
make me cry! But this one was very polite, and I liked her. She asked permission before she left."

By the lidloti pole I listened to the tape, which augmented what I
could remember. I knew the place the spirit referred to. Before I left
America, I visited the Japanese Art Pavilion that had just opened in Los
Angeles. Designed as an homage to the Shinto style, the building contained a collection of eighteenth- and nineteenth-century screens. If one
of these belonged to the spirit's father, then she lived one or two hundred
years ago. I thought of her sad story, the crazed search for her dead lover.
I imagined her wandering the wilderness, a cold, watercolor landscape.
Her dead, frozen baby. She had a knife. She must have known how it
would end.

I felt shaken up. By participating in the shayelwa ritual I had allowed
this tragic woman to come to us through me. But I thought of her mod-
esty and her sweet manner; I felt a tug inside, and I knew I held some love
in my heart for her. I spoke to her at the lidloti pole and hoped she was
finding peace where she was now.

▲　▲　▲　▲

The cramped, dark, hot and dusty room where I stayed was now infested
by rats. I woke one night with a shout when one ran across my chest.

Rustling around in the dark, rats gnawed through my garment bag for the candy inside. They gnawed a hole in a plastic tub where I washed dishes, they ate soap, ate candles. I set out a trap baited with peanut butter and in two weeks caught eleven rats. The largest had a six-inch body and an eight-inch tail.

The only way to escape them was to build my own house that would not be attached to an old, filthy kitchen. It seemed a simple matter to put up a round mud hut with a thatched grass roof. I had no idea of the hellish ordeal that would occupy my next two months.

Prince Vovo selected a site behind the Indumba, and I set to work with a machete and rake, clearing the area of giant weeds and prickly bushes. A man named Phesheya came by and claimed to know how to build a hut, and I paid him half the price he wanted for the job up front. Phesheya was dour, paid little attention when someone spoke to him, and wore a peevish expression on a round face mounted pumpkinlike atop a tall, narrow-shouldered body bloated by a beer belly. But the money I gave him for the job put him in a good mood, and he and his "crew" spent much of their time drinking home-brewed beer in a tree's shade. After several days, they had managed to raise only seventeen wall poles in a circle in the ground. A week later, with only a half-completed framework erected, Phesheya announced that he only intended to do the framework. I refused to pay him more money until he finished the hut as promised, and he shouted to the skies at the white man's treachery before storming off with the threat to have me deported.

I was dismayed by this unfortunate beginning to a house that, requested by White Feather, would be the dwelling for all my lidlotis. I vowed to build it myself.

The wall poles set in their circle were already half covered by thin rods bent and nailed in place to create outer and inner wall frames. I attached more rods and filled the cavities between with stones. These would catch the mud when the time came to slap it on.

I knew nothing, however, about thatching a roof. One of the drinking men at the beer hut claimed to know the work. He had an erratic nature that signaled trouble ahead: one moment he had a superior, contemptuous air toward me, the next he was so hyper his eyes and smile seemed crazed. He drank as much as Phesheya. But Gogo Ndwandwe was fatalistic, saying, "Who else are you going to get?"

I realized I was on my own with this house. Also about this time, my wallet and its contents were stolen from my room when a robber took advantage of a faulty door lock. Gogo Ndwandwe unleashed the wrath of her hot temper when I asked if I should file a police report. "Are you mad, Lusiba! The police will come here! The police must never come to the king's place!" This was how she referred to Prince Vovo's homestead.

Fearing for my "luck," elderly Gogo Mabusa suggested that I sit for a divination ritual she would do. She was a small, thin woman and possessed considerable dignity. I thanked her, and the session that followed was elaborate, almost ceremonial, with several people coming to the Indumba to chant, shake rattles, and in the end, beat the drums. I sat on a grass mat while Gogo Mabusa, in a trance, attempted to locate my troubles by "sniffing" about my body with a cowtail brush dipped in medicine. She was a capable sangoma and executed the divination with energy and style. At the end she reported that the curse which had been put on me so I could not have children could be removed by performing a river ritual that involved a black chicken. Following this, an important cleansing ritual had to be performed so my lidlotis would work to make me a father and also fortify my luck. Gogo Mabusa did not say whether or not the curse had been placed by the cleaning lady MaZu had once spoken of when she first read the bones for me.

There was no biological evidence that I could not have children. I wasn't impotent, or sterile, as far as I knew. MaZu said that from her experience the curse would have prevented me from ever finding a woman to be my wife; hence, no children. I couldn't really believe this, but I agreed to undergo the river treatment because MaZu also wanted to do it for a sexual problem she chose not to divulge, and she suggested we treat each other to learn the technique. Although we were supposed to be celibate throughout kutfwasa, ailments divined by the lidlotis were best treated as soon as they were diagnosed.

The second ritual Gogo Mabusa had spoken of would require the sacrifice of a goat. My mentor, Gogo Ndwandwe, suggested I give her money to send to her mother, an aging but still active woman who lived in a part of the countryside where goats were plentiful. For the river ritual, MaZu and I purchased two jet black hens from a neighbor, and just before sunset, we headed for the little stream a mile away. I now knew enough of the SiSwati language to understand MaZu when she told me that every time a sangoma sacrificed an animal, the carcass was given to people to eat. But the ritual we would now perform in the water was unique: the chickens would be buried. A patient's condition was transferred to the bird in this rite, and no one must eat the spiritually poisoned flesh.

Sunlight angled through green tree branches covering a secluded bend of the shallow, quietly flowing stream. I would go first. I removed my clothes and stood naked, legs apart, in the water. MaZu made "African injections" on my wrists by pricking my skin with the tip of a razor blade. She was good at this, and I felt less irritation than I would have from an injection with a hypodermic needle. MaZu pinched the tiny cuts until a drop of blood appeared and then rubbed a fine powder into them with her finger. She then made tiny cuts on my scalp, shoulders, back, sides, hands and knees. Blood began to trickle down each wound until my body was streaked with red. I felt like St. Sebastian.

The bleeding stopped when MaZu rubbed in the medicine, which acted as a coagulant. She dropped the razor blade with my blood on it into an empty milk carton that contained the heart and other organs of the chicken she had slaughtered with a pocket knife a few minutes before. She had me spit into the carton, and still naked, I walked upstream with it. The ritual required that I remain in the water until I finished my task. I dug a hole through the coarse sand where the stream was most shallow, placed the closed carton in the hole, and covered it. Soon the current would wash away the sand, open the carton, and sweep away its contents, which now contained the condition that was said to hinder my fatherhood. I recited the SiSwati words to end this ritual, saying I was leaving my problems there and they would bother me no more. "I am turning my back on you."

I did, returning to MaZu and not looking back until the river had done its work. MaZu held her black chicken. I put on some shorts, took the knife, and with its sharp blade cut off the chicken's head with a stroke. I had done this with other chickens back at the homestead, but this was different and presented a dilemma: this chicken was not being killed for food, and this bothered me. As MaZu urged me to hurry, I cut open the carcass and removed the internal organs she wanted. She undressed, and with a new razor blade I pricked her skin from head to knee and rubbed medicinal powder into the cuts. MaZu went upstream to finish the ritual while I buried the bird carcasses along the river-bank.

The sun had set by the time we left the river. MaZu said I had done the ritual well. But I was still disturbed; the chicken that had been slaughtered for MaZu was her business, but mine seemed like a gratuitous killing. Even the prospect of slaughtering a goat for the next ritual did not bother me as much because the homestead people would be able to feast on the meat, a rare event for them. I had felt ambiguous about the "curse" that may or may not have kept me from having children. I didn't understand it. Until I did I made this vow: that I wouldn't slaughter any more animals unless they went into someone's pot.

It also bothered me that I had no way of knowing if the ritual we just completed had any legitimacy at all or was simply superstition. When I accepted the lidlotis I at least had the personal evidence of visions and the psychic powers I was beginning to display when I studied the bones. How would I ever know if the curse that was said to have hovered over me had ever existed?

Brooding over this, my eyes rose to the darkening sky. I saw there a rare thing, and with it seemed to come the answer I sought. The full moon was rising bright yellow over the hills, but a large piece of its bottom was missing. It was a lunar eclipse. I smiled and pointed it out to MaZu. She squinted at the moon and said there was a cloud over it. I was about to explain about the earth's shadow when it struck me that she was right, only for me it was a metaphoric cloud; this was a sign. Within minutes, the shadow was shrinking. By the time we arrived back at the homestead the moon's disc was whole, and by then I understood the message from my lidlotis. The earth and moon would have aligned themselves in that manner whether I or anyone else existed or not, but what was important was that I had noticed and understood: the moon's face had been partly obscured but now shone unobstructed, just as my own life, once partly cast into shadow, would be whole. The sangoma's insight had transformed a physical event into a nicely timed communication, and if I read it right, it meant the ritual we had just performed was a success.

Gogo Ndwandwe agreed with my reading. "The lidlotis they speak to us in strange ways. But you now know how to listen to them, Sibolomhlope."

Perhaps it was that growing ability to listen that enabled a new spirit to emerge. It would be the strangest and most demanding lidloti that would ever appear. And it would change my life as completely as kutfwasa had.

By the end of March, my fourth month here, the days in Swaziland were growing shorter, but the land was still green and the nights warm. We decided to hold the evening's drum-beating ritual in the courtyard before the Indumba, under the stars.

On a grass mat placed over the hard ground, I slipped under the white sheet once more. Close behind me the women and girls beat the drums, and soon I saw the familiar vision of running zebras. Gradually, my mind was drawn into a tunnel of darkness.

I was fully aware of my body, but my awareness seemed to belong to someone else: someone who had come into my body but found it wrong. This person did not seem to be a fully developed human somehow, and its consciousness was a vague, impulsive thing.

For the first time, I "came back" during this ritual. One moment a new lidloti was present; the next I was myself. But the spirit seemed able to communicate to me, and I somehow knew that the drums' rhythm was not to its liking. I turned, the sheet half-falling off, and took the drum sticks from MaZu's daughter, Doyenne. The others stopped beating. I began to pound a slow, steady rhythm. *Thump-thump-thump* . . . Doyenne took the sticks and duplicated the rhythm exactly. I went back under the sheet.

I did not submerge entirely; something was happening, and I knew what the drums were now saying. Their slow rhythm was meant to mimic the human heartbeat. But now my body felt cold.

For a second time I reemerged. I stuck my head out from beneath the sheet, feeling excited by what was happening. "Sam!" I called to him. "Please, take a couple of blankets from my room and cover me."

I spotted Gogo Ndwandwe seated nearby, and I smiled, "You're not going to believe this!"

She gave me the thumbs up sign. I slipped beneath the sheet once more. Sam returned and covered me with two blankets. They were heavy, and I felt pleasantly warm.

Again I sensed what the spirit was feeling. It was distressed. It had to use my body, but I was all wrong, and it was confused. Its own head, with sightless eyes, ears that could not yet hear, and a nose that could not yet smell, was several times the size of my own in proportion to the rest of its body. Its stomach was enormous; its legs and arms were dwarfish.

I felt more confusion: why was its head up? It should be down. But this lidloti did not know how to move itself. Very slowly, gravity took its toll. Like a sigh, the spirit fell until it was resting on its side. Its hands rested on either side of its head. Its legs were tucked up, knees nearly touching its head, the way it used to be. Through the cushion of the blankets, its back touched the largest drum. The steady rhythm nourished the lidloti. The spirit drew comfort and life from this, its mother.

It was a fetus. It lived in a sac of warm fluid. Underneath the hot, airless blankets my body was wet with sweat, and I felt as if I were in water. Its mouth gaped, but it breathed through an umbilical cord that seem to coil from my stomach.

It had no thoughts. It had no feelings. Only sensations. Only impulses. But it wanted.

I knew its wants. I knew its story. I knew what I had to do for it. But now I was inside a womb. I knew what it was like to be inside the womb again. It was restful, being completely dependent and cared for. But this was my own reaction as an adult. The fetus spirit had a different desire. I knew what its desire was, and of my responsibility to assist it.

Through an act of will I reemerged. It took time. My muscles were flaccid. I had to breathe again through my nose and mouth. From where I lay, I pulled aside the sheets and blankets as the drums beat around me. The amazement I felt toward what had happened was tempered by the bittersweetness of what I had learned from the lidloti: that the impulse of the unborn is to grow and be independent and to carry on the business of all organisms, which is to live.

But that was the tragedy of this new lidloti: it had been unable to live. It had died before birth. How the spirit of this fetus put its story into my mind was a mystery, but much of a sangoma's knowledge is acquired beyond the senses. I stood and went to Gogo Ndwandwe. I asked if I might speak with her alone. We entered the Indumba, I closed the door, and we sat down on the dirt floor.

"Baba, what did you see?"

"Nothing. You were very still, and then . . ." She flipped her hand over to one side, indicating falling.

I explained that the lidloti had been a fetus. Gogo Ndwandwe's brow wrinkled as she searched her memory. "That explains it! You know, when I was in kutfwasa we once had a woman whose spirit was a little baby. When it emerged, we had to speak to her with hand language. What did your spirit want?"

"It didn't know—so I don't know—if it was male or female. It didn't communicate with thoughts using words. But I know it never saw life outside the womb. And it wants to, because it was denied this."

Gogo Ndwandwe nodded her head quietly. I thought for a moment, then spoke. "The lidlotis seem to experience life again vicariously through the people they attach themselves to. This spirit wants to know the life it never had. It can't rationalize. It can't think, really. It can only want. You've told me I must do all that's in my power to fulfill a lidloti's requests."

"You must," my teacher affirmed.

"What if I were to tell you that this new lidloti wants me to have a baby, not so it can be reincarnated but so it can witness life vicariously through my child?"

"Then I'd say you must have this baby, by all means."

"Gogo Ndwandwe, I am in kutfwasa and I'm celibate."

My teacher gave me a wry, almost wicked smile, as if to tell me that if I were in kutfwasa and celibate, I was one of the few who were. She replied, "Lusiba, as you know the kutfwasa years are long and they are lonely and hard. MaZu and many others cannot do without company. It's not that you are married to the lidlotis and they punish you for cheating on them; it's that you can get sick from sleeping with someone who may have a bad spirit. But the real danger is at the end, when you undergo the tests to finish kutfwasa."

She explained that the tests were physically and spiritually exhausting, and an "impure" student could die trying to endure them. The chief sangomas threw the bones to see which students had broken celibacy, and he or she had to pay a heavy fine and undergo treatment with special medicines. These medicines were always available because so many students were unable to remain pure.

"Then I have your permission to break the rules?"

"It is the lidlotis who make these rules, not I. If this lidloti wants you to have a baby, it will protect you and you won't get sick. But even so, at the end I advise you to undergo the medicine treatment if you want to finish kutfwasa." I had the feeling my teacher believed that if I were to break the celibacy rule, it was better that I do so like this, sanctioned as it were by the spirits.

"You seem happy, Sibolomhlope," Gogo Ndwandwe smiled at me. "You want to be a father?"

I *was* happy, and excited by the prospect. I would never consider having a child on the basis of a spirit's request; it was ridiculous. But I had always wanted to have children, and I realized now how deep this desire was. Naturally, I also wanted a wife, and this would grow more urgent if I became a single father. But now the issue was the child: did I want one, and if I could make arrangements for a woman to bear my baby, a wet-nurse, and then a nanny if I were still unwed, would I willingly assume the enormous challenge and responsibility of raising a child? Yes, again, I thought—yes, with enthusiasm!

"When you find the woman to be the mother, you must introduce her to me because you are my son and I must approve," Gogo Ndwandwe was saying. "You will pay two cows to the woman's family and the child will be yours and legitimate in the eyes of all the people. She can bear your name."

"Of course, she'll bear my name," I said. Gogo Ndwandwe and I looked at each other with startled smiles when we realized what we were saying: *she?* My mentor's seasoned sangoma's "insight" and my still-inchoate ability had both hit upon the same conclusion: my firstborn would be a girl.

six

"Accidents"

A YEAR HAD passed since I first visited Swaziland, when Yvonne and Timothy Motsa brought me to this homestead where I had been living now for four months. From time to time I visited Yvonne. After the fetus lidloti appeared, I told her of its request and of my desire to have a child. I emphasized that I did not want a child to fulfill a spirit's wish as much as I wanted to fulfill a desire of my own to which the spirit had alerted me, and if the lidloti was also happy with the outcome, fine. Yvonne understood, and strongly urged that I consider for the baby's mother her friend Thandaza. A few days later, Yvonne arrived at Prince Vovo's homestead with this friend, and I was introduced to a slightly plump, light-skinned woman whose docile manner was offset by hard and shrewd eyes. I was not immediately attracted to her, but I was looking for a woman to bear my child, not a wife. She agreed to the arrangement, and that was all that mattered.

But after Yvonne introduced Thandaza to Gogo Ndwandwe and they had left, my teacher was doubtful. "You cannot love this woman, Lusiba! You can see she is selfish. She says she has three children, but they are all being raised by her mother in Johannesburg. How can she care for your child?"

I was inclined to agree with her, but replied, "I am not looking for a wife, baba. I want one, and my life's not going to be complete without her, but until it happens, I'll be raising my child myself."

"You are right, Sibolomhlope," she said. But it was clear she did not care for Yvonne's choice. My own instinct was to go slowly with Thandaza. When she wanted to go to South Africa to tell her mother about me, I gave her money for the trip partly to allow myself time to think.

Gamedze, my alcoholic roof thatcher, was dawdling along, putting in ninety minutes of work a day, hanging out at the brewing shack the rest of the time, and begging me to advance him more money. I yielded so he would finish placing a line of grass along the roof's outer edge, sheltering the walls so we could apply the mud. This was the fun part: Jabulani, Sam, and I stood around the circular hut and threw handfuls of red mud at the wood and stone framework.

Another painful infection caused my foot to swell up to twice its size, and I spent two days hobbling about. Gamedze seized the chance to disappear entirely. The man I hired to do the plaster work, Mabizweni, could not start until the roof was further along and capable of shielding the walls from rain. Mabizweni was a short, skinny man in his thirties whose large expressive eyes were often mournfully sad. He was constantly trying to ingratiate himself with me, and spoke English as if he had learned it from a Victorian novel: "Do not let your heart be sad, Mr. Sibolomhlope. We will find this Gamedze, and we will *thrash* him!"

We did find Gamedze after a search of the area's drinking shacks. Alcohol was used socially in Swaziland, but for a few people like this man it was a ticket to oblivion, and what they wanted from a brew was to take them there fast. I was shocked to find Gamedze drinking a concoction that had gotten its mind-numbing kick after the brewer tossed in some radio batteries. This poison had brought Gamedze to the oblivion he sought: his head jerked as if pulled by an invisible string, and his rheumy eyes were blank. I left with a hard look at the stone-faced woman who was selling the brew, returned to Prince Vovo's place with Mabizweni, and was surprised when Gamedze returned late in the afternoon and finished enough of the roof so the plastering could begin.

Construction was entering its second month on the simple mud hut that was proving to be a classic money pit. Bags of plaster sand and cement were brought in by truck to make a strong interior and exterior wall coating. The wall and roofing poles and framework rods had also come from a supplier. To economize, I made dozens of trips with a wheelbarrow down to the river to collect sand for the plaster mixture. Pushing a wheelbarrow full of wet sand one mile uphill under a broiling African sun was the most difficult work I had ever done. When I arrived with the load, I stuck my head under the yard tap and prayed that the water supply had not been cut, which it occasionally was for hours on end without explanation.

Then, Mabizweni the plasterer disappeared. After two days he showed up at my door, red-eyed from crying. I had gotten to know Mabizweni, he seemed to like me, and I felt my gut drop when he said his daughter had died of heart failure. He looked weak and tired. I offered him food but he shook his head, his eyes releasing large, round tears that rolled down his cheeks. "Thank you. When I eat I vomit. My head is going 'round and 'round. God, He took my first born!" He drew a wheezing breath. "I loved her. I put her through all her levels at school. Please, Mr. Sibolomhlope, I have used up all my money. The ambulance to take my daughter's body charged me forty rand. And I gave all my money to the man at the mortuary. But I am still owing him. Please, if I could have the money for her coffin, I will work *hard* for you."

I gave him the money but was unable to speak. He must have read my condolences in my expression, because he nodded his thanks and left. That was the morning Thandaza returned from South Africa to announce she was going back immediately to sell Swazi-style garments made by a friend who lived not far from the homestead in the town of Manzini. Thandaza suggested we all have lunch together so I might get my mind off Mabizweni's tragedy. I agreed, but the trip had to be made surreptitiously. Gogo Ndwandwe had agreed to my plans for a child because the baby would also fulfill a lidloti's desire. She felt the celibacy rule would not be broken so much as stretched in my case. But she feared gossip. People who knew nothing of kutfwasa assumed we were celibate to show our devotion to higher powers, when in fact it was simply a health measure: we did not sleep with or even shake hands with anyone for fear of contracting a spiritual contagion that might manifest itself as a physical illness. It had nothing to do with sex.

But we did not discuss kutfwasa with outsiders, who knew of it only in general terms. Gogo Ndwandwe was fearful that people would criticize her for allowing her student to break the celibacy rule. These malicious gossips, she said, didn't care about reasons. Gossip is a damaging force everywhere, but in this insular tribal society it was particularly harmful. People were driven from their villages on the basis of gossip; people were accused of witchcraft and innocent people suffered retribution on the basis of rumors. Gogo Ndwandwe's medical practice could be compromised if people jealous of her reputation learned what I was doing.

I promised to be discreet, and I made Thandaza promise to be discreet as well. I was therefore dismayed when we arrived at her friend Evah's house, and she knew all about our arrangement. But Evah, as I discovered, was one of the most pleasant and understanding people I had met in Swaziland, and I soon relaxed in her company. There was always a tension between Thandaza and me; she was a mystery, telling me little about herself, and always seemed to be angling for something. Right now she wanted me to pay eight months' back rent on a flat she kept in the capital town of Mbabane. In contrast to Thandaza's closed expression, Evah's was like an open book, and on it I read a calm confidence and quiet intelligence I was attracted to at once. She was a year older and several inches shorter than me, with a mature, womanly frame, but I principally noticed her bright, humor-filled eyes above wide, round cheeks. She smiled with pride when she showed me the dresses she made. She had a skilled hand, and colorful garments with elaborate embroidery were piled up in her one-room flat that was as small and orderly as an ocean liner stateroom.

Evah was also an excellent cook. We spoke English over lunch, and I longed to ask her about the mystery that was Thandaza. Evah seemed sincere, even wise. After two hours, though, kutfwasa duties beckoned, and I had to say good-bye and leave the women.

Work on the house continued fitfully. Mabizweni returned, ill from sadness and the flu and unable to work. He found someone to finish the plastering work. But the roof thatcher Gamedze had disappeared again. All that was left for him to do was to install a special broom-shaped cap woven of grass, which went on the roof's peak. When Gamedze finally showed up, he claimed to know a woman who made these caps. She lived far away, but he'd go to her if I gave him the bus fare. Hoping that it was not a trick, I agreed.

Word reached me that Mabizweni was seriously ill. I went to the house where I was told I could find him, found a dilapidated hut with a collapsing roof, and knocked on the door. A faint voice answered, "Enter." I stepped into a cramped, windowless hovel; brown mud walls were damp and moldy, a rusty bed frame and plank table were the only furnishings. Mabizweni lay on the dirt floor, one blanket under him, another upon him. He looked haunted and emaciated; he looked like he was dying.

Without greeting me, he reported in a flat voice, "I went walking last night. I was not in my right mind. They had to tie me down to the bed frame."

"Mabizweni, you're more than a workman to me. You're my friend. I'll be back." Determined not to let him die in that hole, I went out to find one of the battered cars that worked as informal taxis. I returned with one, but there was no sign of Mabizweni. A neighbor said he wandered off delirious shortly after I left. I searched in vain for him for several hours until I learned he was in the government hospital. I went to see him the next day.

I found Mabizweni lying listlessly in a bed in the men's ward, a long, pale blue room where men were dying in a blaze of sunshine through wire-mesh windows. He saw me, but his expression remained that of a man resigned to a hopeless fate.

"They 'witch me, Mr. Sibolomhlope."

"Nonsense," I assured him.

He grew agitated, raised his head from the pillow, and looked at me through frightened eyes like round, yellow moons. "I tell you, it's true! They killed my father. They killed my mother. They killed my daughter. And now they kill me."

I took hold of his shoulders and gently eased him back down. "Why would they do that, Mabizweni? Why would anyone want to harm you?"

The eyes upon me narrowed. "It is because of *you*, Mr. Sibolom-hlope. They 'witch me because of you."

"Me? Why?"

"They are jealous. They have no job. They are jealous that you help me."

"Because I gave you a job? I've given many men jobs on the house."

"They see me working, those men drinking the tjwala beer. They call me over. 'Why do you work so hard for this white man? Why don't you play him for the fool, like Gamedze? There's nothing he can do.'"

So, I thought, that was why it was taking forever to build my house: a little conspiracy I had suspected but hadn't dared admit to because those men were right; it had been proven that I could be robbed and there was nothing I could do about it. I felt angered and dismayed by this confirmation of my fears.

But my duty now was to calm Mabizweni. "You're very ill, my friend. You've lost your daughter. You're worrying yourself. Suppose there is something to this bewitchment business? It's a sangoma's job to set it right, isn't it? We can fight this. We can beat it."

He shook his head in a pitying way at my naivete. "You are new here. You do not know. It is already too late."

"Don't think that, or it will be too late."

I promised to return the next day after consulting with Gogo Ndwandwe. When I saw her, she told me Mabizweni could be treated, but not at the hospital. Swazi medical doctors, she said, were trained in the U.S. and Europe, and had turned their backs on the ways of their people. Instead of working hand in hand with traditional healers, they were thoroughly hostile to the sangomas' medical practices. "Do you know where half your patients will come from, Lusiba?" she asked me. "They will come to you after the doctors have tried to cure them and failed."

I returned to the hospital in the morning but found that Mabizweni was not in his bed. Another man occupied it. Was Mabizweni now better? I sought out a nurse, and she told me that he did not go home. Mabizweni had died the previous night.

I left. Among my thoughts was this: Although I was training to be a healer I had been powerless to help him because his belief in his own destruction had been too great. But what was worse was that I was going to have to live with the knowledge that this man went to his death believing he was bewitched because of me.

Struggling through that day was like swimming against a viscous, dirty current. I thought how once upon a time when I was depressed I'd watch a video of some old Hollywood confection like *Gentlemen Prefer Blondes* or *Holiday Inn*. How innocent that life now seemed, when all it took to cheer me up was Bing's crooning or Marilyn's vamping. But how much innocence was still in me, I wondered, that was yet to be torn away like a scab, layer by layer, on days like this?

I decided to cook one of my favorite meals, and went to a nearby butchery where I could roast a piece of fresh beef over a coal fire kept burning in back. Swazis liked their beef "on the hoof": never refrigerated, let alone frozen, and cut from freshly slaughtered carcasses hung in the butcher shop. I had never tasted beef so delicious and succulent.

I was standing at the fire in the cooking shack, turning my piece of meat with a long wire, when a man spotted me. He smiled with delight and shouted, "Well!"

I greeted him politely, but I was on guard. He was drunk. But he seemed happy to see me. Although I wore my sangoma-in-training attire and was somewhere I'd never seen another white person, he acted as if I was a tourist just off the plane. "Do you like Swaziland?"

I assured him that I did. "You speak SiSwati? Do you like our humble language?"

Again I said I did. He giggled, "We have many stories in SiSwati. Many stories! But do you know something?" He leaned close to me, nearly bursting with pleasure. *"We won't tell you any!"*

He went off into the night, laughing, and I felt as if I'd been slapped. Not only did this fellow sense my isolation and vulnerability, he was thrilled to be able to rub it in. I told myself that, of course, Swazis told me stories. They never stopped telling me stories. But Mabizweni, who revealed the men's desire to cheat me and their contempt for anyone who didn't do likewise, was right when he pitied my naivete. Kutfwasa put such demands upon my mind, body, and spirit, it was so hard, that I felt I needed allies to get through it, and for my allies I took the entire Swazi nation. Since these were their beliefs and their culture I was embracing, surely they would respect my undertaking and want to help me? But now I was forced to admit that there were cynical and racist people here as there were everywhere else, and they didn't give a damn about me and my kutfwasa. They saw only a white man, and they hated me on sight. It was not that they blamed me for all the evils of colonialism and exploitation—racism wasn't that rational—it was that my skin was pale compared to theirs, my nose and hair were straight, my eyes were blue, I spoke SiSwati like a backward child: I was different. And being different, I was an object of contempt. There was no shame attached to cheating me; as an inferior, what right did I have to things native Swazis had to do without? Stealing from me was not a crime; it was considered correcting an imbalance.

It wouldn't have mattered to them to know I was broke. My accountant had written that he used all the money in my bank account to pay my taxes. He said I could expect to starve where I was unless he sold my IRA certificates. I had written back with my permission, numbed by a fatalistic wonder at the price I was paying to do what I thought I had to do. I left the butchery without an appetite after the mocking stranger departed that night. I gave the grilled meat to a boy I met along the way and sank into despondency, wondering how it would all end.

Gamedze, the alcohol-crazed roof thatcher, delivered the coup de grace to the difficulties of the house construction the following morning. It was the end of April, and after more than two months the hut was still unfinished, though the walls were mostly plastered and a carpenter had installed a door and window. Over two weeks had passed since Gamedze had begun his trips to the woman he said was making the traditional grass roof cap he needed to finish his job.

He showed up with a bundle of grass under one arm. My assumption that the finished roof cap was within seemed confirmed when Gamedze told me triumphantly that he would finish the job that day. I was relieved. It had been a long wait, and I felt like a prisoner who was finally told he could leave his cell. A few days before, a radio I had bought and kept in my room had stopped working. I opened up the back and dozens of roaches fell out from where they'd grown up feasting on wire insulation. They scrambled over my hands and arms and I dropped the radio in surprise and disgust. It smashed to pieces on the floor.

I was looking forward to my move out of there while I worked with MaZu and LaShonge that morning. Our job was to store harvested maize cobs in an elevated wire mesh storage bin. Throughout the upcoming winter, the people of the homestead would grind the sun-dried kernels into meal. I stood knee-deep in cobs while the women handed more to me in boxes I'd empty and hand back out. Gamedze approached, his smile unnatural, almost hysterical. His eyes were saucerlike, and he looked high on drugs, a condition the local brew sometimes brought out in him. At his side was a drinking companion he said was his "assistant," a grim, square-shouldered thug who gave me a challenging look. They had been working at the hut for all of forty-five minutes but not once had they climbed the ladder to the roof. My gut tensed; I knew what was coming.

"We're done!" Gamedze shouted up at me. "Pay us!"

He had come today only to drink, I saw, and to fortify his resolve to announce that he was tired of this job and was leaving. I climbed down from the bin and walked to the house. The "assistant" yelled, "Didn't you hear? Pay us!"

In fact, through advances I had paid for nearly the entire job already. I entered the round hut. The smell of damp earth was strong. The walls would take many more days to dry. I stood in the center and looked up. A hole at the top, five feet in diameter, let in the sky, as it had done for weeks. I went back outside.

"How," I said, "even drunk, can you tell me this job is done?"

Gamedze began to speak rapidly, angrily, much faster than I could understand. Gogo Ndwandwe was absent, and from all over the homestead people began to gather. The men at the brewing shack abandoned their beer tins and came over. Nobody wanted to miss a minute of this. I suddenly remembered the thatched grass roof cap that was to surmount the hut. I located the bundle of grass Gamedze had brought with him and unwrapped it. Inside I found—more grass.

I saw what had happened. My thatcher realized that he had run out of schemes to get more money out of this job—his last was this fiction about the woman who could thatch the roof cap; the money I'd been giving him for long-distance bus fare had all gone to the beer shack—so he announced the job was done. It didn't matter if it was done or not; he knew I was helpless. He acted as if all the loyal Swazis within earshot were his allies, and just as when Phesheya had pulled the same stunt not a soul told him to shut up, no one said Gamedze was a crook. Instead, as he ranted, people from the neighborhood appeared and pressed around, seemingly thrilled by the humiliation of the white man.

I thought of all the months of tricks while I'd been breathing the dirt of my rat-infested cell, my kutfwasa compromised for lack of a consecrated place for my lidlotis. I thought of the conspiracy of the workmen, the apathy of everyone else, and I blew up. I shouted at Gamedze's haughty, sneering face, "I'll see you in hell before I pay you any more!"

I turned and left quickly before I struck him. The other man screamed after me, "We'll beat you up! When you leave this place, we'll be waiting!"

In my room, I sat down on the floor, trembling. "I can't go on like this," I admitted aloud. "I can't handle the contempt of these people. What did I do to deserve it?"

There was a knock at the door. "Who is it?"

A deep, familiar voice answered. "It is Sam." He entered, knelt down, and looked at me worriedly. I asked him why he wasn't at work.

"I will go late." His expression remained grave. "I know how to thatch. We can finish the roof. Gamedze said if I tried to help you he'd break my arm. But I have a club, and we can defend ourselves."

"Sam," I murmured. I was overcome. How quickly things changed. "My God, Sam."

We set to work at once, climbing up to the roof to begin thatching. Gamedze and his hit man showed up, threatened us, and stole the ladder so we couldn't get down. But some people made them put it back: as long as it had been Gamedze versus me it had been no contest because the word of a foreigner didn't count to them, but with a fellow Swazi on my side, they could no longer assume that I was automatically wrong. I hated Gamedze and I hated all of them, but I loved Sam and vowed I'd do anything for him.

We worked for two days finishing the roof. Gogo Ndwandwe said that all along my lidlotis wanted me to build their house myself. With Sam below and me above, we thatched with a foot-long wooden needle threaded with twine, which we looped around rods attached to the sloping roof poles that formed the hut's cone-shaped top. We worked quickly, shaded by cloud cover from the sun, and after applying a mixture of mud and cement to secure the peak, we were done.

I moved my things in, too disillusioned by its construction to enjoy the new house. Mabizweni's assistant came by to put some finishing touches on the gray walls inside. He finished, and after paying him I left to do chores. I agreed to keep the window open because the plasterer complained the walls wouldn't dry properly otherwise; he promised to stand guard until I returned.

I awoke the next day in my new home and went to my locked suitcase. I had just put in the money I'd be living on for the rest of the month. I found a slash on the side large enough for a hand to fit through. I hastily opened the case. Not a penny remained inside.

The plasterer wasn't a suspect. He had stayed by the house but sat on the west side, while the window faced east, where anyone entering would be hidden by high weeds. News of the robbery spread quickly. It was heard by Thandaza, the woman who was to have my baby, when she returned from South Africa with new requests. Her last letter stated her need for a monthly allowance and a house in town with a garden and servants' quarters. Sam now told me he had seen Thandaza in town and he'd told her I'd been wiped out. After that she did not come by and I never saw her again. I wasn't surprised, and I wasn't sad to see her go. Still, what would I do about the baby? And how could I reverse this stretch of endless, demoralizing bad luck?

It was May now, and for two months I'd been trying to locate a goat for the luck ritual Gogo Mabusa had prescribed for me. Gogo Ndwandwe had suggested I send money to her mother so she might find a goat for me, and I had done so. But when I asked her how the search was coming along, my high-strung and prickly teacher saw the question as a criticism and an affront to her authority. She flared up. "*Hawu!* My mother is old! How can she get a goat?"

"But then why did you suggest—?" I stopped, not wanting a fight. I was also bewildered; not being able to find a goat in Swaziland was like not being able to find a bottle of Bordeaux in Paris. Why was it proving so difficult?

But I knew: being a stranger here, I had grown dependent upon other people. When I did that, they took advantage of me. There was an ever-present danger that I might become hypnotized by the impassive face of Africa that stared back at me wherever I looked, and a danger that I too would become passive and fatalistic. I had to fight this. And I would start by going out and finding my own damn goat.

I carried a sleeping bag and some gear in an overnight bag when I spotted Gogo Ndwandwe in the courtyard, and I went to kneel before her. Her eyes widened with alarm, and I could tell she thought I was leaving kutfwasa. She was relieved when I told her that, on the contrary, I was seeing to it that I could continue kutfwasa. With my finger I drew the egg-shaped contour of Swaziland in the dirt. "We are here," I said, stabbing the map's center. I then touched the very top. "And a town called Sipiki is up here. That's sixty miles. I'm going to start walking, and somewhere between here and Sipiki I'm going to find a goat!"

The trip worried her. She asked where I'd sleep and I said I'd ask for a place along the way; she said there were robbers and I said the way I was feeling I'd beat the shit out of them; she said there were wild animals and I said I'd *eat* them. I was angry, and it was anger that propelled me out of the homestead, past the astonished looks of the men at the brewing shack, past the good-bye waves from MaZu, LaShonge, and Gogo Mabusa, and past the knots of people who couldn't believe that a stranger with no friends in their land would be so crazy as to simply start walking into the unknown.

Well, I thought through the fury that pushed me forward, for six months I'd been cooped up in that homestead and it was time for this adventure of mine to expand its horizons. I traveled quickly out of the narrow Kwaluseni valley with its farms of mud huts and branch cattle enclosures slumbering, always slumbering, in the late afternoon sunshine. A road the color of dried blood brought me up into the hills, and the further I traveled the less angry I became. I was doing something, I was moving; the clean air filled my lungs, my leg muscles seemed strong and happy to be in use, and the scenery of Swaziland began to lull me with its pastoral, dawn-of-time beauty.

For the remainder of the day I inquired at the gates of tiny homesteads that clung to the hillsides, but no one kept goats. Toward sunset, the people I met began to ask when I'd be returning to my valley. But I was serious about going as far as I had to until I got what I needed, even if I had to sleep in the bushes. When dusk approached, I asked a sympathetic-looking widow living with her sister and three children if I could pay her something and spend the night in the kitchen or an outbuilding. She seemed doubtful, so I thanked her and continued on my way.

I hadn't walked far on the narrow road winding through the hills when a small voice hailed me from behind: "Mr. Sibolomhlope!"

I turned and saw a boy with a large head and a thin body clad in torn shorts and a shirt several times too big running breathlessly up to me. "Yes? And what is your name?"

"Timkhosi, sir."

"Hello, Timkhosi. And how in the world do you know my name?"

"You were in the newspaper! We have it at home." I hadn't been able to hide from the local reporters forever, and when they found me they had put my face on the front page of the *Swazi Observer:* "WHITE AMERICAN HERE FOR KUTFWASA."

I walked back along the narrow road with the boy to find the widow whom I had recently met. She turned out to be Timkhosi's grandmother, and waited at the gate with her sister, Timkhosi's great-aunt. I saw by their faded dresses how poor they were, and by their sinewy arms and the sun wrinkles around their eyes how hard they worked the fields. "I did not mean to send you away," the widow apologized. "But what would you eat?" I saw the responsibility of housing an American was heavy on her mind: I probably slept in a bed and ate meat! I wanted to hug her for her worry, and I opened my bag for her to see. "I bought some bread along the way. Look, an apple! Two!" I handed her one, and she, her sister, and the boy laughed. Two smaller children were sent scurrying into a guest hut to sweep it out for me. "I will cook for you some real Swazi beans!" the widow promised.

Before setting out, I had addressed the lidlotis in the Indumba to ask their protection on the road ahead; now, at dusk, I found a secluded place to kneel, cover my head with a cloth, and speak to them again. On

a cliff above, round huts were set like boulders. It was the first night I had
been away from the Indumba since starting kutfwasa, and I explained to
the spirits what I was doing out there.

I emerged from the cloth into a warm, mellow evening. The valley
stretching out below, where candles glowed in the windows of distant
houses, was quiet and peaceful compared to the place I had left. When I
returned to the huts, Timkhosi was waiting to show me the family's avocado tree. Its fruits were the size of cantaloupes. I said, "Why, in the U.S.
one of these, if you could get it, which you can't, would sell for five
bucks!"

"Five emalangeni!" Timkhosi marveled.

"Dollars. That would be twelve and a half emalangeni."

"Americans are rich!"

"That depends on how you define 'rich,'" I said.

The boy proceeded to do so. "Do you have a car?"

"Yes."

"And a TV? Does it play tapes? I think you have a computer!"

"Sure I do. But let me ask you something. Do this." I inhaled a deep
breath until my chest expanded with air. "What do you smell?"

Timkhosi inhaled with a serious expression of concentration. He
looked puzzled. "Nothing. The trees?"

"Yes. And the grass. And the earth. Little boys like you in American
cities, where most of us live, smell chemicals and car poisons when they
breathe."

In the twilight, the stars were coming out. "See those?" I said. "In the
places I lived in America, you can't see them at all."

"Why?"

"Too many lights. Too much apathy. I want to ask you one more
thing, my friend. Have you ever seen an elephant?"

"Yes!" Timkhosi replied. "Many! In the wilderness preserves."

"In America, the children never see elephants in the wild, in their
natural homes, the way you do."

His gaze drifted away. He said quietly, "But I like elephants." He was
thinking of the dream that was America, where everyone was rich but
where, he now learned, people lived without roaming elephants and
stars and sweet-smelling air.

When I went to the guest hut, a girl told me brightly, "Granny gave
you a candle! And she left something for you!" I entered the hut to find a
complete dinner set out on a small table: a pot of tea, a bowl of sugar,
some sliced bread, and a covered plate. I lifted the lid, and the delicious

aroma of a peppered bean dish rose with the steam. And I had wondered how I would survive on the road! It seemed as if my lidlotis were rewarding me for taking the initiative of this trip. That night I said to them, "You know, I'm discovering a Swaziland out here that's very different from that mess I left back in Kwaluseni. Thank you for showing me the way."

I met the widow outside, and she told me of a place in the mountains where goats were to be had. At dawn she would be headed that way with her two grandsons to attend a prayer service at a relative's homestead, and I could accompany her.

I rose early, and we set out as an amber full moon descended over the valley to our left and dawn was breaking in volcanic red to our right. We soon encountered a dozen members of a Christian sect along the hilly road. They sang as they walked and were led by a tall elder with a gray beard and a brass cross raised in powerful hands. The men were attired in tight green knee-length coats over white trousers and the women wore white robes with green sashes. The men crouched and leapt and shouted as they sang, a vestigial spirit of pagan ritual in them as strongly as the Holy Ghost. All were smiling, happy to see us, happy to be alive.

The widow refused the money I offered for the lodging; she seemed content to tell me of her life and her long-dead husband as we walked briskly for hours through fields and forests. We didn't rest for a moment; the old woman was tireless. She only hesitated when we came to a forty-foot gorge where a bridge had been swept away. But she eventually found the courage to follow after the boys and I proceeded single file across a girder set between cliffs, while two crocodiles, motionless in the river below, appraised us for our food value through yellow eyes. After three hours we began to climb a steep mountain trail that soon brought us to a homestead, where a rectangular main house was set between boulders as large as trucks. The people of the place saw us ascending the path, and came out to greet us. The widow introduced me to the owner, a middle-aged man in traditional loinskins, and his three wives. They invited me to join them in the sitting room of the main house where tea, bread, and fruit would be served.

I entered to find a room crowded with legless sofas and, sitting upon them inches above the floor and smiling broadly as they looked up at me, three young men in shiny shirts and black trousers. The eldest announced they were born-again Swazis. I noticed he affected the smooth manner and aggressive geniality of an American televangelist. With a preacher's studied hand gestures he indicated his two grinning companions, their long legs sprawled out before them. "This is Dumisane. He is a preacher. This is Mduduzi. He is a preacher. I am Joseph, servant of the Lord. And you are the American who is to be a sangoma?"

"Word gets around," I said with a small sigh, sitting down. I knew what was coming: many such good-hearted folk had tried to convert me to one of the dozens of churches that sprouted like mushrooms along the Swazi spiritual landscape. The preacher named Joseph blithely told me that all mankind was destined for hell if they were not saved; meaning, of course, baptized into his obscure sect. These men were obstinate and closed-minded about their religion, but at the same time boyishly cheerful and, I suspected, capable of skipping over to another sect at any time. When they casually informed me that I was damned because I did Satan's work by curing people in the Indumba, I replied that they had their facts wrong: a sangoma does not worship the lidlotis, who are not divine. This impressed and worried them, for they were not used to a reasonable discussion of religion. Their minds had been filled with the propaganda, intolerance, and fanaticism that too often accompany religious zeal. One of the men closed his eyes and began to chant "Praise Jesus! Praise Jesus!" as protection against me, Satan's representative in their sitting room. Joseph had lost his smooth manner and persisted unhappily, "But you pray to your spirits!"

"We talk to them, the way I'm talking to you."

This bothered them further; it wasn't what they had been told by their fundamentalist Christian elders. The room began to fill up with about twenty men and women from nearby homesteads, and they decided that the only thing to do was to pray for me, for not only did I communicate with spirits but I was Catholic and therefore doubly damned. They were so pleasant and enthusiastic in their desire to save me from hell's fire that I grinned and knelt down on the floor with them. The tin roof shook with the cries of the faithful and the wails of women possessed, they said, by the Holy Spirit.

When it was over, I thanked them, and a girl led me up a path to a neighboring homestead at a higher elevation. I found goats there, but the head of the household was away. No one could say when he would return, and I proceeded to the next place. And so it went through the day: stops at places that had no goats or places that did but where no one was willing to part with one. I could not be discouraged because my resolve was firm: it felt as if I had all the time in the world, and I was passing through pretty mountain scenery and interesting little homesteads ingeniously situated on narrow, rocky ledges. Fruit trees were planted as windbreaks before them, and the crops that sustained these homesteads were reached by quarter-mile vertical trails leading to fields below. At regular intervals I'd come to a single-room shop similar to an old-fashioned general store. No matter how inaccessible a place was, fresh bread and milk were somehow delivered to these shops in the mornings. Canned goods, candles, soaps, and matches lined plank shelves along the walls, separated from the customers by a broad counter. Bored-looking men or young women, resentful that their daydreaming was interrupted, gathered goods from the shelves when a customer pointed to them. I bought half a loaf of bread to eat with an avocado Timkhosi had given me, and a pineapple soda. With no electricity at the shop for refrigeration, the soda was room temperature, but tasted good against the hot noon.

I stopped and chatted with people along the way, and by late afternoon received a tip about a place where I could definitely find a goat. I'd had false leads before, but this one proved legit. The owner of a homestead built over a ledge of rock and populated by a half-dozen shy and ragged children said his brother would part with a goat from his herd. He lived far away, however, and it would be best if I unrolled my sleeping bag in a hut for the night, and in the morning he'd have one of his sons show me the way.

I was far off the beaten path now, and exotic strangers were so unknown in these parts the children were too timid to come near me. Their father had to hand them the candies I offered. A crimson sunset flared over the sharp peaks of mountains that pressed in close to us, and an acid-green meteor streaked over the horizon like a UFO while the children peeked at me from behind mud walls of stick huts, disappearing the instant I returned their look.

The next morning, there were chores to do before the son could be spared as my escort, and I helped by scraping kernels off maize cobs using a stone's rough edge. Women poured the buckets of kernels we filled into a large circular bin of corrugated iron. The sky was clouding over when I finally departed with my guide, a twelve-year-old boy. For two hours we followed roads and paths that meandered up the side of a slender, triangular peak.

When we arrived at a compound of gray huts set in a circle, we found in the middle of the central yard a half-naked old man washing his feet in a tub. He had a nasty disposition, and when I told him the purpose of my visit, dropping respectfully to one knee, his eyes grew wide and he reacted as if my request was outrageous. *"Imbuti! Nanini, nani, nani!"* ("A goat! Never, ever!") I thanked him, and suppressed a sigh; with rain threatening, the trip seemed less fun. But once I left and was descending a path, a young man wearing patched trousers, a striped shirt, and a black beret ran to catch up with me. "Sir! I can get you a goat! There is a homestead up there."

Seeing only rocky outcroppings and a peak above, I asked how anybody could live up there. He gave me his name, Bongani, and assured me that goats were to be found. All I had to do was wait until a boy brought one down. Two hours later a boy did show up pulling a small, shaggy white goat at the end of a rope. I paid Bongani, who had the boy accompany me to a road where I could find a bus. We managed to pick up a dozen other boys from the area along the way, and when we came to the road an hour later I gave them all shiny coins with wavy edges that bore the likeness of their youthful, feather-crowned king. They stood and gazed at the coins in their hands, and I doubted that anyone had ever given them money before.

The children left and I waited, the goat tied to a tree and munching grass. Perhaps one bus a day would travel a little-used road like this one. It was four o'clock in the afternoon, and when two more hours passed I was certain no bus was coming. I spotted an abandoned hut a few hundred yards away. The first fat raindrops hit the ground, making splattering sounds like insects striking a car windshield. I untied the goat, and when we made it to the house rain was coming down hard. A plank door hanging from one hinge opened onto a dank, single room. A section of grass roof had fallen in, but in the opposite corner I was able to build a small fire from sticks and loose planks. Outside it grew rapidly dark. Angular mountain peaks disappeared into the black clouds of the sky. There was no traffic along the road, no sound but steady rainfall. I felt strange and sad being there all alone, with only a goat munching fallen roofing grass as company. I addressed the lidlotis, observing that evening ritual. I opened a tin of meat and a can of juice from my bag, ate an orange, and then lay down in my sleeping bag over a mattress of grass. The rain fell harder, and came through the hole in the roof to splash into the fire's embers, which hissed when struck. Then I remembered: I had forgotten what day it was. I knew this day was coming, but with no newspapers, TV, or radio to remind me of the date, not even a calendar, it was hard to remember if it was Tuesday or Wednesday, much less the sixteenth or the seventeenth.

"You know something, goat?" I said aloud, and for once the horned animal with pupils in its eyes like two vertical slits looked at me. "It's my birthday."

The goat had been fussing and kicking all afternoon, but it now lay demurely on its bed of grass as if auditioning for a role in a Christmas crèche.

Cold rain fell, the red glow of the fire's coals was dying under a blanket of ash, and in the blackness outside no life stirred, as if the world no longer existed. I had to hear something, even if it was only the sound of my own voice. "Do you know how I always spend this day, goat? Depending on where I am, I'll go to that nice art deco bar on the Queen Mary, which is tied up, sort of the way you are, down at Long Beach. If I'm in Chicago, I'll go the bar at the Drake Hotel, or if I'm in New York, to the bar at the Waldorf, where the harpist plays. And I always order the same drink: a Manhattan—sweet vermouth, bourbon, and a cherry, straight up in a chilled cocktail glass. At the Drake they serve them in crystal snifters."

For a long time, I stared bleakly out the hole in the roof at the rainy darkness beyond. "It doesn't get much lonelier than this, does it."

▲ ▲ ▲ ▲

My arrival at Prince Vovo's homestead after a two-hour trip with the goat tied on top of the bus was greeted by hand-clapping and the women's high-pitched ululations. They knew they were about to have a feast.

The goat was slaughtered and I was quickly washed in its sticky, warm blood. Sam skinned the animal, gave it to the homestead's women, and they started cooking.

But the cleansing ritual was a serious matter, and Gogo Ndwandwe, MaZu, and LaShonge worked in a no-nonsense, businesslike manner. I sat naked on a mat behind the Indumba, covered head to toe with coagulating goat's blood, and they worked quickly to give me a second bath with the contents of the goat's stomach: a green pungent chyme of half-digested grass and guava leaves. I had washed patients this way, and to me it was the latest step in my kutfwasa development: a difficult and unpleasant act but an important rite of passage for a prospective sangoma. I wasn't squeamish and I knew the rite was necessary, but my one contrary thought was there is never only one way to do something, and if I or a patient had to be cleansed and made to "shine" for the ancestral spirits, my job would be to find another method. But for now this was it: a blood and chyme bath that had served these people well for ages.

I was not permitted to wash until the following morning, and I spent the rest of the day swatting away a swarm of biting flies for whom I, covered with blood and stomach debris, must have seemed like housefly heaven. At dawn I had a bath of medicine laced with goat's blood. I also steamed and vomited with the mixture, and repeated the process the next day. I reminded myself that the procedure was not meant to cure a conventional ailment but to correct a spiritual malaise using supernatural powers. But it was hard for me to feel cleansed when I was covered with crud. Nor did I feel peaceful inside when the procedure was finally over on the third day; I was agitated. I felt so strongly that something unexpected was about to happen that I was concerned. The medicinal baths had washed away spiritual impurities which had shrouded me. The lidlotis could see me clearly now. But what, I wondered a bit anxiously, would they see?

Inside the new hut a few days later, toward the end of May, I climbed a ladder workmen had nailed together from old roofing poles. A ray of white sunlight cut laserlike through the interior, striking my cheek as I moved toward its source: an opening I intended to patch with grass so rain would not come in. I was ten feet above the ground when the bottom of the ladder slipped backward as if yanked by an unseen hand.

I held on as the ladder dropped. The end by my head tore at the roofing grass, which flew like chicken feathers, and when the ladder hit the top rim of the plaster wall my left wrist snapped. Now the ladder's end was scraping against the wall as it dropped, tearing loose pieces of plaster. It struck the table where I did my cooking in an explosion of flying pots, utensils, and breaking bottles. My knee broke through a rung; my left wrist snapped a second time.

I pulled myself off and looked at my left arm. The wrist was bent at an odd angle. In the moment before shock was replaced by pain, I opened the door with my right hand and tossed the ladder outside in disgust.

"You need pictures, Lusiba!" Gogo Ndwandwe cried when she saw my wrist. She meant X rays, and these were available at the hospital in Manzini. A bus got me there in twenty minutes.

The doctor, a white volunteer from Oklahoma City who admired my Swazi attire, inspected the X rays and found my wrist fractured in two places. I returned to Gogo Ndwandwe at sunset with my arm in a cast that extended to my shoulder.

"I'm stuck in this thing for six weeks," I reported bleakly. "I don't know how this will affect my kutfwasa." My teacher was also concerned but urged me to continue with all the rituals to the best of my ability.

I did not ask Gogo Ndwandwe how this accident could follow an elaborate medical treatment intended to boost my luck, because from the moment it happened I was haunted again by a concern I had been living with for two weeks. Shortly after a thief cut open my suitcase and stole my money, Gogo Ndwandwe came to the hut and applied a secret ointment to the case. "The person who stole your money, his hands will get all swollen up," she said. "Only I can treat him, and I'll charge him a lot of money."

I was puzzled. "You mean we'll be harming this man?"

She nodded with a smile that suggested the thief would be getting what he deserved. I had serious reservations about the ethics of doing this. I saw the sangoma's role as one of curing people, not using supernatural potions to injure them for revenge and then shaking them down for a lot of money. Wasn't that black magic? Wasn't that bewitching someone for vengeance and profit?

My opinion was not sought on the matter, and I knew better than to incite my teacher's anger by questioning her judgment. But looking back following my accident, I had to wonder how much I also wished revenge. The ointment still glistened on my suitcase, and my wrist was badly fractured. Now whose hand was "all swollen up"? It was the hand that belonged to a person who had just undergone a cleansing ritual so his lidlotis could see him clearly, and what the spirits had immediately perceived was my willingness to do something I knew was wrong because I was angry about a robbery.

I was beginning to learn about Indumba ethics, about a sangoma's responsibilities, and, it might also seem, lidloti teaching methods that included corporal punishment.

I had these things in mind one morning a week after the accident. Mornings were the most difficult times because I was unable to dress myself. Jabulani stopped by after his night shift as a security guard and tied my loinskins and undercloths for me. We chatted; I fumbled with one hand to make coffee on the stove.

"I don't see why the dead can't be left alone," I complained. I told him that Gogo Ndwandwe had been visited by a woman who claimed my dead plasterer Mabizweni was a thief: he had worked at her place by day and said flattering things, and at night he came back and stole anything he could. "She said they hadn't been able to find him. Maybe they should try the cemetery!"

"Ah, he is clever!" Jabulani muttered darkly.

He said nothing more. I sensed something, and I asked him what he knew. Reluctantly, he allowed, "This Mabizweni was not true to you."

"How?" I asked.

"He was working for another man, but he quit that man so he could work for you and get more money. But that man threatened to call the police, so Mabizweni lied to you and went back to finish his job."

"When was that?" I was puzzled. "He was with me the whole time, except when his daughter died."

Jabulani's slightly crossed eyes dropped to the floor, and he answered slowly. "It was not his daughter who died. It was his brother's daughter who died."

I stood still and stared at him, trying to rationalize: many Swazis took their brother's or sister's children as their own. Perhaps Mabizweni felt that way. He was too distraught when he came to me to be lying. Or was he drunk? I gave him money for the girl's coffin. Did he just pocket it and then go off to finish this other job Jabulani spoke of?

I didn't want to believe it. I told Jabulani, "I saw him in the hospital. He was dying. He knew I had come to see him because I cared about him. No man can look another in the eye on his deathbed and not tell the truth!"

Jabulani continued to look at the floor, he was so embarrassed for me. "I am sorry, Sibolomhlope. We did not know he was dead, like you said, so we were not surprised when we saw him that day. He was on the back road, talking to his assistant."

"When was that?"

"The day you were robbed."

My eyes clamped shut as if I had been struck. Then it had been Mabizweni, with the cooperation of his assistant "guarding" my hut, who had entered that day, cut open the suitcase, and made off with all my money. He knew it was there because he once saw me withdraw money from the suitcase to pay him. His talk of bewitchment? A plot to make me feel guilty and uncertain. Our friendship? In my loneliness I had accepted his overtures as friendly, but I now saw he had been ingratiating himself to avert my suspicion. Had he bribed the hospital nurse to tell me he died, or was she simply uninformed, as so many were? But what cut deepest was that Mabizweni had me believe that he went to his death thinking he was bewitched because of his association with me. He'd have me live the rest of my life carrying that guilt.

I had to shake my head in grim wonder: he had been brilliant. He played upon my trusting nature (or my naivete), my ignorance of his culture, my loneliness and vulnerability like a master. I had never felt so betrayed or helpless in my life. Even if I could locate Mabizweni—and other than Jabulani on the day of the robbery no one had seen him in a month—Gogo Ndwandwe would not let me file a police report for a crime that occurred at "the king's place." Perhaps it was best I didn't find Mabizweni; the way I was feeling I'd crush his skull in my hands. And that, I thought darkly, might not be the most suitable act for a healer.

That evening we were visited by a sangoma, a large woman with close-cropped hair from a nearby homestead who always had a sympathetic and motherly fondness for me. She performed some divination rituals in our Indumba, and I sat with my arm in its L-shaped cast watching her use an oxtail brush to "sniff out" her patients' problems as she circled them on her knees. She was very good at this, but my mind was elsewhere, on Mabizweni's treachery.

I was startled out of my thoughts when the sangoma finished prescribing a cure for a patient's illness and, still on her knees, turned toward me. Her eyes were closed, her face was wet with sweat, and she swished her long oxtail brush back and forth beneath her chin. In rapid, rhythmic phrases, she spoke to me, "You are angry about your injury. You are saying, 'Why are they doing this to me?' You want to beat the people. Because you are angry."

She told me I must seek an answer from my lidlotis. I must go to the river, at night, now. I must bring a candle to light my way and draw the spirits to me, and beside this candle at the river I must speak to them.

Yes, I thought, what do the lidlotis who brought me here have to say about all that's happened to me these past months? I took a candle from the house, lit it, and carried it outside in my good hand. I headed down the road toward the river. It was late. I encountered one couple who looked startled at what must have been the ghostly appearance of this tall, candle-lit white man with a long white sheet draped over his shoulders. There was a small breeze, but the candle flame did not go out.

At the edge of the little stream, I pushed the candle's base into the gravel at its edge. Everything was cast into darkness beyond a circle of light that touched the transparent water flowing noiselessly before me. I covered myself completely with the sheet. Clapping my cupped hands twice for each name, I greeted the ancestral spirits who had come to me thus far in the evening drum-beating rituals, and then I greeted the African tribes whose lidlotis inhabited the Indumba: the Bandzawe, the Timzmzu, and the Benguni. This done, I shook my head resignedly, and spoke.

"This may be the last time I talk to you this way, lidlotis. I can't go on like this, and I think I need some encouragement from you, some acknowledgement at least that what I'm going through is for a good reason. I need *something*." I told them the first months of kutfwasa had been wonderful, but that had changed. The physical injuries and the isolation I felt didn't seem as painful as the loss of something: the loss of an innocence I once had about this venture. "I know I had no right to expect anything when I came here, but I did. I realize this now. I suppose what I wanted to find was love and understanding between people, and prove that we can all respect one other in this world. And either I'm blowing it, or it's not to be had."

I reminded them that I had been at that river at night once before, the time I admitted to myself that they, the lidlotis were real and not imaginary. Now it was a different crisis: my kutfwasa was overwhelmed by problems. I listed them: Gogo Ndwandwe seemed to be in a perpetually irritable mood, the people of the homestead were increasingly reluctant to beat the drums to bring out new lidlotis now that the novelty of my arrival had worn off, MaZu was frequently ill or absent with her boyfriends, LaShonge was often drunk, there was crime and noise, and finally the homestead's neighborhood was depressingly ugly now that winter had stripped away the greenery to reveal a dusty, garbage-strewn landscape. Many of my kutfwasa problems centered around the rowdy homestead of Prince Vovo, and if I were to continue this venture I would have to consider finding a more suitable place to study, even if it meant leaving Gogo Ndwandwe.

I clapped my cupped hands in conclusion. I pulled the sheet off my head and sat up. A great, painful sadness ran through me, because I knew my kutfwasa was over if things continued the way they were. It was up to the lidlotis now: they had to communicate with me somehow. I didn't expect a sign to arrive as fireworks in the sky, but, still, I couldn't help but look up. Perhaps a shooting star? None fell.

Two days later, on Sunday, I still hadn't made up my mind whether I would stay or go. To think things through I went for a walk, my arm cast banging against my chest with each step down the dirt road. It was June, and only a few days remained before the southern hemisphere's winter solstice. Shadows were long, but the sun was out and the day was mild.

I decided to rest underneath a tree; I liked the view. I sat with my back to the late-afternoon sun, and ahead the valley and all it contained was burnished by a golden light: the greens of trees were dark velvet and the cloudless sky was deep blue. The coats of cattle grazing on white maize stubble were lustrous brown and black. To my right was a large tree with low, heavy branches occupied by herd-boys. They sang in boys' voices a man's work song. They saw me but paid no mind, for I was gazing out over the valley, the blue mountain peaks, the golden sunshine— the type of orderly rural arcadia that Gainsborough or Constable once painted.

The boys were gone from the branches of the tree. There was a stranger standing ahead of me, facing me. I couldn't see him clearly, but it appeared he was wearing a suit. His entire figure was in shadow, as if he were silhouetted against the sun. And yet the sun was shining upon him. Suddenly he was before me, standing a few feet away, looking down at me as I sat with my back against the tree trunk. I still could not see him clearly. But I knew who he was."

"How's the kid?" he said.

"I'm tired, Harry," I complained to my lidloti. "I'm disgusted"

"So you've been saying. It hasn't been easy."

"How come, Harry? Why? Why was building the house such a fiasco? It was your lidlotis' house! Why was I everyone's patsy? Why is there this artillery barrage in my head all the time?"

"Why?" the midnight-black figure before me said with humor. "Why? Why? Why? Why do you think? Or did we choose you because you're stupid?"

I thought, then I said with wonder, "I do *know* why! I've always known, haven't I?"

"Well, sometimes it's hard to see clearly when you're in the thick of things . . ."

"I've been set up!" I said, not in anger but in awe. "By you and the others. To see what I'd do!"

"Naturally." His tone became serious. "But don't think it's just you. It's what life is all about. That's why you're there."

"Then life is just a test?"

"A series of moral choices, actually. If you pass, then one day you'll find your peace."

"That's . . . so simple!"

"Really?" Harry said this with a wryness that made me feel that it was I who was simple. I thought of all that had happened, and I felt ashamed. If I had known I was being tested, I would have acted better. Instead, I got angry and made mistakes.

He read my mind. "You can't 'act' your way out of a moral dilemma. You make a choice, right or wrong, and reap the rewards or pay the consequences."

I looked down at my plaster-swathed arm, which was the consequence of having agreed to injure someone with the lidlotis' medicine. "This was no accident."

"Accident?" I felt his smile burning into my downcast head. "There are no accidents."

Still looking at the cast, I said, ashamedly, "I failed this test."

"The bewitchment medicine? Yeah, you flunked. But give yourself credit for figuring out what you did wrong."

I looked up into the shadowy face. I knew he was about to leave.
"Don't go."

Harry laughed. *"I just told you the meaning of life! What can I do for an encore?"*

"But if you leave, then I'll awaken, and it'll all seem dim. I'll forget, and start to doubt. And I'll lose the message."

Without moving he now stood twenty feet away. "Time dims real life experiences, too. Dreams and memories are all the same in the end. You'll need reminding from time to time. Everyone does. That's just the way we're made."

I was in a panic, desperate to keep him. He could tell me everything. Everything! I shouted, "Made by who, Harry? God?"

"Who else?"

He was gone.

"HARRY!"

The chilly cry caught in my throat, and my eyes opened. I was alert and realized that I hadn't been asleep. Once before I had had a vision while awake, when I saw John MacDonald's Scottish farmhouse in the place of that Swazi hut in the predawn blue one morning. But this vision was more profound: I had entered it, was taken over by it. I had become what was called *Indlu Yemaphupha*, a "house of dreams."

Across the way, the herd-boys were dropping from the tree's limbs like ripe fruit. The sun was setting, and the golden light had acquired a brasslike hue. I stood and walked quickly, with no direction in mind but with a body full of energy. I felt wonderful. Harry spoke little but had said so much! He certainly shot down moral relativism. Things were either right or wrong, and human equivocating suddenly seemed like childish play to me. My shame at the mistakes I had made was offset by Harry's compliment that I had understood my failure with the bewitchment medicine. I felt he was endorsing not only my pursuit of the sangoma's calling but the need to understand what was behind it.

I wasn't out of the woods yet, I knew. Challenges remained, and, I suspected, more moral tests. But for the first time in weeks—months!—I felt I was thinking clearly. And clear as the valley air I inhaled into my lungs, a name came to me, and I thought of the person who might be able to see me through at least one of my problems.

"Of course! Evah!"

seven

Zebras

WHEN I SHOWED up at Evah's door in Manzini town, her eyes shone with concern at the sight of my arm cast. She made tea while I sat on the sofa in her cramped one-room flat, and from time to time she glanced at me with a small and, it seemed, knowing smile.

I had visited Evah once after my first lunch with her and Thandaza. Her son Sandile had come to my hut with the message that Evah needed to see me, and I had arrived to find her upset over Thandaza. Evah had entrusted Thandaza with some of her dresses to sell in South Africa, and she had disappeared with them. I hadn't been able to give Evah any information about Thandaza, but we had enjoyed another lunch together, one of the few moments of peace I found during those difficult weeks. Evah had been open and friendly, even slightly flirtatious, which reminded me what Thandaza had indiscreetly reported: after that first lunch, Evah had confessed, "If only *I* could find a man like James!" That knowledge had given me the courage to come back this day.

Evah placed the tea tray before me and sat down with the same knowing smile. I crossed my good arm over the one in the cast, and gave her a wry smile in return. "Do you know why I'm here?"

"I think so," she said softly.

"Thandaza told you what we were going to do together, I know. She told you about the lidloti who wants me to have a child." Evah nodded her head. "You don't think that's crazy?"

"No," Evah said with quiet conviction. "I know about kutfwasa. I respect the lidlotis."

"Well, I should tell you that for those three months Thandaza was here, I never slept with her." But Evah knew this, too. I explained, "The truth is, I just couldn't have as the mother of my child someone I didn't love. Thandaza turned out to be a shady character. I know more about you than her, and I've only seen you twice." I knew that Evah had a seventeen-year-old son, who had been born during her last year in high school. The father had been a fellow student who couldn't support a son and had refused to marry Evah. Sandile was raised by Evah and her mother. His father married someone else, went into business, and later sent for his son to live with him until Sandile returned to his mother a year ago, when he assisted her with what Evah politely called her "problem."

In fact, it had been a tragedy. Evah had a South African lover who had been a good man, and she was distraught when he disappeared one day. She learned he was in jail, and then discovered she was pregnant with his baby. Evah did not specify his crime because she was afraid to discuss the politics of that volatile region, but I was able to learn he had been involved in the liberation movement, had been picked up at a

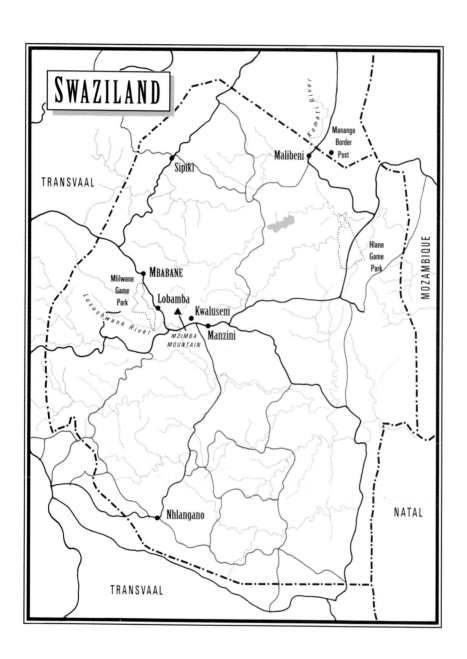

(above) Myself before kutfwasa: In Beverly Hills, California, with the 1937 Cadillac I owned then. (left) Attired as a kutfwasa student.

The wooden superstructure of my Kwaluseni hut comes together.

Digging medicinal roots along the Komati River.

Preparing herbal medicine: chopping roots with a machete...

...and crushing pieces to powder in mortar on the stoop of my hut.

Administering medicine (kugata) on patient.

The ematsambo
"divination bones."

*My little mud hut in
Malibeni.*

Evah.

Vusi in April 1990.

Nomoya at five months old, December 1990.

Imigato strings worn over the shoulder are cut from medicinal roots.

Sangomas in ceremonial finery dance before the Indumba "spirit house."

In 1991, a sangoma now, I'm visited by Miriam Makeba.

border crossing, and disappeared into the gulag of the apartheid state. Evah endured a difficult pregnancy with Sandile and her mother at her side. Another son was born to her, but the baby lived only a few minutes because of the hospital staff's negligence.

It was a poignant thing to watch her pull out of a high cupboard all the baby things she had collected but was never able to use: a bath tub, diapers, a bib, some clothes she and her mother had knitted. "I saved all these things. I always knew I would use them again," she said with a smile. When she sat down beside me, I took her hand.

"Evah, are you saying you'd be willing to have my baby?"

"You must meet with my father and tell him how you intend to support the child and me, because I and not you will be raising it. A child needs its mother. If my father is satisfied, I will do it."

"But let me ask you something: why *would* you do it? You don't know me at all."

She replied pleasantly, "I know you have two brothers who followed you, and a sister who is older, and your parents are alive and still working even though they're elderly . . ."

"Well, they're not *that* old."

". . . and you like the music of Philip Glass, and you think he should beat the Indumba drums, and you wished you had *Time* magazine to read every week. Oh, you talked when you were here!" She grew serious. "But mostly I know that I respect you for working to become a sangoma. I too can see things, and I know you are not a bad type who will run away and leave me with a baby."

"I like you, Evah," I said. "I like being with you, very much. But I almost made a terrible mistake with Thandaza, and I think we should be careful." I indicated my bulky arm cast. "This thing's scheduled to come off on the Fourth of July—my own day of independence. Then I want to consecrate my new house, and Gogo Ndwandwe is taking us on a trip for some important ceremonies when MaZu finishes her kutfwasa." I told Evah it would be August, a month and a half away, before she and I had to make a decision, and in the meantime I'd like to come by and see her so we could get to know each other better. "Unfortunately, it's got to be done in secret. Gogo Ndwandwe supports my desire for a child, but she's afraid of gossip. I don't like it, because I'm excited about having a child and I want to tell the world, but I have to respect her wishes."

"She is right," Evah affirmed. "Swazis can kill you with their gossip."

Twice before Evah had been pregnant out of wedlock, which seemed unusually common in this country where polygamy was practiced by only a few men who could afford to keep multiple wives, but where the idea of polygamy seemed strong in the minds of young men who impregnated girlfriends they could not afford to marry. Swazis disliked birth control, and abortion was against the law. Consequently, the tiny kingdom had one of the world's highest population growth rates. And perhaps because children were traditionally raised by their mother or grandmother, with the father a distant figure enthroned in a homestead's main hut, no scandal was attached to this arrangement. Evah's son Sandile had never hindered her attracting other men, and she might have married her last lover if he had not become another of apartheid's victims. As for any child I might have with her, it would be considered legitimate if it bore my name, and if I publicly declared my fatherhood by honoring Evah's family with a gift of two cows, called an *imvimba*.

Evah wanted me to meet her father, who proved to actually be the uncle who had raised her. Her own father died when she was young, and her mother now lived with a second husband in Mozambique. Evah and I traveled by bus a week later to the house where she had grown up outside the capital town of Mbabane, and there I met a gentle, quiet, and polite man whose brown eyes nonetheless held a wryly humorous gleam. Evah's manner was identical to her mother's brother, down to the mischievous sparkle in her eye. Mr. Kunene had a shy smile set in a long face, a balding head with small ears, and large, veined hands which he clapped together twice when he saw me, giving me the sangoma's greeting. He knew not to shake hands with a person undergoing kutfwasa. From Evah he had learned who I was and what we were considering.

I was nervous at this meeting, but Mr. Kunene was warm and friendly, and he soon put me at ease as we sat in wicker chairs on the veranda and spoke SiSwati, he with a slight stammer. We discussed the sangoma's arts of healing and divination. He asked me if I intended to support myself in the future as a sangoma, and I replied that even if I succeeded and became one, I didn't see how I could earn money as a healer. The female sangomas I had seen like Gogo Ndwandwe lived on their husbands' farms, while the male sangomas I knew had farms of their own that supported their families. The income earned by healing was extra. I told Mr. Kunene that I hoped to return to my writing one day. He said that in the old days, sangomas traveled from village to village and were fed and housed while they treated people and lifted spells. They'd sometimes be given livestock when they left. Sangomas always had great prestige in Swazi society, but they were never rich.

Our meeting went well, Mr. Kunene accepted my pledge of two head of cattle if Evah and I had a baby, and I relaxed and joined Evah, her cousins, nieces, and nephews for a Sunday dinner along a long table piled with vegetables gathered from a copious garden and chickens raised in the yard. I drank Heineken beer with Malume, as Evah's uncle wished me to call him, and earned the kids' devotion by giving them a deck of cards, the plastic-coated kind that was always in demand.

Being accepted by Evah's family made the prospect of having a child by her more real. Her son Sandile had not been at the dinner. She hadn't told him of our plans and was grateful when I suggested that I have a talk with him. But first, I wanted to have my arm cast removed.

For the past six weeks I had been treating myself with the sangoma's bone fracture medicine called *umhlabelo*. I went to the river to find the small plant with the enormous, onion-shaped brown bulb. I peeled away its layers, pounded them in the mortar with my good hand, and boiled the paste into a foul-tasting mixture which I drank faithfully. At the hospital, new X rays showed the bones were thoroughly healed. When the cast was removed, my arm had shrunk to half its size, the muscle was soft as putty, and the hand was swollen and discolored. But it felt good to have it back, and medication brought the swelling down. Gogo Ndwandwe had lots of roots for me to pulverize to strengthen my emaciated arm.

I made a date to meet Evah's seventeen-year-old son, Sandile, at a restaurant in Manzini town. I waited outside and watched him walk toward me with the loping, loose-limbed walking style of young Swazi men, his skin luminously brown and his wide smile showing perfect teeth of unusual whiteness. Physically, Sandile resembled a Masai warrior: he was tall and broad-shouldered, with long, wiry limbs, muscular thighs, a narrow waist, and stern and proud facial features. His charming smile, amiable good humor and modest manner reflected his Swazi origins. He wore a shirt and tie and dress trousers to meet me. I imagined him running home to change out of his school uniform. He was finishing his last year at the Catholic high school, and had learned to speak English with precise, mellifluous diction.

The meeting went better than I could have hoped. Over tea and cake, he listened quietly to my explanation of the way kutfwasa worked, and the story of my lidloti who was never born. I said that just as my lidlotis were attuned to the mortal world through me, so, too, would this spirit experience life vicariously through the new life of my child.

Sandile smiled brightly, and said, "It's like an operation to get new eyes from someone else!"

But like Evah's uncle and family, and I suspected like all Africans I've met here, Sandile was not really interested in my explanations or my plans. He was attuned not to my words but to my voice, and his judgment would be based on the sincerity he heard there. I was therefore very touched after our meeting was finished, and Evah later confided to me, "Sandile told me, 'I do not just like Mr. Hall. I *love* him!'"

Though Evah was unable to attend, Sandile joined my friends and the people of Prince Vovo's homestead for the consecration of my new hut. The night before the ritual, tradition was observed inside the empty hut when I slaughtered a chicken that would be served to the guests, and LaShonge brewed a special batch of beer. About fifteen people crowded the circular room beneath a high cone of yellow, straw-like grass that glowed gold in the lamp light and smelled of the meadow. The sangomas brought in the drums and beat them until I, seated beneath the white sheet, was replaced by my lidloti, White Feather, who commandeered my voice and my body.

He did his intense but slow, bent-over dance, raising his knees high and howling like a wolf. The people seated at his feet cheered and clapped their hands. He knelt down, declared himself satisfied with the house, which he claimed for himself on behalf of all my lidlotis, and then cryptically warned that anyone who entered it with thoughts disrespectful to the spirits would be "unhappy." Someone set a tin of freshly brewed beer before him, and the spirit emptied it with a single long drink. The people cheered again, the spirit knelt close to the ground, and as the drums beat once more it departed.

I regained full awareness with my head buzzing from the strong alcoholic drink, LaShonge having brewed the beer to her taste. Sam reported what had transpired while my consciousness had been swimming like a goldfish deep within the dark tank of my body. Blinking my eyes, I looked around to find the party in full swing—a "hut warming" with people drinking beer and dancing to a cassette of the American soul singer Luther Vandross.

I slept well on my foam mattress my first night in the consecrated hut. It was a comfortable place, fifteen feet in diameter with an eight-foot-high circular wall of rough gray plaster surmounted by the ten-foot conical roof of thatched grass. A plank door opened onto a raised, half-moon step, and a single window with red curtains sewn by Evah looked out onto a field and a banana grove. I could hang my clothes over two long rods suspended from the roofing poles, eat at a brightly varnished handmade table with matching chairs, and cook on my small gas stove, which sat atop a plank table. There were two wooden benches for guests, four wall shelves for my medicine bottles, diaries and radio, and hanging hurricane lamps for light. Grass mats covered the floor, and no matter how hot the sun burned outside, the hut remained cool.

▲ ▲ ▲ ▲

After four years, MaZu was preparing to finish her kutfwasa. Students knew they were ready to undergo the graduation tests when the lidlotis took possession of them in the middle of the night and sang the *Inkhan-yan*. The song was heard only at this time. For weeks I had been coming out in the cold winter air at midnight to beat the drums while MaZu, in the grip of her spirits, sang and did her small-stepped swaying dance to the Inkhanyan. Then she departed for the homestead where Gogo Ndwandwe had done her kutfwasa and where her teacher, Gogo Sim-elane, still resided as one of the most powerful and respected sangomas in northern Swaziland.

The last Friday in July, a cold, gray, and windy day, we journeyed north to join MaZu and participate in the graduation rites. I had a bad feeling before piling into the back of the pickup truck with LaShonge and two female sangomas who made the trip with us, Gogo Ndwandwe seated in the cab with her cook and the driver. I knew enough now to trust my instincts, and soon a cold rain fell. Exposed in the open-air truck bed, I caught a cold that was my first illness of kutfwasa, though it hindered me little during the days of discovery that lay ahead.

We traveled for three hours until it was night and we reached northern Swaziland's border. The driver parked the truck at a small police station beyond which stretched the ominous dark fields of South Africa. We would not be entering that country. Our destination was a homestead that touched the border. Under the starlight we descended the steep banks of the wide Komati river and forded its shallow waters with our gear on our heads. It was so dark we could locate each other only by our voices. This was dry, flat country where a multitude of stars shone brightly in the clear sky. We had left the clouds and cold behind. Ahead in the darkness came what sounded like an army of drums beating the same rapid dance rhythm. It was dramatic and portentous, and as we drew closer to a col-lection of huts ringing a giant bonfire, I grew nervous. What lay ahead would be my public debut as a kutfwasa student. The people knew I was coming and had all heard about the white man who was studying to be a sangoma (and by all accounts was doing reasonably well). But now they would judge for themselves. Sangomas from all over the country who were present for the special graduation rites would watch my lidlotis dance; they would scrutinize how I dressed and observed ritual, and they would decide if I were fit to be accepted into their society.

We entered the homestead in silence, walking up a dirt drive that smelled of fresh cattle droppings. Orange light from the bonfire rose above a long main house where LaShonge, another sangoma who had just arrived, and I changed into our dancing skirts. In a small, candle-lit room, we knelt and fell into the trance that enabled out lidlotis to emerge. Then our lidlotis propelled us out of the house, and we burst into the courtyard where the hundred people ringing the log fire were beating drums, shaking rattles, and singing. I was later told that my sudden appearance was sensational.

People gasped, pointed, and were so startled by my arrival—a kutfwasa student who was a white man—that half the drums stopped sounding and the noise level dropped off for a moment before resuming with even greater force, inspired now by this in-the-flesh confirmation of the wild rumors the people had been hearing. Before the fire, the spirits possessing LaShonge, the new sangoma, and me danced side by side as if choreographed, with the same back-and-forth steps interspersed with jumps. Some women rushed up to me and placed a long peacock feather in my hair. A man tied leopard loinskins around my waist. Our spirits knelt and greeted the people with ritualistic phrases. They danced some more, then ran back to the main house and into the little room where they released us, and we reclaimed our physical selves.

I discovered the peacock feather in my hair and the loinskins tied around my dancing skirt, and I knew that these were gestures of acceptance and approval. I felt very happy and proud, and when I went out to the bonfire to help beat the drums, I was gladdened by the many faces I knew. Sangomas who had visited Prince Vovo's homestead were here, as well as friends like Sam who came to see the special graduation rites that would determine who would become a new sangoma. MaZu and three other women would be tested this weekend. Throughout the night we stayed awake beating drums as the four women emerged from this homestead's Indumba, a large circular hut with zigzag designs painted on the wall and a low, conical roof. In the throes of their spirits, they danced until dawn with only brief breaks to allow newly arriving sangomas to release their spirits and dance the greeting song.

Halfway through the night I located Gogo Ndwandwe wrapped in a blanket and seated before a fire that burned in a small, walled cooking courtyard behind the main house. As I joined her, I heard a booming voice with a babyish lisp loud within the house. I could not tell if it belonged to a man or a woman. In either case, the owner had to be an unusual character. But as the voice approached and grew louder, there was no doubt that it belonged to the *boss*. Gogo Ndwandwe smiled, and said her teacher, Gogo Simelane, was coming.

I moved from a sitting to a kneeling position. A stout woman with a broad, rubbery face, small, round eyes and a wide, thick-lipped mouth came within range of the flickering fire light. She was short but had a presence that made her seem huge, especially from my position on the ground. If she had been Gogo Ndwandwe's kutfwasa mentor, she'd be about sixty now. She sat down heavily on the only chair in the courtyard, adjusted the shiny cloths that swathed her bulky body, touched the scarf over her hair, and only then did she notice me at her feet.

Her eyes enlarged, and she threw wide her arms. *"Nkhosi 'ami!"* (My God!")

She never took her astonished eyes off me as I greeted her ritualistically by clapping cupped hands. I could see at once that this woman had a sense of humor, and she was playing the scene for all it was worth: clapping her hands loudly in response to mine and uttering words of wonder. Gogo Simelane leaned forward, placed her two hands on either side of my head, drew me toward her, and touched her forehead to mine. In Swazi custom this rare and intimate gesture of an elder to a younger person meant that we were now one.

She quizzed Gogo Ndwandwe about my kutfwasa. My teacher delivered a good report, saying I went to the river in the darkness of the winter morning every day to do the vomiting ritual, and my lidlotis had begun to spontaneously emerge in the afternoon to dance. Each SiSwati utterance of mine evoked more exclamations of wonder from Gogo Simelane. I couldn't stop grinning, and impulsively I took her hand and kissed it. This floored her. No white man had ever done *that* before. She grabbed my hand and delivered a wet smack of her own.

And that was generally the reception I received from the sangomas during a week of rituals, dancing, feasting, and trips to dig medicine with some of the finest herbal practitioners in Southern Africa. MaZu and the three others passed the exhausting tests, finding little sleep and looking wiped out at the end.

I wondered how I would endure if in a year's time I underwent these ordeals, which included locating hidden objects through divination ability. But all students and sangomas in attendance that week were tested at some point, and when someone hid a thing for me to find, I was able to locate it using my inchoate sangoma's insight. Kneeling in the dirt before the Indumba and speaking with the incessant throaty voice that a sangoma acquires when the lidlotis are working through him, I drew in my net by giving ritualistic responses to the young woman who was testing me, saying first what had been hidden *(Something from God's realm . . . a living thing . . . a person . . . a female . . . a girl . . . someone's daughter . . .*

a sangoma's daughter . . . MaZu's daughter . . . Doyenne!), and where
*(At the homestead . . . outside . . . close by . . . with us . . . right there,
hiding behind you!)* It was a small triumph, but an encouraging one.

I got to know the red clay huts, flat landscape, and thorny, dry shrub-
bery of the hamlet of Malibeni, named after the cemetery where the
Mahlalela clan was buried. The clan's current head was Gogo Simelane's
husband, "Lion" Mahlalela. He was a short man in his late fifties, with
a big belly, dark eyes, jet black hair and beard, and a kind manner.
Malibeni was prone to drought, and a difficult place to farm and raise
cattle. Years of troubles and worry seemed etched in deep furrows on
Mahlalela's brow, as if his oxen had plowed there.

The presence of up to three dozen sangomas attired in their finest
beads and feathers made Malibeni a magical place. Three students were
undergoing kutfwasa there, and they invited me to join them. I was
tempted: I would not have to go to the river alone in the morning, and
here the drums to bring out the lidlotis were beaten faithfully every
night. My spirits seemed to like the large Indumba, and two new lidlotis
emerged as I sat beneath the white sheet that week. There would be no
tape of either of them; I hadn't anticipated doing this ritual and had left
behind the cassette recorder. My recollections were frustratingly hazy.
But the sangomas in the Indumba swore that both spirits were black African men. If I was indeed possessed by such lidlotis, it might provide
another piece to the puzzle of how I came to do kutfwasa.

On my final night beneath the sheet, as expert drum beaters made
the powerful instruments sing like a primitive chorus, a vision arrived
that I did remember clearly:

A herd of zebra grazed in an expansive field of tall yellow grass.
No one owned this land, I sensed; it was Africa of long ago, a
time when tribes roamed, conquering or being conquered by
others. In the distance was a blue mountain range. The view
was low to the ground, as if I were looking through the eyes of
a hunter stalking the vast zebra herd moving slowly beneath a
bright blue sky. I felt a human heartbeat racing in anticipation.
Ahead were food, skins to wear, and bones for medicine . . .

That was all for now. It appeared that one of my lidlotis was an African hunter who knew medicine. He might have been of the Swazi tribe or
of a tribe that preceded today's Swazis. Perhaps I now had an explanation for the affinity I had felt at once for this land. The zebras? The image

of the running herd that had been appearing in my visions from the beginning of kutfwasa now stands revealed as the prey of this hunter lidloti.

Among the several sangomas I got to know was a slender, thin-faced man with a wispy goatee and a sweet disposition who lived over the border in South Africa. Just as I was known as Sibolomhlope, he went by the name of his most prominent lidloti, a name pronounced with two tongue clicks and a phantom consonant: Nqo(f)nqo(f). His eyes turned inward as he sang the ritual songs with a jazzy inflection, and he beat the drums with impressive power. He taught me to beat the three-drum setup; drums of different sizes and tones that called forth the Timzmzu river spirits from sangomas seated beneath white sheets along the riverbank. When playing a single drum, I had trouble keeping a constant rhythm for any length of time, but the three-drum setup was easy for me (the sangomas said I must have had Timzmzu spirits to accomplish this). I was called upon to provide the beat for some of these ceremonies. I felt proud to be entrusted with this task, and I was aware of the irony of myself perched on the riverbank, flailing away at the drums: a white man providing the rhythm for this black African ritual.

But this task seemed a part of the acceptance I was shown by the sangomas there. They were not moved by any spirit of charity, but by the work I had done in kutfwasa for eight months and the respect I held for the Indumba.

It was with real regret that I said good-bye to my new friends at the end of the week. I promised to return soon. But first I had important business at home.

▲ ▲ ▲ ▲

Evah was ready. I was ready. We had made our decision. We wanted our child. By undergoing kutfwasa and accepting the lidlotis I felt cut off from my past, but I also felt free from the constraints of my past. Having a child by Evah did not seem alarming or bad to either me, Evah, her family, Gogo Ndwandwe, or Gogo Simelane, who had been told by Gogo Ndwandwe before she could divine it through her own superior precognition. I would inform my family back in America in due course, as I put it in my diary, meaning, I suppose, at about the same time I told them I had acquired the powers of divination and necromancy!

Evah arrived at the homestead late Sunday afternoon, two days after my return from Malibeni. She went straight to Gogo Ndwandwe's sitting room, where she conferred for an hour with my teacher. Neither of them would tell me what they discussed, but I gathered part of the conversation concerned medications Gogo Ndwandwe prescribed for pregnancy. Gogo Ndwandwe had met Evah once before, and thought highly of her politeness and intelligence. She also liked "my cousin," as she called Evah's son Sandile when he had once come by. Sandile bore his father's name, Nxumalo, which was also Gogo Ndwandwe's clan name. With the clans as extended as they were, it was not unusual for a Swazi to run into a total stranger and find that he or she was a relative.

Gogo Ndwandwe called me in at the end of their conversation, and we both briefed Evah on the drum-beating ritual that would bring out the lidloti. Gogo Ndwandwe said she should wait in my hut and, when she heard the drums, blow out the candle, undress, open the window curtains to let the moonlight in, and lie down on the sponge mattress. Beyond that we were stumped; anything could happen.

I looked at Evah; she was nervous. "What if it is a lidloti that comes to me?" she whispered. "It might be angry finding me in its house and beat me!"

"Impossible!" cried Gogo Ndwandwe, overhearing. I squeezed Evah's hand reassuringly. She certainly had courage, doing this.

I was nervous myself. I had never made love to a woman expressly for the purpose of conceiving a child, and it felt strange. But I was excited, and after almost nine months of celibacy my body was nearly trembling at the prospect of finding release. I hurried about, seeing to Evah's comfort in my hut, checking the drums to make sure they were dry and pitch-perfect, collecting the rattles in the Indumba, and watching the sky darken.

Evening came, and it was time. LaShonge, Gogo Ndwandwe, and two other women positioned themselves behind the drums and began to beat them. The children shook rattles and sang. I slipped beneath the long white sheet. I thought of Evah alone in my hut, lying down on the mattress, waiting.

The lidloti emerged with a howl from my throat. The spirit caused my body to throw off the sheet, jump up, and do a slow-tempo, bent-over dance. Kneeling, it announced itself. Gogo Ndwandwe greeted it with enthusiasm, "Oh, White Feather!" The other women ululated happily; they liked this warrior-medicine man, who MaZu said was "strong and handsome." Clearly, they wished he were not just a spirit.

White Feather said nothing more. He rose and left the Indumba. Spirits frequently ran off to dance in the field under the moonlight, and Gogo Ndwandwe kept the drums going to accompany him. But the lidloti circled the Indumba and headed for my hut. Arriving there, it knelt on the stoop,

*breathing hoarsely. (I was vaguely aware of the movements of my com-
mandeered body. But even with the little awareness I still possessed, I was
in suspense: would it be the lidloti who made love to Evah?) The spirit
clapped his hands together twice, stood, and opened the door. He entered
the hut, dark but for a square of moonlight on the floor cast from the window. There was only the sound of its hoarse breathing and the Indumba
drums, which softened when the spirit closed the door and made its way to
the mattress. Directed by its will, my body knelt beside Evah. It pulled off
the long buck loinskins I wore, and slipped onto the mattress beside her. My
body was strong with the spirit's desire. It lay atop Evah. Then, with a
smooth liquid motion like a wave that had broken on shore and was flowing back to the sea, its hold over me receded, and then . . .*

. . . and then I returned, and I felt so self-conscious finding myself
there, in the hut, lying atop Evah's warm body and fully aroused that the
post-possession drowsiness I usually felt was gone in an instant. Self-
consciousness was *not* the right frame of mind for lovemaking, and my
body's desire also went slack. I looked around, saw the romantic square of
moonlight on the floor of the African hut, smelled the lavender from the
ointment Gogo Ndwandwe had given Evah to wear to attract the spirit,
heard the beating of the drums . . . it was all so perfect, and all so *funny!*
I grinned, and below me Evah, her lovely face etched with silver from reflected moonlight, giggled. I laughed; she laughed. We broke up.

"Oh, God," I groaned. It was then, when I should have felt mortified
by my impotency, that I knew I loved Evah. Our shared laughter at the
whole improbable setup was like a weight lifting from both of us. "I guess
you wished the lidloti had stayed, don't you?"

She gave me a hug. "No! I want you! I was frightened until you returned!"

"And look what happened!" I said, and we laughed again.

▲　▲　▲　▲

We eventually did conceive a child toward the end of August, at Evah's flat
in Manzini town, also accompanied by pounding drums. It was in the
afternoon, and a boys' dance troupe practicing on the playing field of
St. Paul's school directly behind her flat were doing the traditional Swazi
sibhaca dance steps while powerful cowhide drums kept rhythm.

I had a good amount of time to spend with Evah during August and
September, and these were the only happy moments during those gray,
wintry months. It had become increasingly evident that I could no longer
continue kutfwasa at Prince Vovo's homestead in Kwaluseni. With MaZu

gone, there was no one to perform the daily rituals with me. LaShonge was still my friend, but was often inebriated and didn't seem to care if she was still doing kutfwasa in ten years. Although roots could be easily dug in winter when obscuring foliage was sparse, Gogo Ndwandwe took us on only one medicine dig during those two months. She was suffering from kidney trouble, and was either resigned and withdrawn or else shrilly angry with the people around her. The drums no longer sounded in the Indumba at night to bring out the lidlotis; the absence of MaZu's enthusiasm and Gogo Ndwandwe's firm hand silenced them.

Despite all this, my skill at reading the bones, though still new and imperfect, was bringing in my first patients. One gray day I was washing clothes in a plastic tub on the trunk of the disintegrating black 1965 Pontiac, when a young, surly-looking man approached. He wore a torn leather jacket and jeans decorated with hieroglyphic-like designs drawn with a ball-point pen, and in English he curtly identified himself as a Mozambiquan who wanted my services.

We entered my hut and he sat on one side of a small grass mat where I would throw the bones, while I knelt on the other side with a red cape over my shoulders. I placed a lit candle on the floor, burned and inhaled a medicine to sharpen my insight, and murmured an incantation to call for the lidlotis' assistance. Then I cast down the bones and scrutinized them while holding a staff in my left hand.

I immediately noticed the bone representing home. It was on its side, indicating trouble there. Such trouble could be anything, but with growing confidence in my sangoma's insight, I told him flat out, "Your house was broken into last night. You were robbed."

"Yeah," he shrugged, unimpressed; he already knew this, of course. But I still marveled at such results, and a part of me wanted to say with amazement, "But don't you find that remarkable? I look at these things, and I know what happened?"

But angered by the robbery, the man glowered at me and demanded to know who had done it. It was obvious to me who had: the shell representing his lover was on its side, also indicating trouble, and positioned tellingly between the bone representing the patient and another representing his house. But I did not tell him what I saw, for three reasons. The first was that my insight informed me he already knew, and he soon admitted this was true. The second reason was that I was prohibited by law from implicating his lover in the break-in. There was a statute intended to discourage witch-hunts that forbade a sangoma from naming the perpetrator of any crime, and Gogo Ndwandwe insisted that we obey. And finally, I was inspired by the lidlotis to see that the robbery had merely been a symptom of the man's true problem: his troubled relationship with his girlfriend. He wanted her back, but he was angered by her treachery. He admitted this to me, and because he was a cauldron of conflicting passions he didn't know if he wanted medicine to protect him from her bewitchments *(umutsi vikela)* or a love potion to draw her back to him *(kutstandvo)*. I thought it had been a good session because I had been able to discern the truth of his situation, but the patient left dissatisfied, muttering darkly that I had failed because I hadn't told him where all his stolen things were. In fact, I didn't know; the bones were not a detective agency, and the lidlotis did not care about material possessions, only the physical and mental well-being of the patient. That was what the sangoma's divination sessions were; not idle fortune-telling (I turned down people who asked me to tell their futures), but a means to ascertain a problem in order to prescribe a cure.

I had once misused the sangoma's insight by taking a reading unrelated to a patient's therapy. My brother Tom wrote with news of a job change. I cast down the bones and did a long-distance reading to see how he'd make out. His new firm was Drexel Burnham Lambert, and I saw trouble ahead. But for whom? Tom? The firm? It was frustratingly vague. Naturally, I didn't tell my brother anything. What would be the use?

I reported the robbery victim's dissatisfaction when I gave Gogo Ndwandwe the fee he nonetheless paid. As long as I was her student, I would give her any fees I earned. "People are funny, Lusiba," she said. "They can argue, even if you can 'see.' You told that man what happened. You were not telling lies. But even me, I have been doing this for twenty years. People, they are not happy sometimes. They say, 'She does not know how to read the bones.' "

"Even you?"

"Even me!"

Catching her in a good mood, I thought the time was right to ask her if I could return to Malibeni on my own for a few days or a week at a time, and continue my studies under Gogo Simelane. I did not know if Gogo Ndwandwe would think I was abandoning her or if this was a breach of kutfwasa etiquette. But my studies were going nowhere, and I fondly recalled that my week in Malibeni had been a happy and productive time.

Gogo Ndwandwe looked at me with tenderness, not anger, and I sensed she was even relieved by my suggestion. "Of course, Lusiba. Any time you want. There is no question. I can see that you want to work. No, go. Gogo Simelane is there. It is the same as if you are here with me."

I thanked her, thinking that soon I'd be seeing the zebras again.

I had already discussed with Evah my desire to spend some time in

Malibeni. She had heard enough of my despair about trying to do kut-fwasa in Kwaluseni, and we now planned the new schedule I'd follow. On Fridays I'd make the bus trip from Manzini north to the border, spend a week with Gogo Simelane, and return the following Friday to spend a week with Evah in town and Gogo Ndwandwe at the homestead. I'd go back and forth between the two places, never being long absent from either. My last stop before leaving Manzini and my first stop coming back would be Evah's flat. She planned to be busy while I was gone. "You must remember, I have a business to run with many customers who want my dresses here and in South Africa." She intended to keep herself active as long as she could through the pregnancy and wanted me to respect her independence.

I packed the next day, the first Friday in October. At the lidloti pole I addressed the spirits, informed them of my trip, and asked for their protection and guidance. Gogo Ndwandwe joined me there and asked her own lidlotis to assist me as I continued my studies far away.

I returned to the hut to get my things. My friend Jabulani would be living there in my absence. I gave him the key, and we headed for the road where I could catch a shuttle bus to town. Jabulani spoke of the surprise he found on a trip he had made the previous day, his birthday, to the capital town of Mbabane.

"I went with Gogo Ndwandwe's daughter, Thambize. I go with her to the government building. It is *tall*. Four floors!"

"Yes," I said, lulled by the music of English when spoken by a Swazi.

"We walk up the steps to the top. There is a man there she wants to see, and she talks to him. Then we stop at a metal door. I do not ask why we stop, because I think maybe she can laugh at me. These two men are there. They are talking about Jesus. The door opens, by itself! We go into the room. A small room! The men are talking about getting redeemed. I think that maybe we pray in this room. The door closes, but nobody pushes it! I hear this sound: *Grrrrr!* My stomach feels funny. I wonder if we pray now. And then the door opens. But things are changed. We go out, and we are on the ground! You see out the window, and there are cars! I ask Thambize, 'What was that little room?' And she says, '*Likheshi.*'"

"Jabulani! For your twenty-first birthday you took your first elevator ride!"

He grinned from ear to ear, and we wished each other luck. I was relieved that I had finally taken the initiative to kick-start my kutfwasa out of its doldrums. I looked forward to what lay ahead in Malibeni. A little shuttle bus came chugging out of a cloud of dust up the road. When it arrived, I said good-bye to Jabulani, tossed in my gear, and climbed aboard.

eight

Malibeni Spring

THE SWAZI BUSES had names: *Intamakuphila* ("Trying to earn a living"), *Ukhalelani?* ("Why do you cry?"), and *Sukumani MaSwati Netimela* ("Stand up, Swazis, and be independent!") Aboard one of the large, long-distance buses I experienced the first of the raucous three-hour trips that would take me slowly and with many stops down sixty miles of bone-jarring dirt roads to the low country of Malibeni. Collecting fares, two male conductors, still in their teens, shouted and joked with passengers who shouted back, drank beer in the packed aisles, cradled babies and chickens in their laps, and purchased fried fish and roasted maize from women who rushed up at bus stops bearing trays of food on their heads. The bus's impassive driver, separated from the rowdy passengers by a wire cage, blasted South African township music through overhead speakers. As the party rolled along, I sat back and watched a dusty panorama of small farms and stony hills pass. For a long stretch, the bus drove through the largest of the country's game reserves, a tract of wilderness where visitors saw elephants, hippos, and other indigenous animals in their natural habitat. I peered through the umbrella trees and spotted several running herds of impala.

Suddenly the bus slowed, throwing us forward and causing things to fall from the racks above our seats. The conductors were at the front window, shouting and gesturing as if to shoo away something ahead. I heard the word *bhejane*. Rhino! I wanted to see, and made my way through the other passengers having the same idea. Blocking the bus was a huge beast lying with its feet tucked under itself on the warm surface of the road. He stared back at us through a beady black eye, his horn raised like a curved dagger at the end of a long snout.

The driver honked the horn repeatedly, and the conductors went outside to yell and throw stones that bounced unnoticed off the animal's thick hide. I stepped down. I never thought I'd see a rhinoceros this close in the wild.

One of the conductors grinned at me, but the other, irritated by the delay, said, "Hey, sangoma, chase this stupid rhino! Use your *mutsi* [medicine]."

"Me?"

I looked at the animal. It was resting peacefully. I asked a conductor to tell the driver to lay off the horn, and I stepped forward slowly, feeling a busload of eyes on my back. The rhino's stillness gave me the confidence to approach. When I was ten feet away from it, I dropped down on one knee. The beady eye was fixed upon me, and slow breaths lifted its massive side. I took from my belt a hollow bull's horn that had been fitted with a leather cap to make a container. I withdrew a pinch of snuff and sprinkled this on the road as an offering to the lidlotis. I clapped my cupped hands and murmured to the spirits that I wished this beast would leave so I could go to Malibeni and release them to dance and assist our patients.

I opened my eyes with a jolt, realizing I had closed them and lowered my head while addressing the lidlotis, an instinctive but foolish thing to do beside a rhinoceros. But I saw no anger within the black depths of the animal's eye, only emptiness. Now what? I was tired of this stalling. I arched an eyebrow and spoke into the black eye. "You know, you're giving us the impression that in the animal kingdom good manners are a thing of the past!"

I stood. The rhino abruptly turned its head. That's all it took, and I was back beside the bus as fast as my long legs could carry me. The conductors were clambering aboard. The rhino was up on its stubby legs, rumbling off the road. I leapt aboard the bus, the door slammed behind me, the driver started the engine, and the people whistled and laughed as the rhino disappeared into the bush. The conductors were all over me. They thought the snuff I sprinkled on the ground was medicine. Perhaps they were right. I returned grinning to my seat through passengers smiling their congratulations and slapping me on the back.

Malibeni, on the border with South Africa, was the last stop. A bus conductor tossed me my gear, I pushed through the tall pine trees that separated the road from the Komati river, and descended the steep bank. I forded the wide but shallow water and was midstream when I heard the drums beating their welcome for me a quarter-mile away. No one was expecting my arrival at this place, but someone with keen eyesight—I *was* conspicuous among an entirely black population—had alerted the homestead.

The first thing a sangoma or kutfwasa student did when arriving at the home of another sangoma, often before saying a word, was to put on dancing skirts, release the lidlotis, and perform the *bingelela* greeting song. I went straight to the low, wide Indumba spirit house, and fell into a trance as I changed outfits. Some of the ten or so sangomas living and working there and the three other kutfwasa students were already in the throes of their spirits when they crowded into the Indumba behind me to swiftly put on their own dancing outfits. Our spirits brought us outside, and we danced together in a single line in the courtyard—the simultaneous, high-jumping steps and on-your-toes movements that were executed with chorus line precision—while the twenty adults and fifteen children who lived there beat the drums and sang in accompaniment. Then our spirits, made mobile in our bodies, trooped to where Gogo Simelane sat before the main house, and the eldest sangoma greeted her on our behalf.

Back in the Indumba when the dancing was done, our lidlotis departed and we became ourselves again. The warm greetings I received from the friends I had made during my first visit reminded me why I wished to return. In this Indumba, the daily medicine-taking rituals and the drum-beating rite were observed faithfully and with real enthusiasm by sangomas who considered themselves privileged to be blessed and empowered by the ancestral spirits to perform the holiest of undertakings: to cure humankind. I was judged solely on my own dedication and accomplishments while in the Indumba. My skin color was novel but irrelevant, and my bumbling mistakes with language and customs seemed to bring out the friendliness in the men and the motherliness in the women as they patiently assisted and corrected me. I loved it there in Malibeni among the widely spaced farms far from the shabby and ill-tempered urban centers, amid a primitive landscape of scrub brush and aloes, distant, unformed mountains and the wide, meandering Komati river. Before dawn we went to the river together—kutfwasa students and often a sangoma or two—to perform our morning rites. The drums beat throughout the day and into the night for ceremonies and divination rites. Gogo Simelane's husband, Mahlalela, gave me a dilapidated mud hut to patch up and live in, and because I would now be a part of the homestead, I was expected to help with the chores.

And so it was that with the spring rains falling and the planting season upon us, I became the man behind the plow, and found in tilling the land the happiest and most satisfying work since my arrival in Swaziland. What I felt inside was more than the vicarious enjoyment of a long-dead ancestral spirit nostalgic for this work—the Scottish farmer John MacDonald—though I sensed he was with me. There was something about the task of driving four giant oxen across a field that put a man right where he should be, solidly on the earth.

The team, yoked in two pairs front and back, was brought out early, when a crimson sunrise cast long black shadows across the ruddy field. Mahlalela's farm workers were two young men in their twenties: an amiable bachelor named Silembe with a puttylike grin and a black beret he never removed, and Willie, who had hair that stuck up like a pine forest, gold rings looped through his earlobes, and an impressively muscled body he corrupted by chain-smoking. Willie's petite and good-natured wife had just given him their first child, a baby girl. The three of us took turns behind the plow, and they showed me how to maneuver it to cut straight furrows.

The rhythm of the work took over: back and forth across the broad field in the cathedral-like silence of each new morning. It was a tough and sweaty job but relaxed in the manner of an endeavor done the same way since the dawn of history. I gripped the wide, smooth handles and the plow's metal blade parted the soft earth, which received maize seeds dropped by boys walking behind. Willie prompted the dumb powerful oxen by snapping a long leather whip in the air, showing off by making gunshot sounds. Silembe urged the beasts forward with warbling, bird-like whistles. The metal chain connecting the plow to the harness clinked languidly. The women of the homestead arrived silhouetted against the rising sun, singing softly and carrying baskets of dry, black manure on their heads which they scattered over the furrows. All was bathed in a timeless, golden sunlight beneath a rich blue dome of sky.

Around eight o'clock in the morning, the smaller boys milked the cows in a circular enclosure, where Mahlalela kept his herd of forty cattle at night. A similar enclosure held twenty goats. Pigs and chickens roamed where they pleased. The nights were riotous with croaking frogs from the river and at dawn in the forest across the road, birds with satin-bright plumage called to each other with such shrill urgency they sounded like commodities brokers.

I spent a few hours each day patching with new grass the roof of the small square hut Mahlalela had given me. I slapped red mud into wall crevices, and installed a ready-made window I had found a mile down the road at the general store, where I bought bread and canned food. At the border station, women sold steamed maize and yams, and the kids brought me wild guavas and papayas the size of coconuts. At this poor homestead where everyone was required to work, the children, some of whom seemed to never go to school, were kept busy from sun-up to late at night driving the goat and cattle herds to graze along the riverbank, doing chores, and running errands for their elders. When they did find time to play, the boys fashioned ingenious model cars and buses out of wire, with aerosol spray caps for wheels, and they pushed these along with three-foot bamboo steering columns angled up through the roofs.

One day I spotted five of the homestead boys along the roadside collecting insects in bags. They were scooping up a swarm of fat, brown and black striped bugs with transparent wings that seemed slow moving and rather stupid, like insect cattle. I helped them out, and we all went back to the cooking courtyard behind the main house. I saw what was up when the boys started snapping off the insects' wings and dropping the bodies into a frying pan atop the fire. The bugs crawled around for a bit and then lay still, cooking. "Lion" Mahlalela sat on a stool made from a tree stump at one end of the courtyard, his Buddhalike belly falling over his loinskins and a large bottle of beer at his feet. The boys brought over a finished batch of insects, and he popped them by the handful into his mouth like snacks. He ordered them to bring me a bowl. I demurred, but there were hundreds of bugs; plenty to go around.

"You like!" Mahlalela assured me in English, smiling with strong white teeth that were marred by an insect leg sticking out between two. My stomach tensed a little when a boy gave me a bowl of fried insects resembling small dates. The other boys were looking at me; they liked me, and I didn't want to let them down. I picked up a cooked insect and looked at it: it seemed innocuous, and certainly was a valid source of protein, I reasoned. As long as something didn't squirt out when I bit into it I'd be all right. I put it in my mouth and bit down. A crisp covering tasting of salt and cooking oil yielded to a fibrous, chewy interior that tasted like cardboard. I survived, and had another, washing it down with beer Mahlalela kept cool in a kerosene-powered refrigerator. I ate some more, finding that the appeal of these bugs was not their pallid taste but the sensation in the mouth of the crisp and chewy—with the bonus appeal of revenge, for we were harassed night and day by their cousins, mosquitoes, flies, and roaches.

The butterflies of the place, though, were varied and colorful. I was indebted to one later that afternoon when I went out to dig medicinal roots in the forest with the youngest of the kutfwasa students there. Going by the name of one of his lidlotis, Inyoni was a short twenty-year-old who was eager and enthusiastic when he wasn't in a dark mood brought on by his recurring illness: a painful bleeding from the urinary tract that no hospital doctor had an answer for. The sangomas divined that Inyoni had lidlotis, and since like his father he was already a "prophet" (a psychic healer in one of the local Christian-Zionist churches), he thought the spirits might cure him if he devoted himself to the Indumba. Generally, Inyoni was fit and wiry; he wore his hair in red-ocher-covered braids, and when he was possessed by his spirits he had a wild, howling singing voice that was pure rock and roll.

Of the other two kutfwasa students, Makhalela was a melancholy woman who often withdrew into silence as she recalled the family homestead she had left for the first time in her life. Matsenjwa was a man in his late fifties, mellow of voice and manner. Age was pulling at the flesh of his amiable face, and he had a resigned attitude toward doing kutfwasa so late in his life: "It's the lidlotis' will."

To find a root she wanted for a vomiting medicine, Gogo Simelane sent Inyoni and me out to search with pickaxe and shovel. In the forest, I recalled that the medicine we sought grew in long, hoselike branches that at first glance resembled vines. We were interested in the roots only but identified plants by their leaves, blossoms, and barks. Inyoni and I searched for half an hour without finding anything. The forest was not yet green and seemed nothing but thistles and gray branches. I spotted a vine and called to Inyoni. Sharp needles bristled along its surface and he scratched between them, past a greenish inner bark and into a white wood within.

"White," he said. We wanted red. Finding a surprising command of English, Inyoni declared, "I am suffering for nothing! I am going."

I ignored this and walked on. It was unlikely that he was tired after only half an hour, or that he despaired of ever finding the root. Most likely, he was testing me. If I agreed and gave up, he was spared both the task and the blame. He could say, "The *umlungu* (white man) was tired."

On a branch I noticed a small butterfly with velvet black markings against snow-white wings. I moved toward it slowly, and it flew away, revealing a bright red underside. I turned, and Inyoni was gone. I could hear him moving in the bushes. Perhaps we'd have better luck if we split up, I thought, noting the position of the sun and walking so the homestead would always remain behind me to my left.

I stuffed my canvas sack with other medicinal plants I found but had no luck locating the medicine Gogo Simelane wanted. I tramped onward for an hour and finally recalled a tip a sangoma once gave me. I knelt on the forest floor and asked the lidlotis for their assistance. Conversationally, I mentioned the stories I had heard about healers who dreamt of places to find medicines: they woke up, went to the place, and there it was. I told the spirits, though, that I didn't expect a miracle.

But one came. I clapped my hands to conclude and looked up. There, resting on a branch, was the same butterfly I had seen earlier, miles back. How did it get there? I smiled to myself, thinking how funny it would be if the lidlotis had sent it to show me the root. I stood up. As I approached the butterfly, it flitted away a few yards. With a pocketknife I scratched off some bark from the branch where it had been. Inside, the wood was red. I shook my head, grinning, but felt the same disquiet I always felt when confronted with such magic: it was changing me, making me feel small and uncertain in the presence of unknowable powers.

I looked to where the butterfly was, but it was gone.

▲   ▲   ▲   ▲

I commuted between the homesteads of Gogo Simelane and Prince Vovo, spending about a week at each but generally spending more time at my new kutfwasa home in Malibeni. The places seemed opposite poles whose equatorial center was Evah's flat, for it was there I would always be at the head and tail of every trip. Evah had let September pass without mentioning her condition, and by the end of October I felt certain that she had some news for me. I did not consult the bones, preferring that she give me the news herself. We sat on the sofa in her crowded but tidy room, and I took her hand. Evah had a fetching way of tilting her head down and letting her eyes smile seductively up at me when she wanted my full attention. "I think I am with your little one."

I pulled her close and hugged her. I felt a furnace of pride and happiness inside, and I wanted to share its warmth. She added, "And I think you're right that it will be a girl. The way it is acting inside, I can tell it will be a her."

"Let's tell the lidlotis," I suggested, and we knelt on the floor, clapped our hands in respectful summons, and gave our thanks.

We went to the doctor together to confirm what we knew—a baby was due in May—and to arrange prenatal care. Evah also consulted Gogo Ndwandwe, who reiterated her own herbal prescriptions which I would prepare. Returning from Malibeni every other week, I brought Evah bags of fresh peanuts I helped harvest, which she boiled in their shells for snacks or cooked in a delicious soup. I brought five-liter containers of her favorite drink: fermented milk called *emasi,* which tasted like yogurt. Gogo Simelane made sure I had plenty of this for Evah's pregnancy, but to obtain it I had to do the milking myself. In the mornings after plowing I squatted beside a midnight-black cow in the cattle pen, wearing rubber boots in the muck, while one of the barefooted boys restrained the cow with a rope around its neck, and another boy held a bucket beneath her udder. I found the right pressure and rhythm to use. Pull left, pull right, left, right . . . False pulls would spray warm milk in my face, and sometimes I'd do this on purpose to hear the free and happy laughter of the boys. It was springtime, with new grass to graze on, and the cow's udder sagged with fullness and emptied quickly into the bucket.

Springtime brought a blossoming of the landscape that I could see, smell, and feel like a massage. It was November south of the equator, and with the arrival of monstrous lightning and rainstorms I experienced nature as I had not known her since I was a small boy in northern Illinois: not as insentient elements but as a living force, a fierce and dominating personality. I remembered the awe I felt in childhood at the black, arctic winter nights that would grab my throat as if trying to throttle me, and as I now stood beside my paltry seeming mud hut watching black clouds boil in a wicked sky I felt that same smallness. There was an elemental power that I had forgotten living away from nature, but kutfwasa had brought me back to it.

The rains also raised the level of the Komati, and it was no longer possible to ford the wide but gentle river. The community was building a footbridge, and steel cables already connected red iron towers sunk in concrete on either bank. But until it was done we were obliged to travel across in two small, leaky rowboats. Here, too, the boys worked, standing in back like gondoliers and pushing against the current with long poles braced against the river bottom.

All the boys at this homestead had parents, I learned, except a ten-year-old named Vusi. His mother was considered unstable when she left him in the care of his great-uncle, Mahlalela, two years before. No one had seen her since or knew if she was alive; no one had ever known who the boy's father was. Vusi was a clever boy with a ready, wide smile, bright eyes, medium brown skin, and an alert manner. I watched him wield the boat pole, which was four times as long as he was high, with graceful, economical movements, and I learned from him how to maneuver the boat. I took over, giving him a rest, and we went back and forth in the warm sunshine. We talked, and Vusi bailed with a plastic bucket and collected fares from the passengers. When we knocked off at sunset, he added up the day's profits, which he would give to his great-uncle Mahlalela, the boat's owner.

"You know how to count money nicely," I complimented him. Vusi looked down modestly, smiled, and nodded his head. "But they say you've never been to school."

His expression clouded, and he shrugged, *"Kutemali."* ("There is no money.")

For a long time I had felt paralyzed in the face of this impoverished country's problems. One of the saddest was the number of bright children who were denied an education because no one could afford their school fees. School was neither compulsory nor free in Swaziland; if a child like Vusi was abandoned by his mother and his relatives could not afford the extra burden of his tuition, school uniform, books, and transportation, he would probably end up as what Vusi seemed destined to become, an illiterate goatherd. And yet, I thought, no one's fate was carved in stone. Mine had certainly twisted unexpectedly. I had come to like Vusi. He was always around, eager and friendly, running to the store to fetch a soda or some eggs, expecting nothing in return but to help me, and making me feel less alone by his devotion.

It would not cost much to enroll Vusi in the nearest school, and in a way it seemed a partial payment for the debt I owed the country that was hosting me. I sought out Gogo Simelane and her husband and found them seated together in front of the main house. Kneeling before my teacher, I proposed to her and Mahlalela that if they gave permission for Vusi to attend school I'd assume the financial responsibility—not just for first grade, but for as long and as far as he cared to take his education.

Gogo Simelane threw her arms into the air, rolled her expressive eyes, and shouted, "Praise Jesus!"

"Oh, Sibolomhlope!" said Mahlalela, who told me they had always hoped to find a way to help their great-nephew. They now sent a child to fetch him. Vusi arrived, and his smile stretched his broad cheeks wider when Mahlalela told him that when the new school term began in January, I would be enrolling him. Up to this time, Vusi had seldom left the homestead. His universe was largely defined by the river and the surrounding fields and woods. Now he would be going to town every school day, and he would wear a clean uniform, be with other students, play games, and indulge his curiosity about the world. When he looked at me I had to avert my eyes in embarrassment; I was not prepared for such emotion. He looked at me like I was saving his life.

▲ ▲ ▲ ▲

Injuries from physical chores were part of country living in Malibeni, and I had my share during November. Passing over barbed wire in my sandals at the edge of the field, I felt a tug on my big toe. I looked down to see it slit down its length. Infection soon set in, requiring a trip to a nearby health clinic for antibiotics. I crushed my other big toe against a block of wood in the courtyard one night. This wound's infection brought stunning pain and a quick return to Manzini town and the hospital there. I spent the night recuperating with Evah and Sandile, and she cooked the best meal I had ever had in Swaziland. (I glanced at the calendar on her wall and saw that it was the last Thursday of the month, the day Thanksgiving was celebrated in the United States.)

Back in Malibeni, my work continued. From chopping firewood, I had developed severe calluses on both hands. The next day as I cut branches with a machete the calluses burst open. When I was finished, I looked down and saw bright red blood splattered artfully in every direction so that my right hand resembled an abstract expressionist canvas. I tried to hide it from Gogo Simelane, but with no luck. Her eye was too sharp, and she also noticed with alarm something I had missed. The hard forest thistles, which could run through the soles of shoes or sandals like nails, had punctured my arm. I recalled one vine clinging to me stubbornly. Now raised infected bumps looked like the measles.

The pain was a nuisance but never really slowed me down or prevented me from dropping off to sleep at the end of a hard day. I was not being stoic, but it was an exciting time, each day bringing new discoveries, and the only thing I feared was a flu that would cloud my head and sap my energy. But one never came, and I recalled with wonder how in my previous life in America I used to drag myself through the fetid environment of Los Angeles for a month at a time like a zombie, in the grip of one flu or another. My stay in Swaziland seemed good for what was ailing me not only spiritually but physically—though I doubted these could be separated.

At night, I took my turn with other sangomas and my fellow kutfwasa initiates beneath the white sheet while the Indumba drums sounded to call forth the lidlotis. Over four months had passed since that remarkable vision of the ancient zebra herd had come to me in this same spirit house. I felt that eventually I would see them again, and the full story would be told. Now, in December, they did appear, while a blanket of sound from drums, rattles, and chanting voices enveloped me:

Four, perhaps five hundred zebras. Too many to count. I again saw them through the lidloti's eyes. Our shared view was from a low angle, looking up from ground level. I saw a swarthy man's hand clutch a wooden spear with a sharp metal blade at its tip. Ahead, the veld stretched for miles. Tall golden grass broken by an isolated dark bush or flat-topped umbrella tree extended on all sides, reaching a range of blue mountains along the horizon. The sun was high in the sky, and the shadow of the man's hand was black against the ground. The zebras ahead moved cautiously closer, apparently sensing the hunter. He, and I through him, could see the wary eyes in their long, striped heads. But these animals lived in a world of danger: snakes, lions, fierce storms; they accepted some peril in order to find food.

Now four zebras wandered closer. We saw them ahead as the hunter rose from the ground and ran quickly forward. Our view was five feet or

*less above the ground: the hunter must have been a short man. But he was
swift. I sensed medicine within him, and I suspected he fortified himself by
chewing a root. I seemed aware of the sensations of his body: I felt
loinskins tied about his waist, and streaks of mud on his face that might
have been camouflage. Directly ahead, the zebras were fleeing, galloping.
The hunter gave chase, drawing abreast of one beast, which dodged left,
right. The hunter's mind seemed to anticipate the zebra's motions. He went
as it went. He raised and threw his spear. It penetrated the zebra's neck. The
beast tripped and fell. It rose again and ran slower. The spear remained in
place, piercing the zebra's neck. Blood flowed back to stain red the white
and black stripes of its coat. I felt the hunter's heart throb in his chest as he
raced forward, scooped up a rock, and threw it. The stone struck the zebra
on the side of the head. Stunned, it fell. It tried to rise on an injured leg, but
the hunter jumped upon its back. He could sense the animal's pain as if he
were one with his prey. His strength was now greater than a normal man's;
he took hold of the zebra's large head, twisted sharply, and broke its neck.
The light faded from the zebra's eye. I felt the man sitting astride the beast,
his hands on his hips and his thighs wet with blood. The lofty sky came
into view as he raised his head, his mouth open and his chest sucking in
great draughts of air. He was finished.*

*During the time of these visions I again knew the sensations of an-
other's body, as I had when the fetus lidloti had come. Now the hunter's
spirit took possession of my body; he cast off the sheet, knelt, and announced himself to the people of the Indumba. He spoke SiSwati and gave
his name: Lidvuba. He said that when he was alive, his life was zebras,
though he stalked many animals and knew how to make medicines from
them. The sangomas in the Indumba wanted to know about his medicines, and he told them of the herbs people took to make them strong and
fast. These were the roots he used to become swift when he hunted. The
sangomas thanked him and he departed.*

My head felt heavy when I regained awareness, and I couldn't shake
the veiled feeling from my eyes and mind. The sangomas recounted for
me their conversation with my lidloti, which impressed them though I
was unable to remember it, although I did remember the hunting vision
in detail. Kneeling, I clapped my hands in thanks and departed for my
hut, where I lit a candle and wrote my recollections in my diary. There
was little time for sleep. The nights were the shortest of the year as we
approached the summer solstice of December 21, and though I was usually in bed by ten I had to rise at two-thirty in the morning. I had an
alarm clock, and also had the job of waking the others who would go

with me to the river for the morning rites. We had to return, singing, to the Indumba before sunrise. The harmony of the acolytes' and the sangomas' voices, the men's deep baritones and the women's high, ethereal tones, made for a hauntingly beautiful return journey from the cool water to the slumbering homestead, which rose above the field like a collection of black cut-out figures of shaggy-topped huts against the sapphire of the eastern sky.

In Malibeni, we lived long days of rites and chores. Sometimes a lethargy set in from the heat and monotony of tasks like cleaning the pig sty. I did this with two other acolytes: spirited young Inyoni and good-natured, gravel-voiced Matsenjwa. We shoveled out muck over the low walls of the wooden pen while obese, slow-moving pigs weighing hundreds of pounds grunted and wallowed at our feet. Old Matsenjwa paused to roll a cigarette with a piece of newspaper and pipe tobacco— he couldn't afford cigarette tobacco—and asked when I would read the bones for him. Inyoni was convinced I did this well and told everybody about my skill with an enthusiasm that made me fear I couldn't live up to the advance publicity. I told Matsenjwa that once we finished with the pigs, I'd read for him.

Beneath a tree beside one of the sleeping huts we unrolled some reed mats on the ground, and I positioned Matsenjwa opposite me. Inyoni acted as my assistant, kneeling beside me as I poured from a woven grass container the shells, bones, and polished stones that were the primitive props of this divination rite.

We chanted an incantation together, and I tossed down the bones from my cupped hands. Matsenjwa had complained to me of back pains, and this was confirmed with the bone that represented this area of the body lay upside down. (Actually, several body bones also landed in this position, but my sangoma's insight allowed me to notice the relevant piece and disregard the others.) The alignment of family, luck, and fortune bones with the bone I had assigned to the patient indicated he had a son who was unhappy because he could not find a job. Matsenjwa reported that this was true, and it was weighing heavily on his mind.

The closeness of a stone representing a religious figure to the Matsenjwa bone was, I thought at first, a reference to Inyoni. The two were inseparable, and Inyoni was a Christian-Zionist prophet. But this interpretation didn't satisfy me. Finally I said, "You have a brother, don't you? He's a minister."

"Yes!" Matsenjwa cried. Inyoni hooted and shot his fist into the air. He got excited when my insight hit a home run. I told Matsenjwa he ought to write to his brother, because they had special news—I didn't know what—to exchange.

My ability to glean from the bones such information as a relative's occupation was important to me. It became difficult when the bones predicted the unverifiable, such as a patient's likelihood of encountering an accident if he or she were not treated with a medicine. By this time, I knew the readings were accurate in my heart and gut, but a vestige of the rational American within me made me invariably more skeptical than my patients, who had no doubts about the veracity of the bones or my ability to read them. It was important to me when some unverifiable prediction was buttressed by factual information about a patient's life that I could not have rationally known.

This was to happen a few days later when a tall, good-looking man of twenty-two came by. Sgidi was visiting his homestead while on holiday from work in South Africa, where he had acquired some of the trappings of the international youth culture. He wore stone-washed jeans and a baseball shirt over his strapping physique, and part of his hair was dyed acid-orange. He was buoyant and courteous, and had the easy Swazi smile. I spotted him while passing by the neighboring farms, sensed on sight that he had a problem, and invited him over for a reading. He accepted at once because he had wanted to consult a sangoma at Gogo Simelane's place and, he said, he wanted to become my friend.

It was while casting down the bones for him in the Indumba that I learned he did not work in Swaziland. "You work in South Africa," I said. He confirmed that he did, down in the mines, and asked if he would die in one of the accidents that claimed African miners every year.

I looked. The bones were unequivocal, and I masked the shock I felt with a studious expression. I had known Sgidi only a short time but I liked him, and for his part he was already proclaiming me his "number one friend!" I could not look this handsome young man in the face, bursting as he was with high spirits, and give him the news. He would indeed have an accident in the mines: Beside his bone lay the widow bone. He would die.

Should I tell him? I didn't see the point after a quick roll showed that a combination of a simple luck treatment, a bodily protection medicine (kuvikela), and supplication to his deceased grandfather would place his lidlotis on his side. They would guard him against what would otherwise happen. (Whether people were chosen to undergo kutfwasa or not, everyone had ancestral spirits because everyone has ancestors.) In particular, the spirit of his grandfather had attached itself to Sgidi and would protect him.

When reading the bones I went by my gut and my developing insight, which were much the same thing. But again with Sgidi, my resistance to predictions—in this case a fatal mine accident—was eased by the discovery of some unknowable facts in his life. I saw that Sgidi had children, but his home life was in turmoil. Sgidi said that this was so. When he was still in school he had fathered two children by the same girl. He had fallen out of love with her, and she was now dating several other men.

There were some bones that I kept in my set for tradition's sake, because all sangomas had them and not because I believed in them. One bone indicated *sidliso,* a "bewitched food" that a vengeful woman was said to feed her man to make him ill or docile, turning him into her slave. Whether I believed in such bewitchment or not, there was the bone now, hard against the one representing Sgidi. And here was Sgidi, quickly replying after I told him this: "Yes! She has given me medicine in my food before, but she was clumsy and I found out! She does not love me, she only wants me to give her money. How did you *know?!*"

I found it was possible to know something without believing in it, and I still couldn't say what I thought about the witchcraft stories common in Swaziland. I gave Sgidi the treatment he needed, and then I told him I wanted to know if he was supporting his two children despite his hatred for their mother. He promptly replied that he was doing his duty out of his miner's paycheck, that he was a real man. With Sgidi pedaling and me sitting on a rack over the rear wheel of his wobbly bicycle, we rode back to his homestead for lunch. I could stay only a short time, because I lived my life enslaved to the tyranny of the drums, as I called it, and I always made sure that, when they sounded I was back: sometimes resentfully, sometimes sick of them, but always faithfully, wondering each time what their summons would bring.

▲ ▲ ▲ ▲

My second Christmas away from the United States, which I had left over a year before, was difficult. I was homesick, I had never expected to be away this long, and I felt more isolated and cut off after sending my return-trip airline ticket back for a refund to finance my next few months of kutfwasa. Next I planned to sell my antique Cadillac. I was in so deep now, so deep I felt stuck and sinking. I had no income, but a baby was on its way, I was close to proposing marriage to Evah, I had just committed myself to sponsoring an abandoned boy, and my life was at a crisis stage; I would either succeed in this venture or fail spectacularly. I hadn't a clue which would happen. I desperately needed the reassurance of the familiar: the snows of Chicago, the brandy Alexander under the Christmas tree at Marshall Field's, even the simplest things—like a string of colored lights or a decorated tree, which were nowhere to be found in this place. It was strange to see red poinsettias growing wild in lush green vegetation beneath a hot sun and not decorating a church altar while the sun hung cold and small like an ornament over a snowy landscape.

Before returning to Evah in town on Christmas day, I spent a starry Christmas Eve in Malibeni. I gave presents to the children of Gogo Simelane's homestead, and their excitement over the little toys and coloring books cheered me up for a while. I watched them play around a fire in the courtyard, then I wandered out beyond the huts while a trio of teenage girls seated on a stoop sang "Silent Night" in SiSwati, their voices lovely in the stillness. But homesickness was an ache inside me that I couldn't shake.

Beyond the last hut was the field and the dark forms of row upon row of maize plants sprouting a foot above the ground. The girls' singing reached me there, and my eyes made out the figure of a boy. He squatted on top of a three-foot mound of earth that was an abandoned ant hill. It was Vusi.

I liked this little boy. A few days before, I had taken him to the school he would attend, and we met the Swazi headmistress. She sternly challenged him to work hard to show his appreciation to the white man, and Vusi, unused to such attention, grinned broadly. At a shop, I outfitted him with the first new clothes he had ever owned: a school uniform of gray short pants, gray shirt, and knee-length socks, and a black sweater and shoes. As a Christmas present I gave him a little school box with a T-shirt, running shorts, and a candy cane inside. The headmistress would keep me informed of his other school needs.

It was odd seeing him alone in the field this evening. Usually, the children stayed together. I felt it was better if I did not greet him just now. He seemed to be lost in very private thoughts. He was looking toward the distant hills, and I wondered what he was thinking about. His mother who left him so long ago? Or school? Did he have any idea how greatly his life was about to be transformed? Soon he would start to read. And when he mastered that, he'd be able to look far beyond those low hills. He'd be able to see forever.

I backed away unnoticed and stopped at a spot in the field close to the river. I knelt on my haunches between the maize plants. The Milky Way was directly overhead. So many stars, and so bright.

"I'm not addressing you formally, am I?" I said to the lidlotis. "But who else can I talk to now besides you?" And that, I thought, must make me seem unusually deluded to those I had left behind in the U.S. I rarely dared to think about such things, and didn't need to as long as I was protected by the absolute convictions of those who shared the Indumba with me. But now I was thinking about my old life and the person I used to be. I had changed but had never really acknowledged the change. I'd just kept going. Kutfwasa would eventually have to end; I'd be a sangoma or I wouldn't be. But how could I return to America as if nothing had ever happened, after I'd seen visions, divined ailments, and cured people? I *liked* curing people; it was hard work, but it felt selfless and good and gave my life a distinction it hadn't had before. But now I felt sad and hollow because it seemed the price I would have to pay was to never know again the familiar things that once defined my life.

"This is hard." I felt as if I was my own lidloti, my own ghost— separated so long and under such extreme circumstances from my previous life that I looked back at it as another existence belonging to a person who was dead. My eyes stung because there in my loneliness I mourned the departure of my old self. I had not been a bad person. If I'd been self-centered and ignorant of spiritual forces I now knew, what type of punishment was this? Becoming a white freak in African clothing that not even Africans wore anymore? Having to face a future of frustration and ridicule because I possessed knowledge that no one from my past would ever accept? I felt a million miles away. It was Christmas, and I couldn't see through wet, burning eyes because I was frightened and it was dark and there weren't any lights anywhere and I was absolutely alone.

"Baba?" It was a boy's voice sounding small and scared behind me. He was asking, "My father?"

I gave a start, and I looked up. Vusi stood a few feet away. All the starlight seemed gathered in the whites of his eyes, which were large with fright. He dropped down beside me, quickly wrapped his arms around me, and clung to me tightly. He trembled. He had never seen me like this. Nobody had. I enjoyed Malibeni so much and I was so energetic and full of high spirits while here that the only thing people ever saw was a happy fellow. I heard Vusi sniffle; I embraced him and told him not to cry because I was fine.

Like Vusi's new shoes and new clothes, I was also something new in his life. He had been shoved around from place to place to do work for people who saw him as a temporary mouth to feed and nothing more. He had never known someone who thought of his future or who had given him hope for a different and better life. He had never known some-one who not only told him he deserved everything all the other children had but that he was special. And now it frightened him to see this some-one alone and unhappy. I rocked Vusi for a bit. I had no idea I meant so much to him.

And I realized that I had come to love this little boy very much. The cold had left me and I felt very warm inside, and I smiled because it seemed that in the midst of my crisis the lidlotis sent Vusi to show me what was truly important.

▲ ▲ ▲ ▲

We did not beat the drums on Christmas, and at dawn I took a bus to Manzini town. Before going to Evah's I attended mass at the Cathedral, a pleasantly landscaped fifties-era building with acid-green stained-glass windows and a large fresco of an epicene Christ facing the street. A de-tached concrete bell tower was the town's tallest structure. The pope had visited this church the previous year as part of his seven-hour tour of Swaziland. (He scolded the king on polygamy.) The Christmas service was said by a short, white Irish priest with the unusual ability to speak SiSwati with an Italian accent. I spent the rest of the holiday with Evah and Sandile. I gave her a new watch and him new shoes, and received a sweater she had knitted in return. At four months, Evah was noticeably pregnant and in good health and spirits. She was happy with the news that her mother would be coming to look after her shortly before the baby was due.

The next day on my way to Gogo Ndwandwe's place, I picked up some packages at the Kwaluseni post office. Back at my hut, Jabulani and I opened them and found dozens of gift-wrapped boxes from my mother. As we unwrapped the presents, my African hut was transformed into an annex of Marshall Field's Gourmet Shop. Wine cakes, nuts, can-dies, crackers, liqueur sweetmeats and snacks were displayed in deco-rated containers and beribboned bottles. Everything was so precious and expensive that Jabulani and I just stared in a kind of a daze. I hadn't seen anything like it since I left America.

Jabulani opened a canister. "What are these?"

"Giant pistachios. Have one."

"Thank you." For a moment, he stared at the nut. "Do you plant it inside this shell?"

"No, you eat it. Remove the shell."

He did. "Oh! *Lintongomane* [peanut]!"

"Try one of these," I said, handing him a Frango Mint, a small rectangle of mint-flavored dark chocolate wrapped in milk chocolate. "This is the greatest candy in the universe."

"I was very small when I was born," Jabulani said, sucking on the Frango Mint as if on a memory. "They said they didn't know if I would live. We were very poor, and we had tea only on Christmas. Now that I am living in your house, I have tea every day!"

I spent the week shuttling between Evah's place and Gogo Ndwandwe's Indumba before returning to Malibeni, where I arrived on New Year's Eve. Gogo Simelane had a tradition of giving a little party for her sangomas in the room where her medicines were stored in several hundred jars, sacks, and canisters. To show our respect for the place, we entered on our knees. When Gogo Simelane, the mentor of us all, came in, we clapped our greeting. She directed me to open a five-liter jug of red wine. We poured the wine into glasses, added soda, and passed them around.

Soon the fun began. Gogo Simelane contorted her rubbery face, shook her bulk, and launched into a favorite pastime: preaching. The women responded by shouting, "Glory, hallelujah!" Hymns were sung loudly, and the room resounded with shouts of "Jesu Christo!"

I slipped out after a while. I had another, private celebration to attend. Near my hut, someone had built a small cooking fire. I stirred the embers, added some wood, and got a blaze going. I retrieved from my hut a prized item I had picked up in town that day: the international edition of *Time* magazine. I was in luck; it was the current issue. I assured my lidlotis that any moments I might spend reading the newsweeklies would keep me away from them less than the resentment or depression I would feel by continuing to be cut off. Wholly devoted to kutfwasa, I hadn't read a newspaper since March.

And so, by the flickering orange firelight, my nine months of media isolation ended. I looked at the cover: "Mikhail Gorbachev: Man of the Decade." I wondered, What's this about? I opened the magazine.

"Oh, my God."

There it was, the Year of Miracles that had transpired without my knowledge: the fall of the Berlin Wall, which had seemed as permanent as Gibraltar, the collapse of the communist bloc and the freedom that came to Poland, East Germany, Romania, Czechoslovakia, Hungary, Bulgaria. "The most significant year in Europe since 1848." In China, massacre and repression. In Panama, a U.S. invasion.

For a moment I was struck by the enormity of the news, and I felt cheated. I had missed all of it.

Then I realized the purpose of my self-imposed news blackout. Had I been following these things, I would have been frustrated even more by my isolation. The momentous events of the year that was now only moments from ending were never mentioned to me by a single Swazi. It was Western news. With whom could I have shared these events? Yes, I would have felt lonely.

Yet how I would have liked to have seen the footage of the Berlin Wall coming down! How that must have looked! It had happened in November. What was I doing then?

I remembered and smiled to myself; I was plowing a field with a team of oxen. I was viewing ancient Africa through the eyes of a long-dead zebra hunter. I was learning that Evah was pregnant with my first child.

Would I have traded any of that so I might sit alone watching electronic phantoms play across a glass screen? The question was chilling, the answer swift: No, never.

Suddenly the darkness beyond the orange firelight erupted in shouting: *"Happy! Happy! NguHappy!"*

Someone banged on a metal barrel, and someone else fired a rifle into the air. I stood and went to the courtyard where shouting people mingled. A radio was blaring sounds of celebration from town. Silembe and Willie, the two young farm hands, high on home-brewed beer, staggered about, arms around each other's shoulders. They hailed me. I embraced them both with a bear hug.

Silembe shouted, "It's 1990! And we're still alive!"

It was not a bad accomplishment, I thought, all things considered.

nine

Vusi

IT WAS AT the *maganu* ceremony at Gogo Simelane's homestead the last weekend in January when my acceptance into the Malibeni community was confirmed. The seasonal drink maganu, brewed from the fruit of the *umganu* tree which grew wild in the low country, was available only during the first two months of the year, and its arrival was eagerly anticipated by the Swazis. The consumption of the first barrel was a social rite.

A senior sangoma named Pashamqomo arrived with two twenty-five-liter containers, and by early afternoon the people of the homestead and a dozen people from the surrounding farms were seated on logs beneath a canopy of woven banana leaves. Lion Mahlalela, as the homestead's head man, sat on a stool surrounded by male relatives and elders of the village. Women sat in a circle twenty feet away, and male and female sangomas sat with either Mahlalela or the women. Young men had their own circle, and I squatted a short distance away with some other visitors awaiting placement if it was Mahlalela's desire that we partake in the maganu.

Willie and Silembe brought the heavy container of yellowish brew to the head man. Mahlalela looked over the assembly, all faces upon him, and began to point to visitors, assigning them to the different groups. He gestured to me and indicated an empty stool on his right side. I stood and quickly joined the circle, happy and honored by this most public show of acceptance. But I kept my expression neutral, for the partaking of the first maganu was considered serious business. Mahlalela dipped a cup into the yellowish drink, sampled it with a stern expression, and passed the cup to the man on his left. The cup made its way around the circle of men, and by the time it returned empty to Mahlalela, another was going around and children were scurrying with cups to the other groups. There was no talking at first. Because I was undergoing kutfwasa and had to avoid utensils used by others, Mahlalela gave me my own cup. The other men didn't seem to mind, and I discovered the drink's yeasty, fruity flavor with a sharp aftertaste of alcohol.

As the cups went around, the effect of the drink set in, and the mood lightened from solemn to jovial. The men became talkative, the women sang, and the warriors back from the Incwala harvest festival at the royal village were inspired by the brew to reenact the ceremony's stately dances. I joined them to the roaring approval of the men, doing some steps Prince Vovo had taught me. Younger men launched into the athletic, high-kicking sibhaca dance, and the party, renewed by more people stopping by, continued for hours. I slipped away, and was surrounded by the homestead children. It wasn't candy they wanted. Jumping up and down, they demanded, "NI-XON! NI-XON!"

They wanted to see their paranoid friend. I hunched my back, rubbed my hands together, scowled and shook imaginary jowls at them, and then, glancing left and right through suspicious eyes, growled, *"Angisilo lisela!"* ("I am not a crook!")

The time had now come when the people regarded me as a familiar presence, and I felt the same familiarity with them. I was no longer greeted with elaborate politeness or the overeager smiles shown to tourists. I was treated naturally, with the informality you show an acquaintance. We grew comfortable together, I with the languid but proud people of this faraway place, and they with the exotic newcomer who was part of the Indumba. Perhaps because of the solitude of my earlier writer's life I had been too much of a loner, and unhappy in the role. Until the barriers of language and culture were surmounted, kutfwasa had been a solitary and lonely journey for me. Now I was part of a community. But there was more: when I left Malibeni I could look forward to returning to Evah. We were never separated for more than a few days, and these separations seemed to enhance our time together. Evah was five months pregnant, and in radiant good spirits. I realized that my solitude was over when I admitted I couldn't be lonely and in love at the same time.

▲ ▲ ▲ ▲

On Monday, Vusi put on his new uniform and we set out together for his school. All the parents accompanied their children to class the first day to pay fees. We went across the river to catch the bus that would take us to the nearby town of Tshaneni. Vusi had scrubbed his face until it shone, and his clothes fit well, but he was walking with a severe limp. I asked him if he had cut his foot or twisted an ankle, but he told me he had sores. Normally, he went barefoot and his feet were covered with dust. He removed a sock and shoe, and on his right heel was a dime-sized crater with a raised rim: a bright red caldron of pain that Vusi tried to ignore in the excitement of his first day of school. But I was appalled. What had caused it? Diet? Hygiene? Parasites? Vusi showed me his left forearm, where a half-dozen similar sores erupted across the skin's surface.

After paying Vusi's school fees I took him to the local clinic, a pleasant green and white wood frame building set in a grove of eucalyptus trees. A white doctor, visiting from the Netherlands, examined Vusi, prescribed antibiotics, and left him with a Swazi nurse who administered a penicillin shot. The nurse explained to me with forced cheerfulness, as if embarrassed by the boy's condition, "These small children, sometimes they are lazy to wash."

I was wondering if this was the case with Vusi when the bus brought us back to the border post, the last stop, from which we walked back to the homestead. We were spotted by a friend of mine, a captain attached to the police guard stationed there. Simon was a short, robust, hawk-faced officer who wore the summer uniform of short-sleeved khaki shirt, black-brimmed hat, and short pants over powerful legs (he was the coach of the police soccer team). He had been impressed four months earlier when I returned to Malibeni to continue kutfwasa. "It shows you are serious!" he proclaimed at the time. Now he waved us over to the black-and-white-striped gate beside a pole flying the Swazi flag. "Mr. James! How's it going with your boy?"

I told Simon of our visit to the clinic. He thoughtfully twisted the end of his thick moustache as he regarded Vusi, "No, it is not his fault. When I first saw this one, he was absolutely filthy. I said, 'You go to the river right now and wash, or I will beat you!' He said, 'There is no soap.' I gave him money and sent him to the store. The next day, he came back and showed me the soap and that he was all washed."

I asked Vusi when the last time was he had soap. Last year, he replied, when Simon gave him the money. I asked if he owned a toothbrush. No, he answered, but he knew what one was. Had he ever visited the clinic before today? No. What did he eat? Porridge, some vegetables, meat and milk sometimes, and fruit when they found it on trees. We headed back to the homestead, and I asked him to show me where he slept.

Vusi brought me to an ancient, soot-blackened shack, a former kitchen off the cooking courtyard. The air was smoky from a fire tended by the children who slept there. Scorpions scaled the grimy walls, though the rats kept themselves hidden until nightfall. Vusi showed me a bat that Willie had killed there, its sharp fangs prominent in a black rodent face. At night, Vusi slept on the filthy floor and covered himself with old canvas maize sacks. He had a request for me: "Please, a blanket."

How, I wondered, had I been able to live there in ignorance of these conditions? Was I just inured to the poverty of the country? Or was it self-defense, closing my eyes to a situation I was powerless to correct? People and their children came and went so often at that homestead that I assumed the children's arrangements were temporary. But this had been Vusi's only way of life.

I took one look around and asked him if he'd like to come and live in my hut. He agreed at once. But first I wanted to take him to the general store. It was time he was introduced to the rudiments of personal hygiene. At the dry goods counter I had Vusi pick out soap, a soap dish, toothbrush and container, cup, toothpaste, towel, face cloth, comb, and blanket. Back at my hut came his first tooth-brushing lesson: "Up and down. Never sideways. Morning and night. Every day!" I showed him how to swirl the bristles at the gum line between the teeth. But I went slow on the flossing after his tender gums bled.

At dawn of the first day of our new arrangement, I prepared eggs, bread, and tea for Vusi's breakfast. This was necessary after he reported his school's food service had not yet started and Gogo Simelane's porridge was never ready until after he left in the morning. I gave him money to buy fruit in the afternoon when he walked the four miles back to the homestead. This soon evolved into a weekly allowance. We ate our evening meal together in the hut after cooking on two kerosene stoves I kept atop a varnished plank table.

I supervised the application of Vusi's skin medicine, supplemented it with a poultice I boiled from fern leaves I gathered along the river, and after a week the sores shrank and disappeared. But there was a cloud on the boy's horizon. Gogo Simelane and Mahlalela had two adult daughters who objected to Vusi's attending school. What was particularly disturbing was that one of them, Mamsie, was a school teacher herself. She lived with her children at Prince Vovo's homestead, which was closer to her job (Gogo Ndwandwe granted this favor to the daughter of her mentor). But when Mamsie had returned to Malibeni and heard of Vusi's school plans from her sister Jabu, she had tried to have her father withdraw his permission.

Mamsie made her reasons plain. When I greeted her one day, instead of greeting me back, she shouted, "What are you doing with this boy? Who is going to look after my father's goats? You?"

"Well, Mamsie," I explained, "Vusi will do his chores when he gets home. That's what your father agreed to. Besides, there are other boys here."

She dismissed them with a contemptuous wave of her hand. "Oh, they will run away any day! They are like animals!"

I didn't doubt she felt the same way about Vusi; I turned away and left her. I was angered that she would deny the boy the education she would never deny her own children, and that she and Jabu would prefer to see him remain an unpaid child laborer tending their daddy's goats. I knew they would continue to object to Vusi's schooling; my only question was, would they succeed in ending it? The last thing I wanted was a conflict with these two stout, imposing women—Jabu with her overwrought, emotional manner, and Mamsie who shouted every word as if I were a backward student seated at the far end of her classroom, so that even an innocuous conversation seemed like an argument. And I did not want to forget that both women had extended helpful hands to me at times over the past year.

But with Vusi I had to stand firm. He was proving a quick and eager learner at school, and the thought of how close this clever boy had come to spending his life illiterate and ignorant filled me with a kind of panic. I might have seen myself in him; how my healing potential had nearly languished unrecognized before my own education via kutfwasa. Perhaps I wouldn't finish kutfwasa and wouldn't become a sangoma. But I could see to it that this boy realized *his* potential. I was determined to.

Meanwhile, powerful summer storms were tearing through Swaziland. One ripped at Gogo Simelane's homestead and scattered tin roofing sheets over the fields. Storms thundered over Prince Vovo's homestead, where I stayed every other week, mainly so I could be with Evah and ease her pregnancy with little attentions like cooking grilled cheese sandwiches for lunch and bringing her flowers and women's magazines from Britain. She was filling out, her smile and skin glowed, she was happy, and I was so happy when I was with her that the hard rain pelting the tin roof above sounded like nature's applause.

On one trip back to Kwaluseni, Gogo Ndwandwe instructed me to give some patients a powdered medicine to protect them from lightning strikes. I pricked their skin with the tip of a razor blade and rubbed the medicine into the incision. I was no longer doing this with my finger; contact with so much blood seemed a sure way to contract AIDS. Though there were only 300 HIV positive cases reported in Swaziland, government health authorities were uncertain of the epidemic's hold on the general public. I began using a porcupine quill after I saw an elderly female sangoma rub medicine into an incision this way. I discovered that my incisions seemed to heal quicker when using a quill, and I wondered if they contained some kind of natural anti-infection agent. Certainly porcupines must stab each other by accident all the time, and they don't get infected. I had LaShonge treat me also with the lightning medicine. Yes, it was magic, if that's what I had to call the unexplainable power of the lidlotis who engineered the protection, but magic was my life now, my business.

▲ ▲ ▲ ▲

For months the men and women of Malibeni had been gathering at the Komati river to build a footbridge. It was a sturdy structure of metal pylons and steel cables supporting a long, thin span of wooden planks. Now at the end of February the intebetebe was done (the name translates, literally, as "it really swings," referring to the span's wobbly motion when a person crossed it). The area's chief declared a feast of celebration and sent a large steer for us to slaughter. At sunset on the eve of the event, I joined the men of the homestead, who were to slaughter the steer under Mahlalela's direction. Willie and Silembe had the steer roped not far from the house of a hunter named Sifundza. He was a lean, rugged, and amiable man who tended a small plot above the river next to the new footbridge. He wore the traditional Swazi male beard that encircled the mouth from nose to chin but left the cheeks and neck clean. Sifundza earned extra money selling the feathers of the birds he shot to weavers of ceremonial headdresses. With ammunition an expensive commodity, he was a sure shot.

It was the first time I had helped slaughter a steer, and the grisly job was an eye-opener. I was aware all the time of the animal's fear and pain, and I realized that I had lived my life thus far as a hypocrite, or at least in a state of willful ignorance. How, I wondered, did I think food came to me in America? Did it materialize in the store meat cases without pain and death?

No, humans were living organisms who thrived on the deaths of other organisms, now vividly illustrated as Sifundza plunged a dagger into the beast's neck artery (I read somewhere that this also severed a nerve, so the animal was effectively anesthetized). These Swazi cattle seemed like such harmless, stupid beasts, ambling along and pulling up grass, and this one expired without a sound or movement of protest as its blood flowed copiously into a bucket held by Silembe. The animal knelt, then rolled over until its legs stuck straight up. The men got to work, using their pocket knives, the only tools they had, to remove the hide and separate the limbs. These were hung from a tree branch. The men worked quickly and skilfully. Out came the heart, liver, and other parts, looking like oversized reproductions of human organs at a science exhibit. Sifundza straddled the head with his legs, and brought down an axe repeatedly with powerful blows to crack open the rib cage. The head was removed and hung, eyes closed and tongue lolling, from a tree limb. I helped lug a side of beef to Sifundza's hut, and I realized again how my culture had protected me from the killing that occurred on my behalf so that I might eat a Big Mac without concern for its origin. I knew I'd be involved in other cow slaughters, and I'd never feel the same about eating meat: I'd still do it, but I'd feel more honest and somber about it. The next day, when we gathered to enjoy the chief's gift, which was roasted over a large fire in Sifundza's yard, it tasted delicious, the most succulent and flavorful beef I had ever had. But eating it meant accepting the way the natural world worked: a beast was slaughtered so I might have the energy to live another day.

Beef was expensive and therefore rare in the diet of the Swazis, and so the steer was the highlight of the day's celebration. Also featured was a traditional women's dance troupe in black skirts, orange cloths exposing one shoulder, and black beehive hairdos. The women formed a line, and the men in their loinskins and fighting sticks danced in homage opposite them to the same slow rhythm and the women's a cappella singing. I did, too, and then joined the others to listen as the old chief spoke in tribute to the community's work: the footbridge that stretched behind us, its slender length dipping in the middle as if to kiss the brown water. No more would we have to ford the chilly Komati barefoot in the winter, or endure the cumbersome crossing in a leaky boat during the summer. We all felt proud: we had built it ourselves, and I had helped when I could, carrying bags of cement and baskets of dirt on my shoulder up the steep clay riverbank.

An elderly man who lived close by, one of the distant and nonroyal members of the Dlamini clan, greeted me. He was on the stout side, the beard encircling his mouth was white, and he preferred to speak English with me when we met. This day his tired eyes regarded me with worry. "I hear you are taking this boy out of the fields and putting him in school. Mamsie and Jabu are saying you are stealing him from his work."

I had always found old Dlamini a fair man. "Do you agree with them?"

He did not answer, which indicated he had only wanted my response. Was I going to attack the wicked sisters and create a disturbance in the community? When I did not, he voiced his own concern, "What will happen to the boy after you leave?"

"You don't have to worry about that," I asserted. "I'm going to sponsor Vusi as far as he cares to take his education, no matter where I am."

He nodded his head and seemed satisfied by my commitment. But his concern remained with me: What would happen to Vusi if I did have to leave? Providing school fees was simply not enough, not if Mahlalela's daughters were determined to keep Vusi home on the farm as a "family member"—in other words, as a lifelong, unpaid employee. Also, how could a child succeed in school without parental encouragement? I couldn't have succeeded, not even at the fine schools of Winnetka, Illinois. And who would see that he got a proper diet, washed, brushed his teeth, did his homework?

All this was on my mind on Monday morning when I accompanied Vusi to school with a present I purchased at an educational supply shop in Manzini town. Vusi and I crossed a playing field bordered by bougainvillaea hedges of neon bright red and pink, and entered a courtyard swept by the girl students. The boys were clearing away debris with shovels. Assembly was called in front of the main classroom building, a single-story structure fronted by a columned portico. The children lined up by class, with Vusi in the first grade. Some had shoes, some didn't, but all were well-scrubbed and groomed as they marched in place with a loose, jivey step, singing "Walking with the Lord" in SiSwati and English, pointing their fingers skyward at each mention of Jesus. The headmistress, Miss Mamba, a dignified, heavy-set woman wearing a pink dress, stepped forward. I had met her when I enrolled Vusi here.

"It's time for school," she intoned.

On cue, the children sang, *"It's time for school, it's time for school, this is the time, the time for school! Hello, brothers!* [A sea of arms jerked stiffly back and forth: wave, wave.] *Hello, sisters!* [Wave, wave,] *Hello, teachers!"*

I liked this song, and grinned as I listened among the teachers standing in a line beneath the portico. Miss Mamba announced, "Today, children, we have a guest, Mr. Hall. He brings us a gift."

She motioned for me to step forward. I carried a five-foot-long, rolled-up world map. I greeted the students and unrolled the map with Miss Mamba holding its other end. Continents appeared in colorful procession from south to north between turquoise-blue oceans that sparkled when the sun struck the map's glossy covering.

"Ahhhh!" the children said.

"I'm from America," I informed them in SiSwati, pointing to the U.S. on the map. My finger moved across oceans and land masses. "Here is Swaziland. It is far!" I looked at my watch. "Now it is ten to eight in the morning. But right now in America it is ten minutes to ten, in the night. Yesterday, Sunday night."

The older students who were able to understand this murmured their amazement. I pointed to the center of North America. "I'm from a city called Chicago. Can you say that? Try. 'Chicago.'"

"Shee-kha-go!"

"Very good! You're smarter than some of our aldermen. Use the map well."

A rhythmic clapping of hands led by Miss Mamba accompanied me back to the portico. The children were dismissed, and they ran off to their classrooms. I accompanied the headmistress to her office and spoke candidly of my concerns. "I'm worried about Vusi. At any time he can be pulled out of school at the whim of his guardians."

I found Miss Mamba a delightful woman, full of warmth and understanding. "Do I know! It was not so long ago when we went around to these homesteads in the bush and asked the head male to send his children to school, and he'd say, 'How much will you pay?' Because the way he saw it he was losing help, and we wanted his children in our schools to pay our salaries!"

She laughed at this. I nodded my head grimly and said, "I've given this a lot of thought, Miss Mamba. It's a radical step for me, but I can see no alternative. I'm thinking of hiring an attorney to see if I can become Vusi's legal guardian. If you could have seen the way he was living: ulcerated arms and legs, not even soap to wash with, a dungeon to sleep in . . ."

"Oh, I do know!" Miss Mamba asserted. "Vusi told me what you are doing for him. And you're right. He's doing very well here. It would be a shame if he had to leave. But why be his guardian?"

"Well, so I can have some legal status in his life when it comes to deciding his future."

"But why be a guardian? That's not the way. Why not adopt him?"

"Adopt Vusi? How? I'm single."

"One parent is better than none. There are single fathers. Look here, Mr. Hall, let me ask you something. What does Vusi call you? When he sleeps in your house and puts on the clothes you buy him and eats your food and goes to the school you pay for, what does he call you?"

"He calls me baba." I said, the SiSwati word for father.

"There, you see? You are his father. He comes from a very nice homestead, but he can't stay there forever. You're all he's got when it comes to a future."

I must have looked doubtful, because she asked, "Tell me something else. Do you love him?"

"Well, he's a sweet boy, of course," I replied evasively. I had never felt comfortable trumpeting my love.

"We all know that Vusi is a sweet boy. But do you love him?"

I looked at her for a moment. If I were to say what was in my heart, it seemed I'd be committing myself forever. But I took the plunge, and it felt good "Yes," I said. "I do."

"There, you see!" She scribbled something on a pad. "I'm giving you the name of someone at the Department of Social Welfare in Mbabane. She will start you off."

The prospect of making Vusi my son struck the right chord within me the instant Miss Mamba proposed it. It felt right, despite the obstacles. I felt as I had when the lidloti awakened my desire for a baby: this was something I wanted to do and could do.

When I returned to Gogo Simelane's Indumba, I knelt to the lidlotis and asked for their guidance. I had never taken kutfwasa lightly and certainly wasn't playing as I prepared to bring a new child into the world. Adopting a boy was no less serious. Yet, in a way, I felt as if the lidlotis had already guided me. They had brought me to this boy. There was no question about what I had to do, or about the certitude I felt toward doing it.

▲ ▲ ▲ ▲

A few days later I returned to Kwaluseni via the capital town of Mbabane and met with Mrs. Gugu Made, Miss Mamba's contact at the Social Welfare Department. Mrs. Made had a pleasant and helpful manner, a round, wide-open face, and small, graceful hands that took down the particulars of my case in handwriting that looked like a series of musical notes. She urged me to bring Vusi to the office for an interview.

But first it was back to Prince Vovo's homestead, where Gogo Ndwandwe always had patients needing treatment. Lately new people had been seeking me there. "We want to try white spirits," they said. I'd help them if I could, or else refer them to another sangoma, each of whom had his or her own specialty. Old and petite Gogo Mabusa handled infants. Gogo Ndwandwe was noted for treating homesteads, protecting them from lightning strikes and attracting the lidlotis to bring prosperity to the fields, the homes, the people.

But there was always general work to do. Evah requested I prepare a medicine she drank every day: *imbita,* which cleansed the body internally. I also needed to regularly replenish my supply of headache medicines, purgatives, and the kutfwasa potions I drank, smoked, and vomited every morning and evening. By far the medicines most in demand by women were fertility potions and, by men, aphrodisiacs. And then there were emergencies. In late March, Prince Vovo's aggressive and cross-eyed dog Emehlobukana ("the eyes that look at each other") broke his chain and promptly bit a visitor. I was called because for some reason the dog was terrified only of me; when he saw me coming he froze in place, peed on the ground, and allowed me to pick him up under one arm and rechain him. I then clipped some of his hairs and burned these atop the fire to destroy fleas and germs. I mixed the ash with a disinfecting herb and rubbed this with a porcupine quill into the bite victim's bleeding leg wound, which closed and in time healed. The part of the dog that was sacrificed—its burnt hairs—was a magic agent meant to reverse the misfortune the dog itself had created.

Evah winced slightly at the bitter taste of the imbita medicine I made for her, but my number one patient declared herself satisfied. We discussed Vusi, and she asked me to bring him by so she could meet him and help me assess his needs. The Easter school break was approaching, corresponding with celebrations set for the king's birthday—a national holiday—and I had received Mahlalela's permission to bring the boy to town to see his monarch.

But now it was time for me to go to town for my own special moment as I accompanied Evah to see her doctor, a dark-skinned, large-headed man from the east African country of Tanzania. The doctor hooked Evah up to an instrument, and we listened to the amplified heartbeat of our baby; a deep, subaqueous throb that vividly reminded me of the hidden life within her. The child was due in two months.

Because of the doctor's visit I took a late bus to Malibeni and arrived after dark. I entered the hut to find Vusi asleep on his mat tightly wrapped as usual in his blankets so only his closed eyes, nose, and bulbous cheeks were visible in the lamplight. Each night he slept like that, and awakened soaked with sweat. But I knew he was cocooning himself against the insecurities he still felt. His new blankets seemed to him his one safe reality. Soon, I hoped, he would think of me as another.

Suddenly, a rustling sound moved along the wall. When I shot a flashlight beam into the corner, green eyes shone back at me from the head of a brown snaked that was coiled and ready to strike. I then knew the reason that no rats had pestered me in that hut.

Vusi's toes were within two feet of the snake, and with my heart pounding I grabbed his blanket and slowly pulled him away. He woke up groggily, unaware of the danger. I slipped on my Levis and rubber boots for protection, grabbed an axé, and cautiously approached the venomous head that stared back at me intently. I kicked my foot forward, and it struck. I felt the impact of the fangs against my heel, and brought my foot down to trap the head against the floor so it could not turn and strike again. I brought the axe down hard, cutting the body in two, but the snake wiggled frantically in pieces, refusing to die until I crushed its head with a stone. At three feet in length, it wasn't a large snake, but Vusi, alert now, stared at it with wide frightened eyes from the corner where he was huddled in his blanket. We both knelt and thanked the lidlotis because we were unharmed. I tossed the snake's body outside, discovered a hole behind the table where it had entered, and plugged the crack temporarily with a can. Vusi was now too scared to sleep, so I laid him beside me on my mat and he disappeared beneath my blanket. In a moment, he was fast asleep against my shoulder.

We had other adventures in that hut. In early April we both bolted up on our sleeping mats at a frightening racket coming from the roof. Some creature was stomping and tearing at the grass. I shone the flashlight up, and in the beam a small, hairy, and inhuman arm tore through the thatch.

"Baboon!" I shouted. Vusi was as scared as if the snake had returned; in Swazi folklore a baboon was a witch's assistant, sent out to do nefarious errands at night. I ran outside, found some stones and, cursing like a New York cabby, started hurling them up at the small dark figure scudding over the roof in the moonlight. It was a baboon all right, as I saw when it dropped to the ground and ran away into the field on all fours.

Lots of creatures seemed attracted to that hut. Birds built their nests in the thatch on top, chickens liked to roost up there, and frogs hopped in to pee so voluminously on the floor that I wondered if they were simply a single large bladder inside. One morning, I dropped a bag of tea into a mug of hot water, felt a thread against my beard, and brushed it away. Another thin thread took its place, perhaps from a towel. I brushed at it as well, but couldn't seem to get rid of it. I went to the mirror and saw a tiny spider diligently spinning a web from my moustache, over my mouth to my chin. I flicked it outside and returned to find a diaphanous cover over my mug of tea. In five minutes, another spider had spun a web over the top of the steaming mug. My last tea bag, too. At least I found some solace when Gogo Simelane declared that it was good luck so many of God's little creatures found me congenial company.

The day I was looking forward to arrived, when I would bring Vusi to meet Evah. At dawn on Easter Sunday, Vusi left Malibeni for the first time in his life. New black trousers, a striped shirt, and brightly polished shoes made him seem like any other boy from Manzini town, where we headed by bus. I enjoyed watching Vusi gawk at the passing scenery.

Every valley was a discovery, and in town everything was new to him: the church with its colored windows and the silk of the priest's frock—it was Vusi's first time in a church—the parade of townspeople in their fine Sunday clothes, office buildings that rose four stories above the hilly streets and sprouted satellite dishes like mushrooms. It was a poignant thing to watch him run his fingers over textures he had never felt before: a chromium office pillar, a door handle of polished brass, the church's smooth marble floor. He did not speak, as if he was now only a receiver of new sensations.

He was shy toward Evah, though she took to him at once with a smile and an embrace. She cooked a holiday meal, and Sandile kicked a soccer ball around with him, but Vusi still said little until he encountered an old friend at my hut in Kwaluseni. Then he smiled and laughed happily, because Jabulani had lived at Gogo Simelane's homestead for five years, a herd boy himself after his father was no longer able to pay his school fees.

I introduced Vusi to Prince Vovo, and once again my patron impressed me with his knowledge. Yes, he knew of Vusi's mother, but out of Vusi's earshot he disparaged her as a promiscuous and disturbed woman, though a beautiful one. No one had seen her in over two years, as someone surely would have if she was anywhere within the tiny nation; therefore, the prince concluded, she had either run away to South Africa or was dead. He encouraged me to press ahead with my adoption plans for Vusi.

"A fine boy, bright like copper. He will work hard for you to show his gratitude. And, you know, God made these poor boys clever so they can escape their lot."

But would he escape? Gogo Simelane's obstreperous daughter Mamsie always spent her holidays at her parents' homestead. But this year she remained at Prince Vovo's place, and when she was joined by her sister Jabu, I wondered if they were spying on us. Mamsie soon waylaid me and as usual said what was on her mind without bothering to greet me. "When is he going back to my father's homestead?"

"Hello, Mamsie. We just got here."

"He's going back when?"

"After the king's birthday," I told her.

"What!?" she shrieked. "He will miss his classes! He will fail!"

I might have told her that Vusi's teacher had excused him from the single day he'd miss between the holiday of Easter Monday and the king's birthday bash on Wednesday, and that her father had given his permission. But, of course, this shrill little woman did not really care about Vusi's education, and wished to see it end. I held my anger and replied, "No, he will not fail."

I turned and left, and Mamsie fired her final shot at my back. "You are playing with Lozangcotho's child!" Lozangcotho was the unfortunate woman who had abandoned Vusi over two years before and disappeared.

Meanwhile, according to Jabulani, during our visit Mamsie's sister Jabu found Vusi, told him I was a bad man, and said he should return with her and Mamsie to Malibeni, where his friends were. Overhearing this, Jabulani defended me, an argument ensued, and when I next saw Vusi he looked confused and frightened by the turmoil. Clearly, I had stepped into a passionate situation pitting an abandoned boy's needs against the greed and jealousy of others, with racist and xenophobic overtones spicing Mamsie and Jabu's antipathy toward me. The two women were already asking their fellow Swazis to side with them against "the foreigner." I learned that many agreed to this test of patriotism because Vusi meant little to anyone and so he might as well leave school and be forever dependent upon the Mahlalela homestead. I knew that if Mamsie and Jabu learned of my adoption plans, open warfare would be declared. I might be kicked out of Malibeni, my kutfwasa compromised, possibly irreparably. It was a real risk.

I reported all this to Gugu Made, our case worker at the Social Welfare Department. Vusi and I went to her office in Mbabane the following Tuesday. She listened cautiously and without expression as I concluded, "I'd rather defend Vusi against King Lear's daughters than those two."

"I see," she drawled in a slow, calm voice. "We must find this Lozangcotho woman."

I agreed, because I did not wish to do anything behind Lozangcotho's back, assuming she was still alive. I told Vusi she would always be his mother. But if his adoption depended on finding her, we were in trouble. I reminded Mrs. Made that she had spoken of finding Lozangcotho the previous month at our first conference. Because of bureaucratic inertia, nothing had been done. I was not encouraged when Mrs. Made would not commit herself to a schedule of further action. But her conversation with Vusi went well. He sat in a chair beside mine, swung his dangling feet in the air, and when she asked him how he liked his first soccer match, which he had seen the day before at Somhlolo National Stadium, he smiled. Did he like school? Yes, he said. Would he like Mr. Hall to be his baba? Yes, again. Could he tell us where his mother was? This drew a blank expression and a shake of his head.

While in Mbabane, a mountaintop town of 50,000 where the banks, embassies, and two newspapers were located, I took Vusi to the open-air market to see a woman who sold traditional Swazi garments. She greeted me profusely and gave Vusi a hug. Did she have a child's *majobo* loinskins? I asked. She did, and brought out a set. I tied these around Vusi's waist. Did he like them? He nodded his head vigorously. I selected child-sized warrior beads and a small fighting stick. Vusi would attend the King's birthday celebration as "a real Swazi."

Back at my hut, Vusi modeled his outfit for his friend Jabulani. After a dinner of roasted beef, maize porridge, boiled greens, fruit, milk, and cookies, he lay on the floor mat, stared up at the thatched roof and sang and chattered to no one in particular. I had never seen him so relaxed and happy, and I was convinced I was doing right by him.

In the morning, we awoke at five to get an early start for Nhlangano, the distant southern town that was hosting the king's birthday celebration. In the lamplight, I tied Vusi's calf-length *mahiya* cloths around his waist, tied his loinskins over these, and draped his beaded necklaces with their colorful woolen tassels over his shoulder. In Manzini town, we met up with Evah and Sandile, and the four of us headed by bus to Nhlangano, passing through dramatic mountainous country. We joined several thousand Swazis for a long program held in a soccer stadium where purple-blossomed trees grew up through the bleachers, obscuring the view of the spectators behind us. As usual, the Swazis did their best with limited resources, and the diplomatic corps arrived in a motley collection of sedans and Land-Rovers. (The American ambassador came in the embassy station wagon, no profligate of taxpayer money he.)

A stretch limo appeared, bringing the crowd to its feet. It could have been Michael Jackson inside, the young black man in a braided uniform waving one gloved hand, tinted blue by the window glass. It was the king, and he strode the red carpet after the Queen Mother's appearance in her enveloping leopard-skin robe.

I held up Vusi, who scrutinized his monarch with a serious look of appraisal. At twenty-two, King Mswati was taller and bigger than most of his subjects, but he shared the incandescent Swazi smile. In his honor, cannons outside the stadium fired a twenty-one-gun salute, sending out shock waves that set off all the car alarms in the parking lot. Military regiments in cardinal jackets marched slowly back and forth across the field for what seemed an hour, and for seemingly another hour a girls' high school drill team twirled batons to the theme of the TV show "Dallas." Finally, the king's warrior regiments marched by with their raised fighting sticks and cowhide shields, bringing the crowd back to life. Then the women's ceremonial regiments wearing bee-hive hairdos and carrying carving knives and wooden cooking spoons went by, singing, and the program was over.

Vusi's first trip away from his village exposed him to much of his country. It had been a happy time for him. Evah liked the boy, and by the trip's end the emotional bonds between us were growing stronger.

The daily rituals of kutfwasa, the digging and processing of herbal medicines, the treatment of patients, the precious time spent with Evah in the eighth month of her pregnancy, the nightly drum-beating rites in the Indumba that saw no new lidlotis but brought the return of White Feather and Lidvuba the zebra hunter, as well as the mundane but often difficult business of cleaning, eating, and staying healthy, all kept me from pursuing Vusi's adoption for the next weeks. I preferred to let the social welfare people do their jobs. But when a month had passed since I brought Vusi to Mbabane and it was clear that they were doing nothing, I called Mrs. Made from a pay phone at the post office.

There was a reserve in her friendly and precise voice that put me on guard, but no amount of defense could have shielded me from the blow she delivered. "Thank you for calling, Mr. Hall. I brought your case up with the department head. She thinks that maybe it is not a good idea that you adopt the boy."

I was astonished. "Not a good idea? What does your department propose as an alternative, that he go back to tending goats?"

"We are only concerned with the child's welfare," the case worker recited. As politely as possible, she informed me, "The problem is you, Mr. Hall." I heard an apologetic laugh, and she explained, "Try and understand, we have never adopted to a sangoma before."

"But you're Swazis!"

"Well, you know the way some sangomas are." Another nervous laugh. "Maybe you haven't gotten to that yet."

"I don't understand," I said, trying to keep my panic in check. "There's been a misunderstanding. I've got to talk to this supervisor."

"I think we've already closed the file on Vusi . . ."

"*Don't!* At least, give me a chance. Five minutes is all I ask. This boy's future is at stake."

I did not say that my persistent desire for Vusi's adoption also had its selfish side: I loved this boy and couldn't imagine losing him. But Mrs. Made probably knew this. A compassionate woman, she at last agreed not to close the book on Vusi until I could make another personal appeal—but she did so with the drawn-out sigh of someone who was being burdened by yet another unsolvable problem.

I hung up, heartbroken and mystified. What did she mean when she spoke of the way some sangomas are? She couldn't have been referring to the sangoma style of dress, which was not too different from traditional Swazi attire. A sangoma's convulsions in the throes of lidloti possession were restricted to the Indumba. You never saw a trained sangoma singing, chanting, or carrying on in public or outside the Indumba ceremonies and divination rituals. And, anyway, Vusi had known sangomas all his life, living where he did.

Evah was also puzzled, and shared my disappointment. To her and the Swazi nation, a sangoma was a healer to be valued. The British had outlawed them during the colonial occupation, but in those days the British had wantonly and indiscriminately condemned all tribal culture, refusing as well to acknowledge the monarchy of the Swazi king. He was merely the "paramount chief" to the British, who claimed there could be only one monarch in their empire, who resided at Buckingham Palace. I knew that in the towns there were many self-loathing Swazis with a little money and a little education who despised their people and their culture, considering both to be backward, dirty, and superstitious. But Mrs. Made at Social Welfare was not one of them. She was fascinated by my kutfwasa, and she even asked that I invite her to the graduation tests I hoped one day to take.

I consulted the bones on this one. Interestingly, when I cast them down they formed a pattern I hadn't seen before: the widow bone, representing death, was hard against a small, smooth, blood red bone that indicated violence. Together they meant murder. My insight kicked in, and I recalled a grisly discovery of some weeks before when a mutilated, half-decomposed body of a middle-aged man was pulled from the Komati, upriver from Malibeni. Pieces of flesh had been cut from the body, and when I asked what had happened, Gogo Simelane looked at me darkly and informed me that witches had wanted human flesh for their medicines. The local newspapers had a lurid if inaccurate description for the practice: ritual murder.

I found Gogo Ndwandwe, and asked her, "Please, tell me about this medicine they kill people to make."

"It is said to bring a powerful luck to your life," she replied. "After you take it, you can have many cattle and many wives. If you are a woman, you will be your husband's favorite wife."

"Don't we have our own herbal medicines that accomplish the same things?"

"Yes! But our lidlotis will not help a person who is bad. They can't help if what you want can be gotten only if others are harmed, like you can be your husband's number one only if the others die."

I had been completely ignorant of this practice, but Gogo Ndwandwe reported that every few years mutilated corpses turned up. I asked if sangomas ever dealt with these murders for medicine.

"They cannot!" Gogo Ndwandwe exclaimed. "And if you make it so someone dies, your lidlotis will kill you! A sangoma's job is to cure people."

I wondered, though, if someone at the Social Welfare Department was not making the distinction between a witch *(umtsakatsi)* and a sangoma. I couldn't afford such confusion, and it now seemed necessary to firmly establish my normality credentials. When I went back to Mbabane for the meeting with Mrs. Made's supervisor, Mary Shabangu, I was prepared with documentation. Ritual murder? Me?

I was relieved to find Mrs. Shabangu easy to talk to. Her manner was on the curt side and wire-frame glasses gave her face a severe look, but she seemed genuinely interested in Vusi's and my story. When I described his life before I met him and the success he was now finding at school—his teacher wanted him to skip the next grade to make up for lost years—I thought I saw some wetness in the eyes behind the glasses. I gave a sales pitch that would have done my lidloti Harry proud, showing her a copy of the Makeba book I wrote that was on sale here and my most recent U.S. tax forms, which my accountant had sent for me to sign and return.

Then the door to the spartan office cubicle opened, and Gugu Made entered with a short, balding man in a tie and jacket. "This is the assistant to the Minister," she said. "He is the one who will be making the decision about your case."

I stood to greet him, and our eyes widened with mutual recognition. I knew him; he had been to Prince Vovo's homestead dressed in traditional Swazi attire at a time when the men were discussing the possibility of my joining the king's regiments. He now smiled broadly and declared, *"Umbutfo wam'!"* ("My warrior!")

I smiled back, relief flowing through me. This man, who held Vusi's fate in his hands, had been treated in Gogo Ndwandwe's Indumba, and he certainly had no objections to sangomas.

The supervisor looked up from my tax returns and inquired, "You say these were sent to you from America?" When I replied that they had been, she asked, "Then you receive parcels from America regularly?"

"From time to time, yes."

"Then, Mr. Hall," she said, removing her glasses and looking at me beseechingly, "do you suppose you could get me some copies of the *National Enquirer?* They are so out of date when they arrive here!"

I grinned as broadly as the little boy I hoped to adopt, for this woman would not make such a request of someone she didn't intend to help. "Why, sure. What stories do you like? The Ghost of Elvis or UFO babies?"

ten

The House of Dreams

IT WAS MAY 1990, and for the first time in a year and a half I wore a suit. Standing in my hut at Prince Vovo's homestead, my legs felt strange confined in trouser fabric, and the collar and tie encircling my neck seemed awkward. But I had received a surprising message from the bones when I consulted them about the trip I was taking by myself to the wild animal reserve: the lidlotis desired that I dress in my old clothes, perhaps for the last time. The trip was for one lidloti in particular: Lidvuba, the zebra hunter. Often in dreams a spirit directed a sangoma or kutfwasa student to a location it desired. Perhaps a medicinal root or spiritual communication awaited there. For weeks my own dreams had been filled with persistent visions of zebras, and Gogo Ndwandwe agreed that I should seek them out at one of Swaziland's game reserves, and address my lidloti in their presence. Even if Lidvuba only wished to see his prey again through my eyes, it was a desire I was bound to honor, for as long as an ancestral spirit was with me and satisfied, it would endow me with the divination ability to heal and comfort my patients.

But putting on my good dark gray suit felt strange; it was comfortably familiar but seemed like a relic from another era. I had bought it two and a half years earlier, and assumed it was now out of date in 1990 America, where people were wearing . . . what? Coincidentally, a letter had arrived that day from a woman I used to go out with in California. When I finished packing my handbag for the trip, I sat down and read the news. My friend reported that I was missing Milli Vanilli, bungee jumping, Dan Quayle, pony tails on men, the New Kids on the Block, Teenage Mutant Ninja Turtles, and the Donald and Ivana Trump divorce. Her advice: stay where I was.

But the irony was that I could never stay in one place for long in Swaziland, and just as when I had gone off in search of a goat a year before, I was now off in search of my lidloti's desire. When Jabulani stopped by to take the hut key, he asked me somberly, "Aren't you afraid of lions?"

"There are no lions in the Mlilwane game reserve," I said. About twenty miles away from Prince Vovo's homestead, a white farmer years before gave his property to the Swazis to be transformed into a wild animal sanctuary by allowing the land to revert to its natural state. Giraffes now roamed where fields were once cultivated, and the Swazi game rangers lived in the old farm house. There were some huts and bungalows for visitors, but it was off-season now, the beginning of the southern hemisphere's winter, and when I phoned for a reservation I was told that after four local teachers had departed I would have the place to myself.

Jabulani shook his head; he was nervous about my journey. "Suppose you begin to see things?" He was worried that I might see visions in the wilderness, and became what was called Indlu Yemaphupha, a "House of Dreams." I had entered this state twice before, when reality and illusion were indistinguishable, during my conversation with Harry in the field that day, and the time I saw John MacDonald's farm house. But I was much further along in my kutfwasa now, and the possibility that I might become possessed by visions for a long period of time was real. If I were alone in the wilderness, it could be dangerous. But it also seemed an enticing possibility if the visions were revelatory.

"You know I have to do this," I told Jabulani. "I've been waiting for a long time until it felt right. Now's the time."

Jabulani stood like a rock before me. "You should know that every day you are gone I will pray for you."

"Thank you, my friend. And remember, I have lidlotis to watch over me."

When I stepped outside, the men whistled and the women ululated happily. No one had seen me in a suit before. Over my collar was one spot of color in my gray and white ensemble: four red, white, and black beaded sacks of medicine hung from necklaces.

As was the custom when a sangoma sets forth on a journey, I knelt before the lidlotis' pole and addressed the spirits, informing them of the trip and requesting their presence along the way. I rose, and Gogo Ndwandwe and LaShonge, seated on grass mats before the Indumba, waved their good-byes. I returned their smiles, but I felt the weight of the moment, for I could never be casual about walking off into the unknown, no matter what discoveries awaited there.

A bus dropped me off a mile from the game reserve entrance, and I hiked up carrying a handbag stuffed with food (but no change of clothes; I couldn't afford to ruin more than one suit), my sleeping bag, and an umbrella. At the guard house I boarded a jeep that took me into the reserve, an area equally divided into dense woods and open fields of high yellow grass.

A camp built for European and white South African tourists anchored one end of a small lake and contained some cabins, a restaurant, a gift shop, and several "traditional" grass huts wired for electricity. There were no tourists today, and as usual I was the only white face around. It was too late in the afternoon to be taken by a guide to see zebra, so I dawdled about until the sun set, wishing I could afford a drink at the restaurant, and watching a family of irritable-looking horned wart hogs bustle by single file and a herd of slow-moving African buffalo come up to the barbed wire fence surrounding the camp to eat grain from food troughs.

A fire burned in the courtyard before the empty restaurant. I waited beside it in a patio chair until midnight, when the camp was still and the night air was cool. I rekindled the fire by pushing together logs a foot in diameter, and used sticks to pull out some red hot coals. I placed these on the ground and knelt over them. I pulled a large red cloth over my head and body, creating a tent with my face above the coals, and sprinkled over the embers bits of dried cow fat mixed with herbal medicine. A sweet white smoke rose up and filled the space. This way of taking medicine was called *kubhunyasela,* and as I inhaled the smoke I clapped my cupped hands and addressed the spirits. Next I burned some small, dried yellow flowers, herbs that also attracted the lidlotis. The burning flowers had a sharp odor of chicory. I blew on the coals, they glowed, I felt the heat on my face, smoke rose and I breathed it in.

I was alert when I emerged from the sheet. I felt as if something was going to happen, and I had no desire to sleep and miss it. I went off to explore the camp, guided by a nearly full moon. In a grove of tall trees I discovered an empty pavilion, open on three sides. The moon shone with sufficient brightness to illuminate the interior, and I saw benches set about. Stepping inside, I felt the invisible presence of children and seemed to hear echoes of their excited chatter. School children would come here for lectures when they visited the park. I extended a hand toward the large animal skulls on display, and though my fingertips touched nothing but air I felt the skulls' coarse texture. It was uncanny, because I seemed to be feeling through the hands of curious children who had examined these skulls. And then, also without touching but merely extending my hand, I felt the smooth plaster and bumpy contours of hills and valleys beneath the fingertips of children feeling a large relief map of Swaziland. These were sensations living spirits had left behind. The moment was strange and chilling but also pleasing and exhilarating. It seemed I was becoming Indlu Yemaphupha, the House of Dreams.

I wanted to address the ancestral spirits; I hadn't actually spoken to them since I left Prince Vovo's homestead. But the camp seemed an inappropriate place. Even though the staff was asleep, the grounds seemed crowded with the same type of spiritual residue that had clung to the lecture pavilion; so many visitors had left their psychic footprints there. I was acutely sensitive to such things, and I felt claustrophobic in the camp.

At the restaurant that overlooked the lake, I hopped over a three-foot-tall stone wall, and found myself on a barren stretch of ground, white in the moonlight. I felt an acute spiritual solitude here, indicating that people were not usually present. I knelt down, still dapper in my suit, and unfolded my red cloth. The lake water was twenty feet away, and two large black boulders glistened half-submerged under its calm, mirrored surface. I covered myself with the cloth and began to address the lidlotis.

But not for long. I sensed something alarming and rose quickly, throwing off the cloth. Ahead, the two boulders were seized by some seismic force. If this was a vision, it was the most startlingly vivid to date. But when one boulder split open and I saw a huge mouth with thick, cylindrical teeth, I knew I had disturbed two sleeping hippopotami. The partner opened its mouth too, and they started coming toward me. One let out a roar cutting like cannon fire into the stillness. I ran, headed for a tree with the thought of climbing it if I had to. I looked back. The hippos had stopped at the water's edge, blocking my return to camp.

I decided to circle around the lake and make my way back from the other side, wondering if it was true that water which was home to hippopotami did not contain crocodiles. There was no path to follow and I maneuvered between trees and bushes, through a moon-bright night shadowed by drooping silhouettes of trees and swaying marsh grass. I sat down against a tree trunk to rest and looked back toward the restaurant on the far side of the lake. A large sloping window through which diners could watch wildlife gave me a view of the room inside, all lit up. A woman stood at a table. I saw her bend over slightly as she performed her work, folding napkins or perhaps sorting cutlery. I was happy for the company, distant though she was. For a while I watched the heavy-set woman whose face I could not make out, though she raised her head from time to time and looked to her left. She repeated her motions precisely, looking to the left, back, and continuing her work, as if she were trapped in a loop of film that kept repeating itself.

There was a distorted sound in my ears like the ocean you hear when you press your ear to a sea shell. With a little shock I realized I was seeing something that was not there. An optical illusion? I averted my eyes, looked back, and found the woman as she was before. Somehow, this moment in which she was trapped defined her. I thought of my Italian-American grandmother, who while not black, had borne a physical resemblance to this woman. My grandmother always personified domesticity and the hearth to me, and I remembered with a jolt that my grandmother was one of my lidlotis. Was this a way of indicating her presence to me? I continued to watch until the vision fragmented, and I could no longer see the woman clearly. I stood up and followed the marshy shoreline.

The African veld in its natural state was a noisy place, I discovered. Nocturnal birds shrieked and whistled like nothing I had ever heard. It was fascinating but eerie, so much frantic activity done in the dark and hidden from humankind. For a long time I thought someone was banging a hammer against a piece of metal, only to trace the sound up a tree. Another bird's call sounded like a rusty gate swinging. I passed within twenty feet of a flock of blue cranes, their color a delicate shade of turquoise by day but gray now in the moonlight as each stood atop a single storklike leg with the other tucked beneath their egg-shaped bodies. Then they rose with a rustling of wings, slowly ascending, their cries mingling with those of a flock of hawks who emerged from tall trees and swirled around in formation, black against silver clouds. In the distance, the hippos bellowed, an intimidating noise.

At some point toward the end of night I knelt and covered myself with my red cloth to speak to the spirits. But I fell asleep, and when I awoke fog shrouded the woods and the rising sun was a silver disc low on the horizon. Mist first revealed then obscured the mirror of the lake's surface; a flock of cranes winged skyward, gray against gray. I walked the short distance remaining to camp, located my unused sleeping bag and my other bag beside a tree trunk, and opened a can of orange juice. My suit seemed as neat as when I first put it on, and after brushing my teeth I felt fine, eager for another day within the House of Dreams.

▲ ▲ ▲ ▲

As soon as the fog lifted, I set forth with a guide by foot into the veld surrounding the camp, in search of a zebra herd. My guide was a short, slight young man in a brown uniform and boots. One milky, blind eye glowed dully in the shadow cast over his face by a floppy hat. Used to dealing with Europeans, he gave his name as John until I asked for his real name. Hearing my SiSwati, he looked startled, and said Dumisane. He had the silent, serious manner of someone who was not only naturally reticent but who had spent his life in the country and now had to confront something beyond his experience: a white sangoma in a nice suit. But we talked as a herd of impala with long, twisting horns pranced by, and soon he was telling me about his life as a game ranger. He told me he'd often pack a gun against the poachers who made the game reserves war zones in their pursuit of rare rhino horns.

Suddenly, we encountered a herd of zebra. I had never seen these animals in the wild, and I was filled with emotion and pleasure. Here were my friends I had seen so often in visions during the Indumba drum-beating ritual. I felt the happiness of Lidvuba, the spirit whose life as an African hunter centered around zebras.

The herd stood in high yellow grass in three groups of five and six. They looked at us as we stood on a dirt path. They were shy, ready to bolt. We retreated into the shade of a tree that was one of the few on a flat plain, which extended to a forest at the base of rugged blue mountains. The air was clear, the sun bright, and the black-and-white-striped zebras stood in sharp contrast to the pastel veld. I knelt, covered myself with a red sheet, and addressed Lidvuba: I was presenting to him his zebras, I hoped he was as satisfied with the sight as I was, and that he'd remain with me through the course of the journey ahead. Though I had finished the task I had come to do, I didn't want to leave right away. I wanted to continue into the wilderness beyond the game reserve.

When I emerged from the sheet, Dumisane was on his knees also, not out of politeness, I sensed, but out of respect for the lidlotis. We returned to camp, passing a pair of giraffes that reminded me there was no substitute for seeing animals in the wild. These beasts were a wonder; they were huge. The Swazis called them *tindlulamitsi,* "the tree passers," and as they passed above the treetops they seemed so ungainly, tall and thin, I was amazed they could stay up.

I tipped Dumisane and checked out at the reception desk. I noticed that some female workers had gathered around my guide and were questioning him. Like most hotel staff, the workers here spent their time speculating about their guests. But the mystery about me was lifted when I went over and greeted the women. We spoke in SiSwati. They wanted to know why I was wearing a sangoma's beaded medicine sack necklace, and they were astonished when I told them I was undergoing kutfwasa. Could I cure this and that, they wanted to know? I told them my reason for visiting them that day, and the women were surprised; no sangomas ever came there. The park was still considered by most Swazis to be a white man's farm, and white people made up a majority of the guests. I replied that I did not object to white people, and that on occasion I had even been intimate with white people. This set them all laughing.

No vehicle was available to take me out of the reserve, so Dumisane volunteered to escort me through the veld. We hiked an hour before arriving at the so-called South Gate, which by some inscrutable logic was located north and east of the reserve. I tipped him again, wished him well, and headed for the winding green Lusushwana river, which I planned to follow up into the hills. I felt I could find an isolated spot up there to address the lidlotis and receive any communications they might care to send me.

I started out at noon, and by four o'clock I was at the bridge over-looking the water, having walked and found rides from Swazis who spotted me along the road. I descended the riverbank and headed upstream. The river narrowed to ten feet across where it cascaded over stones and rocky cliffs, and it seemed clean and virginal, a place for baptisms. I thought of the little girl Evah and I expected in three weeks' time, and then I thought of the baptism by blood and medicine that would await me if the lidlotis considered it time that I undergo the tests to conclude kutfwasa. Their signal would be a song, the Inkhanyan, which the spirits would sing through me late one night, awakening the homestead. But when would that be? The graduation rites were two months away. At this time last year MaZu's lidlotis had been singing the Inkhanyan for a month.

At a spot where boulders as big as cars met the river, I decided to wash. I clambered up and over stones, wearing my suit and carrying my gear, and discovered a subtle but real spiritual energy to the place. I wanted to explore it and decided to spend the night there. After I addressed the lidlotis, I undressed, washed my shirt and left it on a rock to dry, then washed myself. The riverbank was dense with jacaranda and pine trees, I had left people and houses far behind, and the place was loud with water rushing over ledges cut like jigsaw pieces.

I sat on a rock letting the sun dry me, and stared at the hump of an elongated, half-submerged boulder midstream. It began to change before my wide-opened eyes. Like the hippos the previous night that I mistook for boulders, this boulder began to resemble a hippo, with a head facing me and a pair of indentations at the water line where the nostrils would be. Slowly it began to sway, back and forth, moving slightly toward me before pulling back again. I was fascinated by this rock which I knew to be inanimate but which was clearly moving before me as water rushed all around. "All is in flux," I murmured. "Nothing is as it seems."

Which defined Indlu Yemaphupha, the House of Dreams I had become. For me, waking and dreaming had merged. I looked at the rock closely. The microscopic was suddenly enlarged, and I watched granules of stone being chipped away by the powerful, ceaseless, erosive force of the fast-moving water. The noise was tremendous, nightmarish. It was dark. Was this a dream or reality, a violence made visible and audible?

I was so attracted to the rock that I entered the chilly water and climbed atop it, kneeling naked to address the lidlotis. What followed were repeated visions that superimposed themselves on the sun's reflection sparkling over the rushing water. They were visions of flood waters raging up that narrow valley, a tidal wave between the sheer stone cliffs, engulfing and killing me, and while the scenes were disturbing and vivid, I knew that I was still on that rock so I was not so much terrified as puzzled and unnerved. Why was I seeing these things: a huge wave crushing me, and then with a back-flip of time coming again to sweep me under so I drowned beneath forty feet of water? And then again: this time I was swept downstream to be pinned against a bridge pylon until a tree swept along by the flood impaled me with a spikelike branch.

"Hey!" I shook my head as if to dislodge these scenes of my death, which tumbled one after another. My brain felt loose and floating within my skull, I was drowsy and I felt keenly my solitude in that place. Shadows now covered the river; the sun had passed behind a mountain. I left the water, got dressed, and stared without appetite at some bread and canned meat in my bag. I watched finger-shaped clouds change from a flaming orange to ruby against a violet sky, with wispy streams of pink running off. It was twilight, and I made a small fire and burned more medicines over embers, inhaling them in a tent I made by draping a cloth over my head. When I emerged, the evening was cool, with a crispness announcing winter's imminence. A full moon hung above the river and cast deep shadows onto the ground.

I put on a raincoat over my suit, stored my gear between two boulders, and spent a restless night roaming upstream along the riverbank, sensing spiritual presences that never fully manifested themselves, hearing snatches of music and singing that weren't really there, and glimpsing visions that disappeared as soon as I became aware that a figure moving against a tree was not physically present or that a glowing color against the moon was not of the mortal realm. I explored the woods and stony outcroppings that rose like aliens in the lunar light, and several times I addressed the lidlotis and sensed their tentative attempts to reach me. But for the most part I experienced the sensations of the night the way you listen to Ravel's *Boléro:* as a long, sustained crescendo that never quite reaches a climax.

Toward dawn the sky smeared over with black clouds that looked like too much toner in the Xerox machine. I huddled between two rocks, let my head fall onto my raised knees, and slept for a couple of hours. A fine mist was falling when I awoke, but the sky was bright white. I retrieved my gear, drank some juice and ate some fruit, some two-day-old rolls, and a Snickers bar my mother had sent that seemed as exotic and out of place in that wilderness as my now muddy suit. I could have easily spent days more out there wandering through my House of Dreams, but I decided to stay one more night only, hoping that anything the lidlotis cared to tell me would be told in that time.

I also did not want to needlessly worry Evah by too long an absence. She understood why I was out here, and she recognized its importance as only someone raised in Swazi culture could; she was proud of my work in the Indumba, and, of course, she could never forget that it was my kutfwasa and the lidlotis that had brought us together. She also understood that I could not commit myself to a wedding date until I was freed from the burden of kutfwasa and had seen this venture end one way or another. But I had discussed marriage with her, and had learned from a pleased but unsurprised Evah that she had never doubted our relationship would end any other way. "You're not the only one with inhloko," she said, meaning the sangoma's insight, and, of course, she was right. Though grateful to the lidlotis, I felt their invisible fingerprints all over our unconventional romance, as if they had decided to contrive an arranged marriage for the bachelor in their care. A spirit had telepathically expressed a wish that kindled a desire in me for a baby girl, a desire so strong I went out and found a mother for my "spirit baby." But then I fell in love with the woman, and vowed to make her my wife. It seemed like the plot for a TV miniseries: "Indumba! An African Romance."

Not that I had seen a televised image in over a year and a half. Nor had I needed to. Lidloti-vision had kept me enthralled, and was about to bring another surprise as I journeyed upriver on the bank opposite from where I had been the day before. I had found my way blocked in the morning by an ancient and rusting barbed-wire fence that dipped into the water. On the other side of the fence I saw a long brown hawk feather like a writing quill on the sand. It seemed significant, as if someone had left it there for me to find, so I reached through the wire strands, took it, and placed it in my inner jacket pocket. Since I could no longer go forward, I went back several miles to a bridge and headed up the other side. Near the bridge was a handicrafts complex quite isolated in the woods. I found the workers spending their lunch hour at a prayer meeting in a gallery where baskets, pottery, and tapestries were displayed. I was welcomed into the group for some preaching and gospel singing, and I was happy for the human contact before continuing into the intermittent rain of the cold afternoon.

A mile upriver the mountains closed in to form a gorge, and the water rushed through in churning rapids. On my right as I followed a narrow, muddy road, the hillside rose up at a sharp angle with gray rocks covered by bright yellow and green moss vivid against a pewter sky. Across the way was a cliff, and as soon as I saw it I dropped to my knees and clapped my hands together as if to greet a lidloti. It was not stone I saw, but a spirit.

My eyes were open, though from the fatigue I was feeling after two nights with little sleep they were not wide open. But I saw, as clear as if an artist had arranged the folds of rock and the placement of moss, a dragon's head in profile. It was huge, four stories high, and the mountain behind was its body. I saw eyes half-shut as if sleepy or bored, nostrils, a wide, closed mouth. Anything so large was intimidating, but made of stone it also seemed trapped in stone and unable to move.

I stood up; this wasn't a lidloti, so why kneel? I spoke to it, *"Hello."*

"Hi."

The dragon's response was telepathic. Its stone mouth did not move. I had no doubt that it was fashioning its voice, including a rather insouciant American accent, to fit my mind.

"I'm a little tired," I admitted.

"Who isn't" came the jaded reply. *"I've been here for eons. Trapped in stone. Weathering, weathering."*

"You're a prisoner?"

"You can see that. But it doesn't matter. There's no place I want to go."

I thought, How about the beach? A few million years more and he'd be eroded to sand. There was something of the wiseguy about this creature, and he brought out the same in me. I arched an eyebrow and said pointedly, *"You're bigger than big. You're Titanic."*

The voice coming back to me was suspicious, "Meaning what?"

"Meaning, friend, that when the gods moved in to rule from Olympus, they chased out the Titans. Zeus punished those who resisted by embedding them in the rocks of mountains. Sound familiar?"

He replied dryly, *"I do not as a rule answer questions put to me by mortals. It makes you proud."*

"Can you at least tell me one thing?"

"That depends."

"I've always taken Greek mythology to be just that: myth. But meeting you, I wonder. Could it be that the Olympians were lidlotis of some sort, guiding and interacting with the ancients? How seriously should I take them now?"

His reply was tart, *"How seriously should you take your tripartite religion?"* Mountain Face was referring to my Catholicism, which he seemed to know about, and the Holy Trinity of the Father, Son, and Holy Ghost. I said, *"That's a matter of faith."*

"Exactly. The beliefs and disbeliefs of human beings are of absolutely no interest to me."

I doubted that very much, and I said sardonically, "I see why some spirits are free to roam the universe while others are stuck in rocks."

"I take that as an insult."

I smiled. "I try not to stoop to name-calling with Titans. It makes you proud."

He regarded me wryly through a boulder eye threaded with mossy green veins. "Come closer. I've a landslide that's dying to give way."

"Some other time. I've got to go."

"Well, then, good-bye. When you return, you won't find me. I'll have cloaked myself."

"Thanks for the glimpse, anyway. And the chat. It was amusing." I didn't admit that it had also been a sociable break in a lonely journey. But I sensed the imprisoned spirit felt the same way because melancholy shaded his reply, "That it was."

I gathered up my gear and continued without looking back. I had a strong sense that there was somewhere I had to go. After perhaps an hour's walk—my sense of time was vague, each moment seeming to stretch forever while, at the same time, days and nights were racing by— the darkening sky told me the day was finished. There was little time now to locate a place to spend my final night and receive messages from the lidlotis, if any messages were coming.

For some time the river had been largely hidden from my view by a stretch of vegetation. It was a heavily wooded area. On impulse, I cut through the trees and descended the steep bank. The bushes opened onto a wide stone embankment. Rapids between short lengths of fast-flowing black water cascaded down from terraces upstream and disappeared around a bend between cliffs. I put down my gear on a stretch of sand and headed up to explore along the rock shelves overlooking the rapids. The canyon was narrow, with tall trees rising to my right. I climbed over smooth rocks and boulders slippery from rain, and sharply eroded stone steps bordering the rapids. Low, vaporous clouds swept over the mountain tops. It was an eerie place—rugged, isolated, starkly beautiful.

The temperature was dropping, and I was thinking of getting back to my gear when I noticed a structure ahead. I drew closer. It was the ruin of an iron bridge, dating probably from the early years of the century when the British mined the surrounding mountains for tin. Narrow iron girders were set side by side, spanning a ravine, and I went across one, one foot in front of the other like a tightrope walker, arms thrown out for balance. The metal was slick from rain, and water swirled darkly below; it was dangerous and exhilarating, and I was not drawn by curiosity but from a sense that a lidloti of mine was somehow involved in this place. On the other side I found a stone bridge support but no evidence of the road that must have once existed and led to a mine long since abandoned. The cliff rose vertically above, so I returned across the girder, and with the darkness thickening headed for my gear. I felt compelled to look back at the bridge, a solemn relic. A sharp discomfort passed through me. There was something wrong with that place. It was spooky in the truest sense of the word, inhabited by spirits. Some evil was associated with the work that occurred there, involving spiritual dislocations brought by foreign invaders and their schemes. It was horror and anger and madness that I sensed.

In the twilight gloom, I covered myself with my red cloth and urgently beseeched the lidlotis for their protection. Whatever was out there, I asked that it not vent its rage on me.

Yes, rage! A vision of a man naked but for loinskins running at me was so powerful I recoiled. His club was raised high, ready to strike, his face a mask of hate. I closed my eyes against it and came close to shouting that I was not the one he wanted, but when I looked again he was gone. This spot that included the ruined bridge seem to be some kind of spiritual transit point, and I was sure it was the destination I sought. Again I asked the lidlotis not to permit tortured spirits to interfere with our communication, or scare me out of my wits.

Then I was surprised, because the canyon had not gotten darker with nightfall, but lighter. The moon was so bright it shone like a fluorescent light behind misty clouds. I told myself to eat something, and I could even read the words "Apple Juice" on a carton from my bag. I made myself an avocado sandwich, and had some guavas that Dumisane, the game ranger from the day before, had picked.

I felt better and walked to the river without fear. The rush of rapids seemed appealing; they were so purposeful, so efficient, so *professional.* But they emptied into a black river below that seemed bottomless and ominous. Death seemed to be there. The back of my neck tingled. I returned to my gear and wrapped my sleeping bag around myself like a great shawl against the cold. I looked up at the clouds swirling about the mountains. The place was so alive with spirits it was like a neighborhood of dogs barking and yapping at night when a stranger passed through. It was too much, it was unnerving. I sat down against a boulder, and I asked myself, *Who is it? Who's here?*

Then I seemed to know: John MacDonald, my first lidloti, was there. Or rather, he had been there, while alive. Not at that very spot, perhaps, but around the region. This disturbed me even more, because it seemed impossible. What could have brought a Scottish farmer here, so long ago? I tried to puzzle this out for a long time without success. (It was not until two years later that I learned that the name the Swazis used for South Africa, Sikhwahlande, was also their name for Scotland. Evah's son Sandile told me the Swazis of old had considered the neighboring area of South Africa to *be* Scotland because they encountered a sizeable community of Scots there who arrived in the nineteenth century to build a railroad through the Natal province. John MacDonald might very well have been one of them, and a part of his spirit might have remained here after his death. His house that I had once envisioned one morning might have actually existed in Africa, not Scotland. Perhaps he had stayed in the region and had a farm. Others had. Could this explain the connection between my ancestors and Africa, a connection that had to have been made at one point to bring me to the Indumba?)

It was beginning to drizzle. I opened my umbrella and sat under it. My mind was a blank. I listened to the rain drum against the wide, inverted dish above my head until it diminished and the ever present thunder of the river became the dominant sound once more. I stood up. The hills were luminous, and misty clouds seemed to evaporate as if the aggressively bright moon were melting them from behind. I stepped over to the rapids. Along the stone steps the river had carved dozens of holes a foot or two wide, perfectly round, filled with water and pitch black inside. I did not know how deep they were or what creatures lurked within them. But some force urged me to stick my hand down into one. I refused.

Suddenly the moon found a break in the clouds. The canyon lit up as if a switch had been pulled. Wet rocks and cliffs took up the moonlight, glimmering. All was silver and bright, with the black river pouring down in contrast. Cascading water looked like falling ice from where I stood and watched. A white man's voice, quite distinct, said, *"Don't do that."* I turned, but no one was there. But the voice didn't seemed to be directed at me; I overheard it. I felt a physical vulnerability standing on the stone steps above the rapids. I sensed a slight pressure on my lower back, as if someone were trying to push me in. If I yielded, I'd fall. I stepped back but I did not sit down. I felt as if I were already asleep, beyond fatigue, my body weighing a ton and dragging me down to the earth, and yet weightless, floating.

A dream voice, out of the trees, said, *"How?"* Or was it, *"Hawu!"* I dropped down and clapped my hands to the lidlotis. Something was up, but what? It was cold, but I was not aware of being cold. Everything was wet, but I did not notice that I was wet. I saw things clearly; all was real. Clouds like box cars flew over the moon. Tricky lighting in the canyon now. Sections glowed brightly, then dimmed. A flock of large birds in a V formation followed the river, flying straight down the ravine's center. I watched until they disappeared, and there was—was there?—yes, there was music! It seemed to come from beneath the rushing water. I listened closely.

"You will find your song, and you will sing this song until you die." The lidloti Juan had said this over a year before. Now it was coming: the spirits were giving me my song.

So this was the reason my instincts had brought me here! Everyone undergoing kutfwasa was supposed to have a song, which would be added to the sangomas' repertoire. I reached into my jacket pocket and withdrew the hawk feather I found that morning. I squatted above a square of white sand. The moonlight was bright over my shoulder as I used the feather as a quill and wrote down what I heard: a song whose ethereal melody and sturdy rhythm could have been African or Native American. Did the song come from White Feather or Lidvuba? But there were others: the mysterious spirits of the water, the Tmzmzu. As I wrote in the sand, the song took form. I wrote in SiSwati, but in my mind I translated into English.

Run to the river/ It is coming, the sun/ Hurry to the river/ It is setting, the moon. Like an African song, there was a chorus that sang in counterpart: *Run!/ It is coming!/ Hurry!/ It is setting!* A second verse. *Run to the river/ It is flowing, the water/ Hurry to the river/ They are calling you, the Tmzmzu.* Meanwhile, the chorus sang: *Run!/ It is flowing!/ Hurry!/ They are calling you, the Tmzmzu!*

So it was as Gogo Simelane suggested long ago, when the Tmzmzu water spirits attached themselves to me and took my *timfiso* necklace. Around Christmas, I had lost a beaded medicine sack necklace along the Komati riverbank, and I searched long and hard for it without success. A week later, a small boy found it in the river, a yard from shore, unaffected by the water and not even muddy. The sangomas told me the Tmzmzu had taken the necklace, entered the medicine contained inside, and returned it to me. At the time I was torn; my gut thought there might be something to the sangomas' unanimous interpretation of the necklace's loss and return, but my intellect found such a story amusing and fanciful.

I could not deny that all my life I had been attracted to water; lakes, oceans, rapids, and waterfalls. Now I stared at the words in the sand that mentioned the Tmzmzu. Whether this song originated with these particular spirits or not, it was a gift, an unexpected gift, and I was grateful.

I quickly looked upriver, at something I thought I saw there. I smiled at a vivid vision of old acquaintances: running toward me was a herd of zebra, splashing through the shallow water of the river's edge, the spray kicked up by their hoofs silver in the moonlight.

▲ ▲ ▲ ▲

The next morning after greeting the lidlotis, my instincts suggested I should not make the journey back to Prince Vovo's homestead by bus but rather walk the twenty-odd miles from that place beside the mountain river. After three nights with little sleep I set out on foot, took my time, felt fine, stopped often, talked to people along the way, and saw things that were not there but appeared as if they were. Passing over the highway bridge spanning the Lusushwana river, I watched the rocks thirty feet below rushing up at me as if I were falling toward them; another death image, startling and puzzling. Some power in the water seemed to be continuously drawing me in.

The House of Dreams was often a disturbing place. The disorientation and fatigue I felt stayed with me and intensified so greatly by the time I reached Kwaluseni mid-afternoon that when I knelt to announce my arrival at the lidloti pole I passed out. I woke up on my side in the dirt and recovered quickly, though my suit was fairly well finished. I was so glad to be back and in one piece, contrary to the images of my own death I had repeatedly seen, that I made a present of my shoes to Jabulani. As he promised, he had loyally prayed for my safe return and worried until I came back.

My journey to become the House of Dreams seemed like a climax to my kutfwasa. There seemed no reason why the lidlotis should not announce the conclusion of my studies by emerging to sing the Inkanyan. I knew that the song did not necessarily mean that I would succeed and become a sangoma, but it was a signal that the time had come for me to be put to the test.

The next night, the song came.

eleven

Nomoya

WHEN THE SPIRITS decided to sing the Inkanyan for a kutfwasa student, the first time was at night. The day after returning from the wilderness, I sensed the time had arrived for this song. But I felt the apprehension of someone whose fate depended upon powers outside himself. I could not force the song, I could not fake it, because it was a signal from the lidlotis that they would grant me the power to perform the psychic displays at the graduation rituals and that they'd give me the physical stamina to get through those days and nights.

I stood in the center of my hut directly underneath the apex of the conical roof and asked the lidlotis to give me a sign. I didn't know what I meant by this, for surely the singing of the Inkhanyan was signal enough. But a very faint voice brushed my mind, "What time do you want to get up?"

My own voice deep inside myself, also very faint, replied without hesitation, "One-oh-seven."

I went to sleep. I awakened. I checked the clock. Its battery powered display read 1:07 exactly.

"My God," I murmured, seized by excitement. Well, I wanted a sign. I hurried to get ready but I was not nearly fast enough, for even as I was tying my dancing skirts the lidlotis emerged, took over my body and voice, and headed out into the night. From within myself I was aware of running a loop around the main house to return to the small courtyard in front of the Indumba. The moon was high and three-quarters full. No single spirit with a recognizable personality seized the sangoma or kutfwasa student when he or she danced; it was a trancelike condition that made the voice deep and urgent. In this state my arms swung the dancing sticks, and a voice emerged singing from my throat, sounding both powerful and lonely in the night's stillness.

> *Inkanyan, ye Inkanyan!*
> *Inkanyan, ye Inkanyan!*

I was aware of confusion from the surrounding huts; the voices of newly awakened people:

"What is happening?"

"It's Sibolomhlope!" LaShonge said. "He is singing the Inkanyan!"

Gogo Mabusa and the others emerged from their huts, wrapped in blankets against the night's chill. They began to beat the drums, shake rattles, and sing the song's chorus. From the other houses of the homestead, people emerged and joined the group before the spirit house. It was a significant moment for the homestead: the lidlotis of a student were announcing his readiness to undergo the final kutfwasa rituals.

If all went well, soon there would be a new sangoma.

▲　▲　▲　▲

Word quickly reached Gogo Simelane in Malibeni that my spirits were singing the Inkanyan nightly, and that I would be among the Indumba students who would undergo the final tests under her auspices in July. I did not go myself to give them the news because I did not want to be away from Manzini during the final two weeks of Evah's pregnancy. Her mother had arrived form Mozambique, the country that separated Swaziland from the Indian Ocean. I was pleased to meet Mrs. Kunene, a short, quiet woman who, through subtle looks and body movements, expressed her emotions and her will as plainly as a mime. I saw where her daughter Evah learned her own economy of expression, as well as her knitting skills. Gogo (grandma) Kunene arrived with a baby blanket she had made, which we added to clothes Evah had knitted and the other baby things we had bought in Manzini town.

During this time I was feeling emotions I had never known before: a general and indiscriminate goodwill toward everyone I saw and a pride that I was accomplishing something extraordinary. Forget about the world's billions, I was creating a very special person, my own child by the woman I loved. There was a perfection to that formula, and I was grateful to the spiritual forces whose inspiration I had to thank for this event. My two years in Swaziland had changed my life again and again. I could never have imagined it before, but I thought I understood now the compulsion that had brought me here, the instinct that underlay all the myriad reasons to pursue kutfwasa, a voice that said, *"Go, something wonderful awaits you there."*

And then, a crisis. Evah reported to me that the baby had turned within her womb. She felt its head pressing against her right side. We waited a few days to see if the baby would turn his head down again, but no change came. Evah and I consulted a doctor at the Manzini hospital where she would have the baby. Given the nearness of the due date, he advised a Caesarian section. He wanted to perform the operation in a few days on the date he scheduled all his operations.

And that, if I had still been in the United States where only one kind of medicine was available, would have been the end of the story. But I was no longer in America: I was a kutfwasa student whose lidlotis were singing Inkanyan. I now knew of alternatives to the knife.

While I consulted Gogo Ndwandwe, who gave me some herbal medicine for Evah to take that would enable the baby to turn, Evah found her own healer. She told me about him, a so-called prophet in one of the Christian-Zionist sects named Mr. Hlope. Both Gogo Ndwandwe and Gogo Simelane knew of him, and his reputation as an herbalist was widespread. He did not rely on faith healing alone, though his potions augmented his spiritual powers. Evah asserted, "Hlope can do it; he can turn the baby. Many women go to him. My friend's father when she had this same problem, he hired a taxi all the way from Nhlangano, and you know how much that costs. She was already going into labor. But Hlope set the baby right, and it was a normal birth."

By Sunday, the pain on Evah's right side was so acute she could not walk stairs unassisted. But she was determined to go to Hlope, and we made the trip to his homestead in a borrowed truck, accompanied by Evah's mother. The prophet/healer was also a minister, and there was a new stucco church on his property. Services were over when we arrived late in the afternoon.

We found Hlope, a short, stocky man clad in trousers and shirt, seated on a high-backed chair in a dirt yard between square mud houses. He was in his sixties with thinning white hair, and his manner was quiet and inner-directed, as if he were filtering the information around him through hidden spiritual sensors. Speaking to him was much like speaking with a sangoma, who often gave the impression of listening to you through two sets of ears, the ones you could see and a secret pair attuned to some psychic connection. And Hlope, like a sangoma, looked at you in a probing manner that did not seem intrusive but sympathetic.

As per Swazi custom, the elders conferred with each other, and Gogo Kunene explained to Hlope her daughter's problem. The prophet nodded and invited us into a small consultation room/prayer house. Sharing a bench, Gogo, Evah, and I sat with our backs to a wall below a high window through which a perfect rectangle of orange light was cast onto the opposite wall by the setting sun. Hlope sat beneath this light, facing us. The plain, clean room was empty of religious references and contained only a pink bucket and a brown box, both filled with herbal medicines, beside the prophet's chair.

Hlope wrapped a shawl about his shoulders and asked us to join him in prayer. I had never seen this type of healer work before and was respectful of his practices. Leaning forward with his eyes closed, he prayed aloud in a quiet but authoritative minister's voice. Raising his head and looking at us, he stated that the baby's head had been resting against

Evah's right side for the past five days, just as Evah had told me but no one had told him. This insight impressed Gogo. He called Evah to him, she stood and met him in the room's center, and the prophet placed his hands on her belly and prayed. He twisted her shoulders, sides, and thighs while reciting an invocation to God. Then he made his prediction based on the message he had received while praying and through contact with Evah's body: the spirits would help her. "The baby will turn. There will be no need for surgery. The child will be born normally."

Evah's mother closed her eyes and sighed as if to say "Thank God." She and her daughter were both strong-willed people, but outwardly calm and calming in manner. Hlope had a gentle assurance that made a person perfectly willing to believe his predictions. Did I? Hlope looked at me as if to ask this question, and I wondered if his faith healing required my faith as well to succeed. I was swayed by this prophet's reputation—Gogo Ndwandwe and Gogo Simelane's favorable opinions of him impressed me—but I made my own evaluation based on the many sangomas I had known. I thought I could spot a charlatan if I had to, but Hlope never put me to the test; his gifts seemed so manifest to me. I felt them like a signal coming off the bones. There was no pretense or stridency to Hlope. He seemed at home with powers that performed what outsiders might call miracles but which seemed to me healing by other means, not too different from what I was beginning to do myself, only more polished and assured. If my belief was necessary to make the baby turn, then he had it, though I didn't think either he or the spirits whose power he employed needed it.

Hlope now asked Evah's mother to stand. He prayed over her and shook her by the shoulders, hips, and thighs, a ritualistic practice that seemed similar to a sangoma habit of lightly tugging at a patient's hair, fingers, and toes to draw out evil elements.

Then the prophet had words for me. He hadn't spoken to me since we first greeted each other, but he now stated that he saw many powerful lidlotis attached to me. I would become a great healer in his opinion, which he reported in a flat, almost clinical tone. He said, however, that certain spirits—the Bandzawe African tribal spirits that performed the sangoma's *kufemba* divination rite—had not yet emerged. He was correct. I could read the bones, but did not yet perform well the complicated kufemba ritual, in which I symbolically "sniff out" a patient's ailments with special medicines and an ox-tail brush. If I succeeded with the tests to end kutfwasa, Gogo Simelane planned to have me undergo a rite designed to bring forth the important Bandzawe lidlotis that inspired a sangoma to perform kufemba. I was impressed that Hlope had hit upon this. He gave Evah some herbal medicine to drink, handed her a few handfuls of powder to mix with water at home, and the session was over.

The next day, Evah began to feel movement in her womb. Her pain disappeared, and she said, "I feel like something is dropping like a stone inside me." It was the baby, whose head she felt pressing downward two days before her surgery was to take place. Evah sent Sandile to the hospital to inform them that the operation was no longer needed.

▲ ▲ ▲ ▲

The baby was two weeks overdue when Evah went into labor the first Saturday in June. It hardly mattered that I wore traditional sangoma clothing to the hospital; I felt the same as any other prospective father did in those circumstances: the world around me seemed swept up by an adrenal anxiousness and excitement. I wanted to be present when the baby was delivered, but to do this I had to arrange for a private room. Usually babies were delivered by midwives going from bed to bed in the crowded maternity ward, with other women in labor on stretchers in the hallway. No men were permitted inside the ward. A room was available, but our baby did not arrive either on Saturday night or Sunday, and by Sunday night Evah still did not feel the birth was imminent. She sent me to her flat to sleep with her mother and Sandile, a twenty-minute walk from the hospital, and gave me a list of things to pick up in town on Monday. When I returned with the items the next day, Evah's contractions had grown stronger, and the countdown had begun. Our room was around the corner from the maternity ward; it seemed spacious by American hospital standards and contained a second bed for myself and a large attached bathroom with tub and shower. But for the delivery Evah was placed in a room just off the maternity ward itself.

The cries and screams of women undergoing painful deliveries came through the door, unnerving Evah and myself as I sat by her bed, holding her hand while the evening passed. She swallowed some powder to ease the pain of her contractions, medicine I had prepared under Gogo Ndwandwe's direction, and she felt better, which relieved me. The cries of the other women continued, and I was anxious that Evah not be similarly afflicted.

To get our minds off the wait, I started talking about our wedding plans. Following kutfwasa we would have two ceremonies. Evah consented to convert to Catholicism for a church wedding; her Anglican church hadn't interested her in years. But I knew she would not be satisfied or feel like a truly married Swazi woman until she also had a traditional homestead wedding. I had discussed this with Gogo Ndwandwe because I was concerned that the ceremony, which was designed to bring into alliance not just a couple but the couple's families and clans, could not be effectively conducted with a foreigner. I would do all right—the language and customs of this place were second nature to me—but I could not expect my mother to symbolically claim Evah for my family by physically dragging her into a mud and grass hut and smearing her face with red ocher. And how would my father don warrior gear and lead a line of men dancing with fighting sticks and singing Swazi ceremonial songs? Gogo Ndwandwe insisted that she should substitute for my mother—"I am your second mother, Sibolomhlope!"—and Prince Vovo might consent to stand in for my father. My American family could look on from the sidelines, camcorders rolling, no doubt. It would be fun to get them out here; I certainly had lots to show them. I had thought of such a wedding every night for the past two weeks, inspired by the young men and women who gathered after sunset in the field beside Prince Vovo's place to rehearse traditional wedding songs for an upcoming ceremony. The singing, in SiSwati, was a cappella, with whistling as accompaniment. The voices cut through the chilly evenings and reached me at my hut, a chorus of women, a chorus of men:

> MEN: *I will pay lobola [dowry] for my love. Lobola of cattle.*
>
> WOMEN: *You will pay because you love her.*

A song with a lovely melody was next:

> MEN: *When I die first you will bury me.*
>
> WOMEN: *When I die first, you will bury me.*
>
> TOGETHER: *Love, we will bury us!*

An old song, but one still alive in the imaginations (and reality) of the Swazis:

> MEN: *The Boers! The Boers are coming!*
>
> WOMEN: *Mother! Oh, mother, I am frightened!*

And a new song reflecting the men's obsession and the women's lament:

> MEN: *Football! Football!*
>
> WOMEN: *Oh, news of football!*
>
> MEN: *Kick, kick the ball!*
>
> WOMEN: *The men are following the ball!*

Evah smiled when she heard me humming one of the melodies as I sat beside her. "I didn't know you knew those songs." I told her they constituted my Top-10 play-list every night. "Read your magazine," she urged. "You are worried."

"I'm not worried, I'm just concerned." This felt like the most important moment of my life, and I hated being powerless to help it along. For twenty minutes I read without making any sense of the same short list in *Time,* "Summer Movies 1990: *Ghost, Total Recall, Die Hard 2, Dick Tracy, Back to the Future III* . . ."

Softly, Evah said, "Perhaps you'd better call a doctor."

I was up at once, passing the request on to the head nurse. A moment later a light-skinned woman entered, spoke fluent SiSwati to Evah and then English to me with a German accent. She introduced herself as Celeste, the midwife. She was a large woman with a confident smile, straight hair pulled back in a bun, and mild brown eyes. She knew I was undergoing kutfwasa—everyone did at that hospital where I had come to get patched up so often—and she asked where I intended to set up my practice. I replied that I hoped to settle down on a farm in Swaziland, where I would build my Indumba. Celeste, who appeared to be of mixed parentage, had come from Germany to volunteer her services at this understaffed hospital. "The medical establishment is still anti-midwife at home. Whenever something goes wrong, you hear about it, and it's repeated by all the doctors. They never publish the things that go well— like this."

I was glad she considered the delivery in progress a good one. "It seems midwives and sangomas have that in common."

"But we're needed!" Celeste reported, "We will deliver thirteen babies tonight. We're just starting."

To Evah, she said, "This will be easy. That means a girl is coming."

"A girl *is* coming," I affirmed. "And you've observed this in your work?"

"Oh, yes! I guess boys don't want to come out." She directed Evah, "Push, now. Push!"

For the past several minutes the baby seemed reluctant to emerge, so the midwife assisted. I watched with my throat dry and my blood racing as she pressed down on Evah's belly. Evah closed her eyes against the rush of pain, sighed through parted lips, and with a whoosh the baby slid out, face down, body red and black hair slick.

"Oh, a lucky baby!" announced Celeste, noting the twisted umbilical cord. "She turned twice."

I thanked God and the lidlotis. Quickly and with assured hands, the midwife turned the baby and snipped the cord. "She's crying already," I said. "She can't wait!" She? I had been predicting since before conception that the baby would be female, and I quickly checked to see. Yes, it was a girl.

I do not know why the midwife did what she did next, and later she would not be able to say why either, only that "it seemed right somehow," but Celeste handed the baby to me. I was surprised and overcome and hugged my daughter with all the love that was in me, but only for a moment because it seemed manifestly unfair that I should have her after what her mother had endured during pregnancy and labor. I turned the baby over to Evah, who had been quiet and expressionless for the past moments. Only when she saw and touched our girl did her smile and the light in her eyes return.

In an hour, Evah's strength and good spirits had come back, and we walked around the corner to our room in the women's ward. The corridor was freshly polished. I ran ahead in my sneakers, jumped and slid for several feet. I felt playful and alive, and on the floor I discovered a bright copper penny about two-thirds the size of an American cent. "Imali yemadloti!" I declared, "The lidlotis' money!" It was good luck. Smiling, cradling the baby against her, Evah clapped her hands and took the coin, placing it on the baby's forehead.

In our room Evah went to bed with the baby beside her rather than use the Plexiglas crib in the room. "This one," she said of the newborn with the red face and tiny shut eyes, "will only keep me awake all night."

The baby sucked at Evah's breast and then fell quickly to sleep. I gazed at her, feeling the flavor of the moment as something wondrous: my child, my first born, my daughter. If a boy had come, Evah and I would have been unprepared (and I would have suffered a major crisis of confidence at the failure of my sangoma's insight), but we had discussed girls' names and agreed on one we both liked. As per Swazi custom, our child was named to commemorate the events surrounding her birth.

I said her name aloud, "Nomoya."

Nodding, and gazing at the sleeping infant, Evah murmured the English translation, "The child of the spirits!"

▲ ▲ ▲ ▲

"Nomoya," Sandile whispered the next morning as he sat in the hospital room, the sunlight falling on him and his sister. He held her and stared so intently he might have been trying to hypnotize her through her closed eyes. I asked him, "What are you telling her?"

He smiled. "I am telling her she has an older brother!"

The doctor had just left, having pronounced the mother and child fit and free to go. I settled the bill at the desk: baby delivery, private room with bath, meals and special accommodations for me: about fifty dollars. We entered a cab from the line of taxis waiting out front, and in a few minutes we traveled the short distance to Evah's flat.

At the sight of her first granddaughter, Gogo Kunene's face was transformed. Usually she had a passive and sometimes sorrowful expression that had been etched by a lifetime lived in the poverty and disappointments of Swaziland and the brutalities of the Mozambiquan civil war. She gasped and smiled, and slowly held out her arms to receive the child. Then we hurried into the flat, out of public view, because by Swazi custom a new mother must observe a month's confinement. Modern Evah would compromise and not go out for two weeks, while the rest of us ran errands, cooked, and took care of her.

Now Gogo sent Sandile outside with a paper cone. He filled it with gray ash from a cold fire. Evah placed the baby on the bed. Gogo took a pinch of ash, and dabbed it onto Nomoya's forehead and chest, welcoming her as a rare gift to the house and family. I was reminded of the sangomas' gesture of sprinkling ash onto a coin given as a gift to the lidlotis. And the Catholic rite: ashes to ashes, dust to dust. Out of this, all things come; out of this, all things shall return.

But it was impossible to think of such an end on that bright day of beginnings.

▲ ▲ ▲ ▲

Perhaps she was just tired of hearing from me because I would not let up, but Gugu Made at the Social Welfare Department finally made a commitment on Vusi's adoption: "Let's try to wrap this up." No one had a clue as to where his mother was, and we were no closer to finding her than we were when we started seven months before. I had never stopped pushing the case, and the Mahlalela sisters had never lessened their displeasure as Vusi's attachment to me grew.

But now the time had come for my adoption plans to be known. Mrs. Made wanted to bring a social welfare team to Malibeni to interview Babe Mahlalela and Gogo Simelane. Mahlalela was Vusi's great-uncle, and in the absence of Vusi's mother he was his closest relative and could legally sign off on the adoption. My relationship with Mahlalela and Gogo Simelane was strong. I loved and respected them both. And I hoped their desire for a better life for Vusi would outweigh the assault we could expect from their daughters.

I alerted Mahlalela that the social welfare people were coming, then took a bus to Mbabane to meet and accompany them to Malibeni. Traveling in a government van driven by a talkative man named Muntu, we passed through Manzini so I could show them the new house I had just rented for Evah, Gogo Kunene, Sandile, and the baby. I hoped to bring Vusi to live there so he might go to one of the better Manzini schools that had electricity, toilets, and smaller classes. Mrs. Made and the other case worker, Miss Vilane, fell in love with Nomoya, who had now acquired a creamy skin tone the lightest shade of caramel, and Muntu presented to me, the father, her first marriage proposal. "I have many cattle to pay the lobola dowry!" he boasted. Mrs. Made, meanwhile, asked Nomoya in a marveling tone, "How can you be a girl and look so much like your father?" My daughter actually had my mother's chin, and Evah's brown eyes, only enormous.

Malibeni was overcast and drizzly when we arrived, anxious weather that reflected my own nervousness, for I was powerless to influence this major event in my and Vusi's lives. The social welfare team would explain the adoption procedure to the Mahlalelas, and that proud old couple would decide one way or the other. Gogo Simelane directed us to the newest hut at the homestead, a wide one made of cinderblocks with a sturdy metal-frame window and a finely thatched roof. She and Mahlalela sat opposite Mrs. Made, Miss Vilane, and the driver, and I sat mutely off to one side. Returning from school just then, Vusi happened by as Mrs. Made was explaining how adoption worked. I waved him inside the hut, and he chose to sit down beside me as if that was his natural place. His presence made the issue of his fate less abstract to Gogo Simelane, as I could see from the way she gazed at him. The adoption hinged on her approval; her husband would agree with her decision. Suspense tugged at me, because not only Vusi's fate but my own seemed on the line.

Gogo Simelane took a pinch of snuff and inhaled it, deep in thought. Then she stated, "The world is changing. The boy needs things."

Mahlalela told the welfare team, "We have seen how Sibolomhlope helps Vusi."

When Gogo Simelane spoke next, it seemed she was trying to reassure herself, "Because Vusi is nine or ten, he is old enough not to forget where he came from."

I spoke up now and assured Gogo Simelane that I would see that Vusi never forgot; that, indeed, a part of me now also originated from this homestead. Vusi's hand was in mine; how it got there, whether in the suspense of the moment I had taken it or he had taken mine, I didn't know, but I squeezed it reassuringly. Miss Vilane gave Mahlalela a paper to sign and have notarized to indicate his willingness to turn Vusi over to me. With this document, the office could make a date on the court calendar for a hearing with a magistrate. Mahlalela took it and agreed to sign. I smiled, and thought, "*Mazeltov,* lidlotis!"

Vusi and I saw off the social welfare team, then I went to find Mahlalela so we could go to the border post police station. The station commander could act as notary public. I spotted Mahlalela beside the goat pen. I tensed; he was with his daughter Jabu. She was speaking loudly and angrily to him. I thought, This is it. Would his resolve hold in the face of her assault? How, she wanted to know, could he let me steal Lozangcotho's child?

I stopped and was about to retreat when they both spotted me at the same time, just as Mahlalela was raising his voice in reply, "That prostitute ran away years ago . . . !"

He cut short his angry words, and Jabu quickly left. Neither wanted to conduct a family squabble in my presence. I asked Mahlalela with concern, "Jabu?"

He waved his hand dismissively, as if to say there was only so much a man could take from a daughter like her. We proceeded to the police station, and he signed the paper in the commander's office. Mahlalela could not write, but setting his face in concentration he slowly formed the letters of his name, "L-I-O-N." Watching him make this effort for me, I felt great love and gratitude toward the man.

The commander stamped the paper with a flourish and refused the usual fee. I felt physically drained. It had been a tense few hours. But it was done, and when I realized that fact, I was swept by a feeling of elation. The court date might have been far off, and there was always a chance that obstacles could arise, but as far as everyone was concerned, Mahlalela's signature on the paper made it a done deal.

That night I did what I had not previously allowed myself to do for fear of disappointment. For the first time, when I looked at Vusi asleep on the floor mat, wrapped up like a little mummy in his blankets, I dared to see him not as some hard luck case I was helping but as something more: my son.

▲ ▲ ▲ ▲

Even on drizzly days such as the one when the social welfare team arrived, I and the other kutfwasa students still performed the evening rituals. We did them no matter how hot and dusty or cold and miserable it was. Now the nights too were occupied as the lidlotis emerged to take possession of me and sing the Inkanyan. For nearly two years I had lived by the tyranny of the drums. If I failed the tests to conclude kutfwasa I would have to continue that difficult life for another year, or drop out. I had come too far to drop out, but how could I continue kutfwasa with no guarantee that my psychic skills would ever develop to the point where I might pass the tests? I tried not to dwell on the possibility of failure, but it was on my mind.

Encouragingly, the divination drills that I and the other kutfwasa students performed every day continued to bring results. The drums sounded, and the climactic moment would come when I, half in a trance under the lidlotis' spell, turned to the person who was hiding something, ritualistically divined what that thing was, and then rushed off to draw it out as the people sang their congratulations.

Such moments gave me hope. But in the end, they could not foretell what would happen during the graduation rites, known as *kuphotfulwa*.

Only the lidlotis knew, and they would not tell until the very end.

twelve

Breaking Taboo

THE KUPHOTFULWA CEREMONIES to conclude kutfwasa were held each year at Gogo Simelane's homestead during the last weekend in July. When my lidlotis emerged in May to sing the Inkanyan, I targeted that date in my mind. Every night I was awakened by the spirits and their incessant desire to perform the Inkanyan, and by June they were also taking possession of me by day to sing and dance this announcement. All the signs indicated my kutfwasa was headed for its climax.

Then Gogo Simelane, five days before the tests were scheduled to begin, postponed kuphotfulwa until August. This was unprecedented, and a double disappointment when combined with the prospect of enduring yet another month of the kutfwasa life. But I picked myself up and went on with it, knowing that she had good reasons. One was that Gogo Ndwandwe had left to treat homesteads with protective medicines in the Natal Province of South Africa and had not returned. Gogo Simelane herself was scarcely able to move because of swollen legs, the result of a glandular condition. For three days her face swelled up as round as a basketball, and I barely recognized her. As for myself, I was suffering from a swollen bite from a poisonous insect and a recurrent infection in my foot. My toes itched furiously, and then pustules burst open. At the same time, the cracked and callused skin of my feet, worsened by so much dancing on hard ground in the cold weather, split open and bled. My feet were a mess, and Gogo Simelane declared me unfit to go through the physical ordeals of the kuphotfulwa rites. But by then it was academic because she had already canceled them. The final provocation had been the national radio station's refusal to air her announcement calling sangomas to Malibeni from all over the country to participate in the rites. A royal function was taking place on the date she had chosen, and the radio would not announce competing events.

So I accustomed myself to more weeks of the rituals and duties of kutfwasa, and more suspense as to the outcome. If I failed the tests and my work and dreams of the past two years were for nothing, if it was simply not meant to be that I become a sangoma, then at least I had the consolation of Evah and the baby. No matter what the result of kuphotfulwa, Evah and I were getting married, and my kutfwasa venture would have to be judged a success because it had brought us together.

But in truth I was not feeling fatalistic or fearful about the outcome of kuphotfulwa. I had a calm assurance about my abilities and full confidence in my lidlotis. I was more than hopeful; I was looking forward to it: the tests I would be undertaking were so demanding and impossible by my old standards—given their dependence on psychic skills—I knew that one of those rare moments in life had arrived when I'd be pushed to my physical, mental, and spiritual limits. I wanted to see what I could do. And I was ready.

▲ ▲ ▲ ▲

It was small consolation, but the postponement of kuphotfulwa brought the rescheduled date to within a month of the vernal equinox in Swaziland, so the days were longer and milder and the nights shorter, though still crisp. Throughout the month of August I lived in Malibeni, never returning to Kwaluseni. I saw Evah in Manzini town as often as I could, about four days a week, going back and forth by bus. Until kutfwasa ended I could not be with her and Nomoya full-time, and it was ironic that I felt worse about this than Evah, the new mother; she wanted me to succeed, she badly wanted me to become a sangoma. She believed the prophet Hlope's assertion that I had powerful lidlotis, and she repeated this to her relatives. I daydreamed of the time when we could all live together on a Swazi homestead of my own: Evah, Nomoya, Vusi, Sandile, Gogo Kunene, and I, surrounded by herds of zebra grazing on the land, my Indumba prominent among the huts, and separate guest huts for my sister, brothers, and parents. But first, I had to get through the kuphotfulwa tests.

In the month prior to the rites, I met and got to know the four female kutfwasa students who would also undergo the tests. We became the Class of '90. Sleeping together in the Indumba as per custom for a kuphotfulwa group (Vusi had our hut to himself), going to the river together in the darkness of early morning, preparing herbal medicines, and even sticking our heads together under a blanket to inhale herbs burning over red coals, we became close friends. Inyoni would not be tested this year because, like LaShonge back in Kwaluseni, his lidlotis had not emerged to sing the Inkanyan.

It would have seemed remarkable to me prior to my arrival in Swaziland how thoroughly I was accepted into the company of these four African women, and how comfortable I felt when I was with them. But we were linked by a bond that transcended race, sex, and culture. We had done kutfwasa, we were potential sangomas, we had lidlotis and thus we heard, saw, and sensed things known only to the healers of the Indumba. We trusted one another with our lives, and this was no idle expression: there was danger in digging roots in the wilderness, treating hysterical patients, and even moving under the influence of a spirit. We watched out for each other, we cared for each other, and we were comrades in a cause. For this last reason I often noticed that sangomas responded to me not only with affection but relief, because they saw me as a valuable ally. Just as I could anticipate skepticism and hostility toward my work from the Americans I left behind, so, too, were African sangomas increasingly confronting these same attitudes in a continent yielding itself to the material and intellectual hegemony of Europe and the U.S. Other than Gogo Ndwandwe, who could read and write a little, I had never met a literate sangoma, and so they were even less equipped to cope with a changing world. I sensed they saw in me proof that the world was not completely hostile toward their ancient practices. I knew differently, and had pursued kutfwasa not to change the world but to fulfill an inner need, but if my presence could give solace to these brave and selfless healers, then I was happy to be there with them.

And I was happy for another reason, because I was in the company of good people who were unlike any I had met in the developed world, as it called itself. In my previous life I met on university campuses and writers' conferences many brilliant and intellectual people. I had met noted scientists, theologians, journalists, and technocrats, and to be in their presence was to experience hard, sharp intellects as intense and focused as laser beams. But before entering the Indumba I had never before met a wise man or woman. The intellectuals I knew had the facts but no idea of the application of these facts beyond their own disciplines. The sangomas knew about life, how it was lived and what it was for, how the pieces fitted together to balance people and nature, mortal and immortal, the physical and spiritual. Western civilization had once had such individuals (minus the medical knowledge and psychic powers) and they were called philosophers. Then philosophy became semantics and the general population derided it as ineffectual. And so, quite late in kutfwasa, as I was conditioning myself to undergo the final tests, I realized another reason why I had done it all: I really had wondered whether the ancient wisdoms that the people of the Indumba promised I'd find here were real. They were, and they concerned life involved with other life—people with people, people with nature, people with spirits, the old and the young together, the sick and the well together, humankind living with the knowledge that in the end we were all we had as support against powerful nature and indifferent time: men holding hands not out of love but out of reassurance that they were there for each other, women carrying the babies of other women on their backs as if they were their own, and a nation, Swaziland, that might have been humankind in microcosm acting like a giant family, sometimes squabbling but with its members always aware that they were part of a whole that added dignity and significance to their personal lives, and who did not act like fragmented interest groups in a zero-sum game where one person prospered only if another perished.

I had come to learn all this, had embraced it, and had forged my bonds with the others of the Indumba because of it. There was a price, of course. I was breaking the one great taboo of forward-looking America: I was traveling backward in time and place and finding great and worthy things there.

Nevertheless, I knew my heart, and the experience of the past two years would seem hollow if I did not become a sangoma. Maybe I was too goal-oriented, but that's what I had set out to become, and that's what I wanted to be.

I woke up each morning in the round Indumba hut with my four female roommates. I owed them a lot because the good humor and relaxed manner of these women made the prospect of kuphotfulwa seem less daunting. We had fun together.

The oldest of us, Makhanejose appeared to be in her late forties. She was a short, bone-thin but strong woman with bags like oyster shells under her eyes. Her youngest daughter, age twelve, had accompanied her to Malibeni and lived in another hut. Makhanejose was aggressive and demanding, but when she saw I would not chop any more wood for her or take more pictures of her kid, her face would crinkle into a broad smile as if to say, "Well, I tried!"

Mzwane was about my age, mid-thirties. She was about five feet tall, had a hoarse voice, a no-nonsense manner, and large, aggrieved eyes in a narrow birdlike face. She was like our den mother, nagging us with her interpretations of procedure but always with our best interests in mind, so the lidlotis would be pleased and be with us.

The third person hoping to graduate was Longdweshuga, a heavy, young woman with a high, Minnie Mouse voice, large eyes, and a timid manner that disguised quite a strong will. She was the most respectful of us all, the quickest to drop to the ground to greet a sangoma.

The youngest of us, Mkhwzeni, told me she was twenty-six, though she seemed younger. Her lips were a vivid cherry red usually pressed into a slight pucker; she had a shapely figure, a tinkling voice, and a happy, buoyant manner. All four women wore sangoma hairstyles with thin braids to which ocher had been applied, giving them a lustrous cinnamon color.

As a team, we went to the river before dawn and returned singing to perform the morning rites. During the day we did the drills to prepare us for the kuphotfulwa tests. These tests would be a major event for the families of the four other potential graduates, and I listened a little enviously as they described how many of their relatives would be coming. Much of the spectacle of the rites was mounted to impress the public, and Gogo Simelane threw open the gates to anyone who wished to attend. But for the families in particular it would be a moment of pride and celebration when one of their own, chosen by the ancestors, became a sangoma.

As the weeks leading up to the event dwindled to days, the five of us scattered across the countryside to make preparations. We each needed two goats that would be ritualistically sacrificed. To find them this time I didn't have to walk for three days into the mountains; Lion Mahlalela came to my aid by taking me to his sister's homestead. Gogo Simelane's husband knew as much about matters of the Indumba as any sangoma. He would be presiding over the tests with his wife and another senior sangoma. With his expert's eye for livestock, Mahlalela picked out two goats for me. I thanked him and paid his sister.

Though Evah was a dressmaker, she did not want to attempt the elaborate beaded ceremonial skirt I would be needing. Gogo Simelane recommended a woman in far-off Singaneni, near Swaziland's eastern border with South Africa. I went to her when the job was finished and picked up a black cloth with ten different colors of tiny beads sewn into zigzag patterns and flowers. Along the bottom was the legend: "Lusiba Lolumhlope Lutalwa Nguputaza," which translated as "Lusiba Lolumhlope [the lidloti from whom I received my sangoma name] born of Putaza [the lidloti of my mentor Gogo Ndwandwe]." This was to be worn beneath a full, pleated skirt made of a fabric that resembled blood-red leopard skin, which I ordered from a seamstress in Manzini, the sister of a sangoma I knew.

By mid-August, the lidlotis were singing the Inkanyan around the clock. As the date of kuphotfulwa neared, they emerged frequently, and whenever a lidloti of any of us five potential graduates came out, we all rushed to the Indumba and changed into our dancing skirts. Then the lidlotis emerged and took possession of us all. As long as there was daylight, the people hid objects for us to find using the sangoma's insight. For me this was simply fixing a mental picture of something, watching it come into focus, and then telling the people what it was and where it was located, using the ritualistic phrases the exercise required.

At last the government radio station broadcast the date of kuphotfulwa. Preparations went into overdrive, and special sacred medicines were retrieved from the storage room or made anew. The homestead was given a face-lift in anticipation of the hundreds of visitors. We went around with buckets of a green mixture of cow manure and mud that dried to a dull gray on the exterior walls of huts. We replastered them all. A male sangoma with an artistic eye then decorated the walls with brown and cream zigzag and floral designs.

"It's time to get nervous," I told Evah during my last visit to Manzini before the tests. She gave me a serious look, unable to see why I would be nervous. To her I had done everything expected of a kutfwasa student. The prophet Hlope had confirmed for her the existence of many powerful lidlotis within me, and she was certain these spirits would see me through the long weekend of kuphotfulwa rites. If I expected sympathy from Evah I wasn't going to get it, but her wishes for my success were there in her good-bye kiss. She wasn't coming along. She could not endure the hardships of Malibeni with a baby so young, and I would not be able to look out for their comfort or even see them during the three days of tests because I would be sequestered in the Indumba.

Nomoya was asleep in her bed, a big and healthy girl. For a brief time, Evah tied a white button around her left wrist as protection against crossed eyes. She now had Nomoya wear a waistband of small white beads to ward off fatal diarrhea. In both cases the beads had no protective power in themselves; they were signals to the lidlotis, communicating the mother's hope that the ancestors would guard the child against these particular ailments. I also treated Nomoya with herbal medicine after she kept the household awake for two nights with her crying. Evah insisted she was suffering from libala, a pain around her navel. "Sandile and all Swazi children had this. Ask Gogo Simelane." I did and received an herbal powder that I administered to Nomoya. As I said good-bye to Evah that last time before kuphotfulwa, the baby's pains had gone, and I looked fondly at her as she rested peacefully in her cot, storing up energy for the explosion of sensory perceptions she would confront as the world took shape before her.

My mood changed as I descended the hill on my way to town and the bus ride to Malibeni. For the past few days I had been seized by an undefinable disgust and a stubborn depression I couldn't explain. The kuphotfulwa tests were upon me, but I was feeling worn out, almost as if I had the flu. I felt a fatigue I hadn't known since an infected wound sapped my strength several months before. Other things had been bothering me, trivial things. But they now came back to anger me again. Anger, disgust, depression. Why was I still a prisoner to such feelings after I had lived for nearly two years with wonders I couldn't have imagined before? But it still sometimes felt as if there were warfare in my head. And it was fierce as I approached town.

I suddenly realized I was not going to make it through kuphotfulwa.

I was not going to be a sangoma. The reason was obvious: I was just not good enough. In fact, the whole thing seemed ridiculous. I saw this clearly. Earlier that day, as I was walking alone in Manzini, I felt unusually vulnerable and self-conscious in my sangoma attire. And why not? Didn't I look absurd? That seemed to be the opinion of every bored loafer leaning against a storefront who felt like hurling a sarcastic remark at me, and every snickering schoolgirl who felt there was no need for manners before such a "strange" white man. Not to mention the haughty looks of disapproval from the Swazis in Suits. With no more effort than a frown or a sneer, they made a mockery of all I had worked to accomplish, all the difficulties I encountered, and all the insights I had discovered. A quest for knowledge? For whom? Who was going to believe any of it? Would I have believed it before coming to Swaziland?

These were questions I thought I had put to rest long ago, but they tore through me now. I felt disgusted with myself, angry, ashamed. I didn't need the rude opinions of strangers on the street to alert me, because my own failings seemed so enormous. How could I be worthy of the lidlotis when I was still so insecure, defensive, and quick to anger? I was tired of the struggle in my head. I was tired of the warfare. I hated people for being ignorant, selfish, and evil. This hate made me evil too, and I wanted to crush that evil out of me and I didn't know how. I stopped atop a bridge that was almost always crowded with traffic but was now oddly quiet, and I felt the pull of the river below so powerfully that the moment had to have been arranged, *had to have been.*

For so long the Tmzmzu spirits in the water had wanted to take me. That's what they were saying with the repeated images of my death that I encountered in the wilderness. It would be a quick fall, I thought, and a quick impact against the boulders below. Because how was I going to ever find the strength to go on, raise a family, and live a life while being stared at and misunderstood every day? The Swazis were half American already. And in America, if I were to return as I was now, I'd be a freak, good for a half-hour on "Geraldo" and a blurb in the *National Enquirer.* That was your fate now, I told myself: a lifetime of watching all that I held sacred, all that I had grown to love, taken by everyone else as a joke.

And what right did I have to subject my daughter Nomoya to the embarrassment I would bring her? By what conceit did I think I could make a difference in Vusi's life? Wouldn't any reasonable person see the obvious, that they'd be better off without me?

So why don't we just end it, I thought, and cut the crap.

I leaned forward and looked down at the flowing water and jagged rocks. Ever since I began kutfwasa there were people who did not want me to succeed. And forces, too. Call me insane, but I could feel them. I was a threat to them. If I became a sangoma, I'd be even more of a threat. Well, they'd won. Damn them. I leaned forward . . .

"Hey, sangoma, careful!"

I looked up in a surprise. A bizarrely dressed young man was standing on the bridge. He wore a light-brown leather jacket on which he had drawn swirling patterns with colored marking pens. His jeans were faded and patched, and his feet were shod in painted sandals. But the first thing I noticed was his guitar and its strange attachment. A wire hoop about two feet in diameter hovered above the ground, suspended by a string from the neck of the guitar. Dolls made from clothespins and bits of cloth hung from the ring, male dolls embracing female dolls as if dancing around the circumference.

"Look at my children!" he said. He began to strum his guitar and sing. He did both well, and his voice was full of vigor and cheer. I continued to stare at him as if he were an apparition, stranger than any lidloti vision. Then I looked down. The ring close to the ground slowly began to rotate as the troubadour gently pulled its string by lifting the neck of his guitar. The motion caused the doll couples to sway back and forth independently, but seemingly in rhythm with the man's music. I couldn't believe it, and crouched down to look at this wondrous thing.

Other pedestrians appeared, attracted by the ingenious contraption. But this young man sang only to me. He was so full of life it was as if he were pumping air into my lungs, and I felt a light rekindle within me. I smiled up at him. A flash of sangoma's insight told me that this fellow had moments just like mine, that he, too, had despaired. No job, no money, a talented artist in a country that could not afford to support its artists. But look what he'd done! Look at the instrument he had made, an entire dance troupe to accompany his singing. I was filled with emotion, a love for him, and a renewed determination.

When he was done with his song, I bowed low and placed a bank note on the ground before him. The people murmured their wonder at this large tip for only a street minstrel. But he had helped me.

No, I don't think I would have thrown myself into the river, but I had been depressed to the depths of my soul and such moments were dangerous. Then came an ally, and if the incident on the bridge was yet another eleventh hour test of my resolve I bet I passed, because I saw the lesson of this troubadour: never give up. Fight back at an indifferent and hostile world with your own wit and pluck.

"Thank you, sangoma!" he said. "My children thank you!"

"No, thank *you*," I replied. "You've helped me more than you know."

"We'll see each other again!"

I nodded. I was sure we would. "I have to do something now that's very important to me," I said.

"Good luck!"

"Thanks," I smiled. "You've given me some, already."

▲ ▲ ▲ ▲

At Malibeni, where I was now sleeping in the Indumba with the four other potential graduates the kuphotfulwa rites were scheduled to begin on Friday at sunset. On Wednesday I began to disappear to secluded spots in the fields or along the wooded Komati riverbank to address my lidlotis individually. Over the course of my stay in the Indumba they had emerged at night, summoned by the drums while I sweated under the white sheet. They had told us their stories. I occasionally heard from them during the continuing evening rites, and the drums had also drawn out more visions which hinted of new lidlotis to come. I now addressed them, the spirits I hoped would make me a sangoma:

John MacDonald

White Feather (Lusiba Lolumhlope)

Harry

Grandma

Juan

Impunyu ("fetus")

Winter Blossom

Lidvuba

The Scottish farmer. The Native American medicine man. The white American advertising executive. My Italian-American grandmother. The Spanish settler from colonial California. The unborn child. The beautiful and tragic Japanese woman. The ancient African zebra hunter.

And then I addressed the African spirits: the Bandzawe who helped the sangoma perform the kufemba divination rite to sniff out a patient's illnesses, the Tmzmzu water spirits, the Benguni of the African tribe to the north that was noted for its powerful healers, and *bonkhe bokhokho* (all the ancestors).

As I spoke to the lidlotis, I felt the need to not simply request that they find me worthy to succeed in the kuphotfulwa rites but also to recount my kutfwasa experiences with each of them. It felt strangely nostalgic; the roles they played in my life were fascinating and fun but also traumatic; I had been struggling for years now to reconcile the impossibility of their existences with the fact that, well, there they were.

I felt a different affection toward each lidloti. Each was special to me, and each had played a unique part in my adventure. I knelt beneath a red cloth which when struck by the sun glowed brightly above me like a Martian sky, and spent a lot of time explaining. Those moments I was with Evah and Nomoya, I said, were motivated by the lidloti's wish for a child that had awakened the same desire in me. And my love for Evah was their doing, too. There had been no movies for two years, no entertainments, sporting events, or even books. If that didn't show my dedication, then surely my guilt did. I felt guilty whenever I missed the morning or evening rites. My comfort had never been more important than my duty, I reminded them. So please, I asked, judge me worthy. And give me the strength for the ordeals ahead.

But there must have been something about August, the end of the Swazi winter, that disagreed with me. Like the previous year at the same time, I was laid low with a flu whose symptoms were mild congestion, a touch of a sore throat and a lack of energy that made it hard for me to rise from my sleeping mat. Fortunately, I felt better on Thursday, the day before the tests were to begin.

The head sangoma, Pashamqomo, arrived. He was a tall man with an authoritative air, shrewd eyes, and a flair for ceremonial finery, including a cowrie shell and feather headdress and a toga with a peacock emblem that signaled to one and all that he was the man in charge. He was in his fifties and well built (he had constructed his own hut at Mahlalela's homestead, carrying logs two at a time from forests a mile away, one over each shoulder). His teeth were bad but that made no difference because he had the Swazi smile that seemed to originate from some furnace of goodwill burning within.

As soon as Pashamqomo appeared, all the kutfwasa students participated in the usual greeting dance. In the throes of our lidlotis, we formed a line before the Indumba and danced in place with repetitive steps and wooden sticks swinging at our sides. On Pashamqomo's orders, this was followed by a long dancing session done only by us, the potential graduates. Then without rest, I and the others were put into a lengthy drumbeating session inside the Indumba to bring out the Bandzawe spirits. I was beginning to wonder if kuphotfulwa was beginning a day before schedule.

But that would have been wishful thinking. A brief sleep finally came late that night, twice interrupted when those of us undergoing the tests were awakened by our lidlotis calling us to release them via dance and song. And at dawn we began the practice drills. But all this was but a tepid approximation of the sleeplessness and rites that lay ahead.

By Friday morning my flu had returned and I was sick with fatigue. I lay down on my mat and it was if someone had pulled a plug inside me, letting all my energy run out. Then, my closest friend at Malibeni, a young woman named Tablamanzi who after becoming a sangoma three years earlier had remained to work with Gogo Simelane, appeared at the hut door to tell me Mahlalela was calling us together. I loved Tablamanzi, her tireless enthusiasm and unfailing good cheer, her big cheeks always animated by a smile, not to mention her blessed habit of speaking SiSwati to me slowly and clearly. We had spent many hours in her hut sewing the beaded anklets, bracelets, and necklaces I wore while she nursed her baby, whose father was a man who worked at the river pumping station. Tablamanzi had a buoyant mood that lifted up all who came in contact with her, and as she stood at the door I looked up at her from my sleeping mat (the Indumba where I slept at night was too busy with pre-kuphotfulwa preparations), and I rather hoped she could raise me like Lazarus from my deathly fatigue. But I must have appeared as bad as I felt, because her smile stiffened into a look of alarm.

Where were my lidlotis, I wondered? Everything I had worked for would be decided during the next three days. I pulled myself up, dragged my rubbery bones and flaccid muscles out into the courtyard, and dropped down with the others kneeling before Mahlalela. He gave us instructions and concluded by telling us to deliver money for all the special medicines we would be using that weekend. Nobody had told me of this payment, and I was embarrassed to have to tell Mahlalela I hadn't the money and there was no time to go back to Manzini to withdraw it from the bank.

He was understanding, but I was irritated because this was the type of thing I would have known about if my mentor, Gogo Ndwandwe, were present. She had not communicated with me since her departure for South Africa before Nomoya's birth. Someone told me she was ill in the Natal Province, then someone else said she was working in Johannesburg. I had given a woman traveling to see her a note with the news that I would soon be undergoing kuphotfulwa. Gogo Ndwandwe never replied. I could have used her advice, and certainly her encouragement, and I felt sad and a little betrayed that I had received neither. It almost seemed as if she had no confidence in me, that she would be judged harshly if I failed the tests—she was deathly afraid of gossip—and she was purposefully staying away until it was all over. More than ever I felt I was on my own.

Or rather, I was at the mercy of supernatural powers, and here not even Gogo Ndwandwe could have helped me. But I went into the final afternoon before the ceremonies feeling on friendly terms with those powers. My strength was slowly flowing back into my body, and my head felt a little clearer.

The day was mild and sunny, and the first visitors, the families of the other graduates, began arriving at noon. While the drums filled the homestead with their sound—they'd be beaten continuously until Monday morning—the newcomers hid coins and gifts for us to find. Vusi returned from school, walking the four miles as usual through the government orange groves, and I asked him if he were ready for kuphotfulwa. He grinned and nodded; the advantage of growing up on that homestead was witnessing the sangomas' ceremonies, of which the graduation tests were the most spectacular and festive.

While I and the other graduates divined hidden objects through our lidloti-inspired insights, farm hands Willie and Silembe stacked logs for the bonfire in the courtyard.

At the cooking hut, barrels of traditional beer were being brewed for the guests.

In the Indumba, attendants set out all the new dancing skirts, beads, and adornments we'd be wearing.

Mahlalela herded my two large, black female goats into a pen with the other ceremonial animals. Gogo Simelane gave me two chickens that I'd also be needing, and a child looked after these with a flock of other chickens. All these animals would be sacrificed and eaten in a feast for all the people on the last day of the rites.

The most important visitors began arriving by bus in the afternoon, and formed a colorful procession as they left the border station and crossed the river on the long, swaying footbridge. They were the sangomas from all parts of Swaziland and other neighboring countries. The sangomas from South Africa and Mozambique had elaborate, beaded amulets made with skill and worn with style. The sangomas from the tiny kingdom of Lesotho came in woven grass headgear, and from far-off Botswana the healers arrived draped in sashes from which dangled bull horns that held their snuff and herbal medicines. Sangomas and kutfwasa students arrived by pickup truck with cowhide drums they had beaten on the road, singing merrily and chanting all the way. They added their drums to a battalion of others circling the Indumba and in almost perpetual use now because each arriving group of sangomas released their lidlotis and performed the bingelela dance of greeting.

Jabulani's cousin, Sipho Dlamini arrived from town. Sipho was a reporter for one of the country's two newspapers and had come to cover the kuphotfulwa. Short and stocky, with a severe limp, he smiled as he informed me, "It's *you* they want to see."

"Listen, I'm nervous enough—"

He cut me off, consulting his watch, "Two hours. The drums start for real at sunset."

And they would continue until sunrise. As Sipho knew, to his delight, I would be dancing—or rather, the lidlotis in possession of my body would be dancing—the entire time. And as far as the graduation rites were concerned, that was just the curtain raiser.

In the remaining minutes of daylight, Mahlalela called us—the five hopeful future sangomas—together. Gogo Simelane would be spending her time holding court for the visiting sangomas and Pashamqomo would be the ceremonial head, so Mahlalela would be the general in charge, issuing orders and giving instructions. We now knelt in a semicircle before him, and he asked each of us if we had been celibate for the duration of kutfwasa. He reminded us that last year MaZu, despite her well-known escapades with boyfriends, had not been truthful and had gotten sick during kuphotfulwa, scarcely making it through the rites. We would have to be honest with him, he said, and if we did have intercourse during kutfwasa we had to undergo a rigorous cleansing treatment before taking the graduation tests. We'd also have to pay a lot of money for these esoteric medicines. Mahlalela reminded us that if we had picked up any spiritual "germs," they could react negatively with the powerful new medicines we'd be taking during the rituals, so instead of fortifying us these could harm us. We knew we must not lie to him. Nevertheless, one of the women now did, even though we all knew the truth. She would find the tests a terrible ordeal and be ill by their end. I suspected the reason for her subterfuge was that she couldn't afford to pay for the cleansing medicines.

I had picked up no spiritual contagions from Evah; she had been cleansed with medicine Gogo Ndwandwe had provided. Each time I was with Evah, I had treated myself with these same herbs. But there was always the possibility that something might have gone wrong, and I couldn't risk it. Mahlalela turned to me and asked, "Sibolomhlope, did you . . ." He made a ring by curling his index finger to meet his thumb, then jabbed his other index finger through the hole repeatedly. I had to laugh.

"Yes, *umnumzane*," I admitted. "I have apologized to Gogo Ndwandwe, and I wish to apologize to you. I'm prepared to take the medicine."

Mahlalela whistled, as if to say, "This is going to cost you, friend." But then he moved his head close to mine and winked, "You must let us see the baby. I hear she's beautiful."

I gaped at him; I had honored Gogo Ndwandwe's request scrupulously and never revealed the news of the baby. I glanced at the four women who would also be undergoing the tests. They were grinning at me. I exclaimed in English, "Oh, for heaven sake!" It was ridiculous to try to keep a secret in Swaziland. But I'd done my best. I felt a little sheepish that everyone seemed to know. They'd been polite to not say anything until I did.

I didn't explain that the baby came into being because of a lidloti's request, though they'd probably find that out if they didn't know already. I loved my new daughter; like Evah she filled a vacuum in my life, and I wasn't going to make excuses for her existence. I resolved to undergo the medicinal cleansing without protest. I could always use more fortification.

The sun set, and the sangomas seated around the bonfire and before the Indumba, each of them with a drum, let rip with an opening salvo that sounded like artillery fire. The cries of the lidlotis replied from inside the Indumba. Out came Makhanejose, Mzwane, Longdweshuga, and Mkhwzeni, recognizable by their faces and bodies but their personalities lost in a spiritual trance.

But I was not with them. I was in my hut with Tablamanzi, working my way through the treatment Gogo Simelane prescribed when she pulled from her storage room the medicines that would cleanse me of any evil spirits a sangoma risked picking up through intercourse. It was hard work: I washed and then vomited with the medicine, and when I thought I was done and ready to leave for the Indumba, Tablamanzi told me I had to do it all over again with a second medicine. Pashamqomo kept appearing at the door, waving a ceremonial drum head like a tambourine, checking to see what was keeping me. Everyone, the visitors in particular, were wondering where I was. But a third medicine remained. We boiled it in water atop a heated pottery shard, and I dipped my fingers into the hot liquid, quickly plunging them into my mouth and sucking off the ashy residue. It felt strange to be one of the principal actors in the night's drama but away while the others performed. The drums had been beating nonstop, priming my adrenaline. I was feeling an excitement like stage nerves, and I couldn't wait to go on, to get the thing started.

By the time I emerged from the hut it was dark, and a thin crescent moon was already descending over the hills. My energy, which had been so feeble at the beginning of the day, was now revived by the treatment; the vomiting in particular had felt refreshing in the coolness of the evening. It had happened so often before I had been foolish not to expect it again: the lidlotis saw to it that I was well and strong when I most needed to be. This was the surest sign I could imagine that they were with me.

And with me they now had to be, because kuphotfulwa had begun.

The bonfire blazed in the large dirt courtyard between the main house, the Indumba, and a colony of mud huts. Great yellow flames leapt up from logs a foot in diameter. The first wave of visitors were those who would be up all night, watching the lidlotis dance in their borrowed bodies. If they liked, they could help the sangomas beat the drums. There were two hundred people present now, men and women, old folks cocooned in blankets, babies at their mothers' breasts, children scurrying about.

I approached the fire carrying a curving, five-foot log over one shoulder that I had kept by my hut for this occasion. A murmur rose among the spectators when I came within the fire's ruddy light. There were still those who doubted a white person could possess lidlotis, to say nothing of becoming a sangoma. There were skeptics in attendance now, my reporter friend Sipho had told me. I could feel their eyes upon me, their curiosity that felt like a tickle or their hostility that felt like a burning weight. But I had friends there, too, I knew. Many of them. If I had my detractors sending out their hopes that I'd fail, I also had my friends with their good wishes and support.

I entered the Indumba to find the four other graduates lying on mats under blankets, taking a break that might last two or three minutes. As soon as I dropped my blanket on a mat, the drums sounded again. The five of us let out a yell that instantly brought out our lidlotis.

Our five spirit-possessed bodies danced side by side in place before the Indumba. We were illuminated by the bonfire for all the spectators to see. I was at the far left in the junior position, because I had arrived late. It was still winter and cold. Barefoot, we wore our thin, old kutfwasa dancing cloths about our waists, we hoped for the last time, and nothing else. A faint warmth from the fire came our way but was cut off whenever a person passed before us. Only the graduation song was sung: the Inkanyan, the seven syllables of its lyrics repeated endlessly, hypnotically, by our spirits and the people.

It was from within myself that I observed all that happened that night, looking out as if through a long tunnel at images actually around me but which seemed surreal. And things I knew were not there, *could not* have been there, seemed so real I knew I had again become a House of Dreams. But when I saw Vusi, I knew he was real. It was very late and the other children were asleep, wrapped in each other's arms against the night's chill. But I had no reason to believe Vusi was a vision, even if he wore a T-shirt and running shorts; it was hot by that big fire. He stood bent over a drum and with two sticks he was pounding up a storm. All the children there knew how to beat the drums, but I'd never seen him do so until now. I was pleased and proud that he was participating with such enthusiasm.

As the night progressed I saw others I knew seated among the people tightly packed in rings around the fire. "It's Miss Koretz!" I marveled in my thoughts. There she was, my third-grade teacher from Crow Island School, still wearing those Kennedy-era eyeglasses and that bouffant hairdo. She hadn't aged in twenty-five years! She had a bright, excited smile as she watched me. I thanked her in my thoughts for coming.

I spotted someone else from home, and would have grinned if the lidlotis in physical possession of me hadn't turned my face into a blank mask. It was Monsignor Burke, who ran Saints Faith, Hope and Charity church. He had died, when? Five or ten years before? (I wondered about Miss Koretz.) The Swazis seated to his left and right were oblivious to him, even though he was in his silken maroon vestments. A distinguished-looking man, with wavy silver hair. Hey, Monsignor, I asked him in my thoughts, am I committing an act of apostasy by doing this? He smiled, shook his head, and gave me the thumbs-up. I thanked him.

Girls, women, and sangomas came up to dance in front of us, singly and in pairs, their jumping bodies joyful and dark against the fire. Young men, high on home brew or the *insangu* weed, danced like maniacs, pulled by the ceaseless drum beat that affected everyone. An elderly man moved past us with small steps, an improvised dance stick raised high.

The spirits seemed powered by the drums, because when Pashamqomo gave the signal for them to cease and we returned to the Indumba, we were ourselves again—but only for the three-minute break that came every hour or so. The five of us dropped down on our mats and were instantly asleep. A moment later, it seemed, drumbeats like bombs going off awakened us. At half-past three in the morning, the watch I kept on the floor showed our break had lasted six minutes, but it would be our last before sunrise, three hours away.

Though my senses were dulled—all was muffled as I peered out from within—I had never been more conscious of the arrival of a new day. The midnight darkness of the sky slowly lightened in shades of blue until a pearl-gray was above, and all forms, shapeless at first, became sharp black silhouettes against the horizon. Trees, roofs, fences. The booming drums drowned out all other sounds, but I knew that out there cocks were crowing. The grayness dissolved like mist, and the profiles of dancing people grew faces. All the mysterious objects of the night revealed themselves: the drums, the lumps that became people wrapped in blankets. The courtyard glowed orange. The trees showed the first traces of green. A flock of birds passed above through a pastel sky strung with pale cottony clouds. The sleeping people roused themselves and stood. Those who had not slept jumped and danced. Young men jerked about with crazy energy. Everyone was excited. The new day was at last here; a special day, a day of tests and secret rites, a day that would determine which new sangomas would join the community.

Pashamqomo glanced repeatedly at the mountain plateau to the east while striking the drum head in his hand. A laserlike ray of gold light pierced the sky above the ridge's upper edge. He swept his arm toward the Indumba. The drums stopped, but they had been so intense for so long their echo seemed to reverberate in the stillness as we rushed inside the spirit house. The beginning was over. It was half-past six in the morning, Saturday, August 25. The day hinted of the Southern spring to come, warm and fragrant with tree blossoms that fell white and pink around the homestead. I dropped onto the reed mat for a few stolen moments of sleep.

▲　▲　▲　▲

The first test would be a vomiting rite, done in public like all the tests, and using some of the most powerful spiritual medicines ever to enter my body, medicines fortified with the warm blood of a freshly slaughtered goat. Five goats were tethered outside the Indumba, one for each of us. Vomiting herbal medicines on an empty stomach was one of several methods I had learned to administer our herbs, but on this day it would be done as a special ritual, a test of purification. Like a priest, a sangoma must exist in a state of inner grace bestowed by the lidlotis. The speed with which the five of us were able to expel the undesirable element we had swallowed (the goat's blood) would show our state of grace. Retention of the blood or slowness to vomit were considered proof of spiritual disfavor and a public punishment by the lidlotis for some failing during kutfwasa. Such a humiliation had happened to MaZu the previous year when she found the simple act of vomiting a lengthy ordeal.

Mahlalela entered the Indumba to give us the "line up": Makhanejose, the eldest, would be the first to drink the blood of her slaughtered goat, then Longdweshuga, then me followed by the two others. I wrapped a calf-length cloth around my waist, but other than underwear I had nothing else on; even our necklaces and amulets had been removed. We'd be cheating if we wore them. The medicines inside the beaded sacks attracted lidlotis, and we had to do this test ourselves, without spiritual assistance, to display our own states of grace.

We knelt in a line behind Makhanejose at the entrance. Beyond the Indumba's dark interior, the courtyard glared in the harsh sunlight. I could make out a hundred spectators and about two dozen sangomas with raddled hair and draped with beads, who were appearing for the first time in their most flamboyant ceremonial finery. They moved about and danced spontaneously to the beating drums. Those drums were like a second heartbeat to me, and sent my blood racing. Willie held Makhanejose's goat with arms so corded with muscle they looked like ropes, and Mahlalela, holding a knife, gave the signal.

Makhanejose leapt out quickly on her hands and knees. But she was confused, perhaps by the shouting of the spectators and sangomas, the drums, and her fatigue from the all-night dancing. She didn't know what to do, and as Mahlalela cut the goat's throat the first crucial flow of blood was wasted because she turned her back on the goat, expecting to be washing in the conventional way. Mahlalela shouted at her to turn around and drink. She did, and then was directed to go behind and drink some herbal medicine to vomit with.

Longdweshuga went next. I did not watch but murmured with eyes closed a petition to my lidlotis for their support. I wished I was in a trance, I wished they could possess me. I knew what was coming.

I opened my eyes and saw my black goat ahead, ten feet away; Willie held it up by its forelegs. Its ugly brass eyes with their slit-shaped pupils stared out above an opened, panting mouth. The moment Mahlalela severed its carotid artery, the animal would be effectively anesthetized and feel no pain. I steeled myself. Mahlalela held the knife to the goat's throat dramatically, like a Shakespearean actor. He gestured to me with his other hand, and I sprang rapidly out on my hands and knees into the blinding light, as drums pounded and voices shouted, covering the distance to the goat simultaneously with the plunging of the knife into its throat. The blade emerged when I arrived. My lips touched hot, pungent goat hair. A jet of blood shot out, pumped by the animal's frantic heart into my mouth and onto my shoulder. I closed my eyes and tasted hot, salty liquid. I swallowed as much as I could in the few seconds allowed. I felt light-headed and nauseous, and I knew there would be no difficulty vomiting when Mahlalela told me to move on.

On hands and knees I swiftly leapt past the roaring crowd to a ditch, six inches wide, that had been dug in the courtyard. Lined up side by side before it were five large, shallow bowls, each two feet in diameter, one for each of us. They were filled with an herbal medicine of a golden hue that I found lovely even in my febrile frame of mind. Makhanejose and Long-dweshuga knelt at their bowls, drinking their fill in order to vomit. I quickly started to work on mine, not drinking so much as taking large, mouth-filling bites of the liquid. Soon Mzwane and Mkhwzeni were at their bowls on my left. People surrounded us, shouting, singing, shaking rattles, kicking up dust that settled on our faces. The drums boomed. I calmed myself with a sturdy Midwesternism, *"I'm cool as a cucumber."*

I felt no hurry. When my stomach was full, I leaned forward over the ditch and let go. Little at first, then a good gush, followed by lesser ones. But no blood. I stuck my head back into the bowl and drank. My stomach felt bloated. The bowl held five liters. I was nearly at the bottom. Someone poured more golden medicine by my ear; it rushed about, up my nostrils. I was swimming in it and suddenly felt full. The sensation propelled me forward, over the ditch. A rush came, then another huge one. Goat's blood poured out of me. Above, the women ululated in celebration. The pitch of the people's shouting rose sharply in reaction. I let go again. Blood and medicine. More cheers.

An attendant told me to wash myself with the medicine, but I reacted slowly, feeling dim-witted. Then I saw my forearms, clotted with blood. I washed them in my medicine bowl. Hands took hold of me and pulled me up. I was finished. Two female sangomas on either side ran me to the Indumba.

Inside, I wondered why I was pulled away first. The others were still going at it. Several minutes passed before I heard more ululations greeting the successful vomiting of blood. Then I knew: I was the first to accomplish the task. My mind really was muddled, but this was the reason for the all-night dance: our bodies were purposefully exhausted and our minds dulled so there would be no doubt that it was the lidlotis who would perform the divination tests later that day. The attendants led Makhanejose in, and then the others came when they were done. They had had a more difficult time of it and looked worn out. I was glad I had been fortified by the medicine treatment the night before.

We sat together side by side along the curving wall catching our breaths. Mahlalela came in to give us a pep talk. "Hey, thogoza, don't sip, gulp!" Then he smiled and gave me the thumbs-up. "Hey, Sibolomhlope! Number one!"

I was vague about what was to happen next. Although I had witnessed the previous year's kuphotfulwa, my mind was now a blank. The drums still sounded. Sangomas were trading off behind them, each new group of beaters announcing themselves with a thump, thumpa-thump so loud it was a wonder the drum skins didn't break. Mahlalela lined us up on our knees one behind the other, myself in third position, at the Indumba entrance. He waved at us to go, and we rushed out, propelling ourselves forward with leaping movements on hands and knees. Ahead was an attendant, pulling the top of a wicker basket along the ground at the end of a rope. *"Dlanini!"* ("Eat!") she shouted.

The five of us chased the shallow basket top and pushed our faces down into it. Bits of cooked meat floated in a brown, peppery herbal marinade. Nuzzling in, I captured a piece in my mouth, then another. It was like bobbing for apples. We continued to scramble and follow the basket as the attendant dragged it around the courtyard. When I had four chunks of meat in my mouth, I didn't know what to do. I chewed but did not swallow. In the rush and confusion, people shouted at me. I thought they were telling me to spit out the pieces. I did. The attendant yelled, "Eat it! Don't be afraid!" If the meat was evil, as I suspected, I saw we were supposed to eat it anyway, and perhaps purge ourselves later. I plunged into the basket lid again. There were the chewed pieces I had discarded. I gobbled them up. By now, the attendant had led us back to the ditch, where our medicine dishes awaited. I saw now: we were to vomit again.

I knelt wearily at my dish, my weight on my forearms on either side. I drank. It was exhausting. I filled myself, leaned forward, and vomited. No meat. An attendant told me to continue. It was slow going. I drank and drank. On my second refill I felt the irresistible pressure. I let go. Medicine poured into the ditch and flowed away. My throat opened wide, and another gush came out. Ululations! The women were joyous, the men shouted. I looked down. Clinging to the bottom of the ditch were white chunks of meat, twice chewed by me, once spit out, now vomited out, I hoped for good. The attendants told me to wash, and then led me back to the Indumba.

I again found myself alone. The others straggled in one at a time. Longdweshuga was last; she looked like she was about to pass out. When we were reassembled, Mahlalela entered. "Sibolomhlope, you were number one again! Number one!" The buzz was all around the homestead, confounding the skeptics: not only did the white man vomit successfully, which clearly could not be faked, but he was the first to finish, twice! In my obsession with the afternoon's crucial divination tests, I had underestimated the importance of the vomiting ritual. Now it was over, but the biggest test awaited.

The five of us went down to the river by ourselves while objects for the divination ritual were hidden back at the homestead. It felt good to be away from the noise at the peaceful riverbank, just our group. Vusi brought down some bread and fruit from the hut, which I passed around. Makhanejose and the others were so relaxed—Mzwane and Mkhwzeni even washed some clothes in the river's placid flow—they seemed unaware of the make-or-break test that awaited us.

But I was very aware that all of kutfwasa had been reduced to the few moments to come. We changed into our new ceremonial garments, which felt stiff, fresh, and strange to me. The tall figure of Pashamqomo, made taller by his fathered headdress, appeared on the bluff above, dramatic against the sky. He raised his drum head and beat out our call. A nervous tremor ran through me.

We lined up and squatted on the ground, myself in the third position. Pashamqomo beat his drum head to march rhythm, and we stood and moved up the path to the road. Our lidlotis emerged, and announced themselves with cries tearing from our throats. My body yielded to their will, my consciousness again shrunk, and my senses dimmed until I observed what was happening around me imperfectly through veiled eyes. When we arrived at the road, I sensed a strange absence of people. The area was usually crowded on a sunny Saturday afternoon. But no one waited for a bus now. The food vendors were gone. The long span of the footbridge was still. Everyone was at Gogo Simelane's homestead, waiting for us.

We proceeded up the road. Pashamqomo's drum head was suddenly answered by the booming drums at the Indumba courtyard. Every drum in the area and others that had been brought in by the visiting sangomas were being beaten by the best. Their vibrations rolled over the field. At this moment, I knew, the person who had hidden the objects I now had to divine was blending into the multitude of onlookers. I had no idea who he or she was, but when we arrived I would be required to go directly to that person. There could be no delay, no going from person to person. That would be guessing. And even if I eventually located the person and successfully drew out the objects from their hiding places, I still would have failed because I would have shown that my insight was neither strong nor reliable. Who would trust their health and fortune to such a sangoma? I would have lost the confidence of the people, and without their confidence a sangoma could not work.

The drums increased in volume as, shouting in reply, we drew near the homestead. I was vaguely aware of entering the grounds, but it seemed as if we suddenly materialized before the Indumba, where we danced in place in a line. I was not aware of anything to my left, but to my right people were seated, packed tightly along the fence that extended forward from the spirit house. Others stood behind the fence and beneath a tree, and children sat in the branches. Any moment now, my inhloko insight would inform me of the person who was hiding my objects. I'd stop dancing and go to him or her.

But who? And where? I was still in a trance but felt much more in control than I ever had before while in that state. I could not think because the drums were too loud. The people were a blur. They were vague figures in my limited field of vision, as if I had blinkers on with gauze draped in front. Everyone was faceless.

Except for one person.

Twenty feet away, but seated directly in front of me as if placed there by providence and now spotlit by the lidlotis, was Tablamanzi. She didn't look at me. She was looking at something to her left. But I knew: she was the one.

Just as Makhanejose and Longdweshuga, responding to similar impulses, broke off to my right, I went directly to Tablamanzi. Only when I drew near did she look up. She seemed surprised. Was it a test of my resolve? My inhloko held firm: it was her, all right. I dropped down before her. The harsh, insistent voice that came when I was in a lidloti trance shouted, *"Uyangifihlela, 'mngan' wam'!"* ("You are hiding something from me, my friend!")

At once, a second sangoma, a pretty and vivacious young woman who had come for the festivities, knelt beside Tablamanzi. They were partners in this, and together they snapped their fingers and replied, *"Sevuma! Sevuma!"* ("We agree; yes, indeed!")

I had caught Tablamanzi and the other one off guard, arriving as quickly as I did. The harsh lidloti voice that came from me shouted, *"Yebo! Asambe!"* ("Yeah! Let's go!")

"Sevuma! Sevuma!" my team replied with snapping fingers. "We agree! We agree!"

But *what* was hidden? I seemed to know. How? I was told: in visions too quick to glimpse and whispers too fleeting to hear, by impulses I somehow comprehended. Everything was happening fast. It had to, to show the power of my lidloti-inspired insight.

The ritual required that I cast my net over a wide area, then draw it in using ritualized phrases in SiSwati. "You are hiding something from me. Something from the province of God!"

"Sevuma! Sevuma!" Tablamanzi and her partner agreed with enthusiasm.

". . . Something from an animal!"

"Sevuma! Sevuma!" the women shouted.

". . . Something from a goat!"

"Sevuma! Sevuma!" After each new declaration my team shouted back their replies—"We agree! We agree!"—as I tightened the net.

It seemed obvious to me which part of the goat they were hiding; a part used in these ceremonies. But then everything I had said so far seemed obvious, as if it was *a priori* knowledge within me. *"Yinyongo!"* ("It's the gall bladder!")

"Sevuma! Sevuma!"

But where was it? I knew this too: *"Isekhatsi kwendlu!"* ("It's inside a building!")

"Sevuma! Sevuma!" The women trembled with excitement as they snapped their fingers. I hadn't missed, yet. Words tumbled out of me. ". . . In the Indumba!"

"Sevuma! Sevuma!"

". . . On the floor . . . at the *umsamo* [the sacred spot furthest from the door]."

"Sevuma! Sevuma!"

Tablamanzi shouted with urgency, *"Hamba! Khokha!"* ("Go! Draw it out!") She and her partner were in competition with the other teams to see which of their graduates would be the first to draw out the hidden object. It was me. I leapt up, sprinted the brief distance back to the Indumba, passed the pounding drums and dancing sangomas, ducked, and darted inside. There, on the floor, just where I had "seen" it, was a robin's egg blue metal dish. Within it was a goat's gall bladder, inflated like a yellow, pear-shaped balloon atop a soggy hunk of black goat fur. I grabbed it. I spent only four seconds inside the Indumba before I emerged again.

Into pandemonium.

For the first time I was aware of the courtyard to the left of the Indumba. At least five hundred people lined its sides, packed before the houses all the way back to the cooking hut. They were jumping up. They were running toward me. I could not hear the drums, so loud was the shouting, the whistling.

"SANGOMA! SANGOMA!"

The sangomas reached me first. They grabbed the dish from my hand. Everyone tried to touch me. I thought, "But I'm not done yet!"

I broke away and ran back to Tablamanzi. I threw myself on my knees before her and her companion. "But you are still hiding something from me, my friends!"

"Sevuma! Sevuma!"

". . . Something from the white man [a manufactured item]!"

"Sevuma! Sevuma!"

". . . A thing of metal!"

"Sevuma! Sevuma!"

Everything thus far had come to me easily, but now I wondered what this new thing could be? It came to me. ". . . It's a dish!"

"Sevuma! Sevuma!"

Another dish? Then it occurred to me the dish was where the thing was hidden. *What* thing? ". . . It's a round thing . . . a ring! . . . a ring you wear . . . in your hair! . . . It's in the dish for vomiting!"

"Sevuma! Sevuma!"

The dishes were still lined up along the ditch, filled with golden brown liquid. I sprinted to mine. The ring lay inside. I pulled it out, held it up. The roar of voices was like a physical force. A rush of people surged toward me and engulfed me. I was pulled up. There was no going back to Tablamanzi now! Someone snatched the ring. I was in a dream again as colors swirled around me. Two men lifted me into the air, Mahlalela and Sifundza, the hunter. When I was put down Mahlalela held on to my hand and broke into a frantic dance. Poor Mahlalela, I thought fondly, the tension he must have felt. He took a risk when he accepted a white man to study at his homestead, and could have been criticized if I failed. Now he was vindicated. Not only had I done it, I had done it first.

It was all I could do to break through the people dancing around me, the women ululating, the men whistling and yelling. I made it back to Tablamanzi, knelt before her, and clapped my hands in the sangoma greeting. This ritual formally ended with a litany of shouted thanks.

I began, *"Abe sengibonga inhloko yemadloti!"* ("I thank the insight of the lidlotis!")

The two women replied, "Thogoza!" ("You of the Indumba!")

"Abe sengibonga luvela lwemadloti!" ("And I thank the prescience of the spirits!")

"Thogoza!"

"Abe sengibonga nesikhutsato sebangani bami!" ("And I thank the encouragement of my friends!")

"Thogoza!"

I glimpsed Tablamanzi's round, generous face like a moon above. Her eyes were glistening with tears.

I backed away and returned to the Indumba. In a little while all five graduates returned. We had all found the objects hidden for us. Now it was time for informal divinations as we scattered to find whatever might be hidden for us by the people in the crowd. We were presenting ourselves and our skills to the community we would serve. I spotted Sifundza and knelt before him, sensing he was hiding something. He was: a coin in his pocket. A warrior was hiding a coin under the mat he sat on. A woman hid a pin in her hair. Another woman hid a seashell in her bag. I took each find to the drums before the Indumba, tossed it down amid cheering, then danced a few spirited steps to the kukhokha divination song. Then, following custom, I returned to the person who had hidden the object and gave ritualized thanks.

Our shared inhloko insights informed all five graduates that it was time for us to reassemble before the Indumba. We were joined by the sangomas. The drums changed their rhythm. A somber, stately beat was sounded. The sangomas formed a line with us at the end that proceeded around the perimeter of the courtyard. I was still half in a trance, but I was aware of women rushing up to me and placing gifts on my shoulder. A coin. A pecan. A vial of perfume. As they fell to the ground, a child picked them up to save for me.

It was late afternoon. Another night of ritual, another day of arduous rites lay ahead. But I felt fine; weary, but clear-headed as I took full possession of myself inside the Indumba. Vusi came in and sat beside me. Rubbing the sweat from my face with the towel he brought, I smiled and asked him how he thought it was going. He admitted he was scared when I drank the goat's blood and vomited—it must have looked wicked, I thought. But he was looking forward to eating the goat at the big feast tomorrow; everybody was.

Vusi grinned at me "you found the *inyongo* (gall bladder)." And then, tentatively, he touched my head as if trying to feel the sangoma's insight lodged within.

▲ ▲ ▲ ▲

Visitors spent the night around bonfires burning throughout the homestead. I was among the thirty or so sangomas and their children who slept for about five hours in the large, circular cinderblock hut. Several times we were awakened by our lidlotis, and the ever present drums beat out a welcome for the Bandzawe spirits that took possession of us. The final day, Sunday, belonged to them.

As the sun lifted over another clear morning, the five of us went to the river for a special drum-beating rite for the Bandzawe. Thin, gentle Nqo(f)nqo(f), who taught me how to beat the three drums of this ceremony, now set them up on a bluff overlooking a narrow crescent of sand where we graduates sat on grass mats beneath white sheets. When the spirits took possession of us and emerged, prompted by the rattles, singing, and drums, they headed for their element: the river. Unable to walk, these strange spirits used our bodies—we were clad in red cloths tied around our waists—to hop into the water, where they splashed about, mumbling and humming. Though insulated within myself, I was aware of the chilly winter water, the deep greens and blues around me, and the bright white sun above.

Female attendants escorted us back to the mats where we sat wet and shivering, ourselves once again. One by one our second goats were sacrificed by Nqo(f)nqo(f) behind our backs for a medicine bath. Three pairs of female sangomas hands quickly rubbed my body with the hot blood that poured over my shoulders and down my back. The hands were gritty with sand, and irritated my skin as they rubbed hard over my torso, legs, face, and hair. The steamy green contents of the goat's stomach came next, and the same rough hands rubbed the sharp-smelling chyme over my body. This was the second time I had endured such a cleansing, and my ability to accept it made me feel strong and committed. An attendant told me to enter the river, and I plunged into the cold water and swam until the blood and chyme washed off.

For the third and last time I took my place on the mat with the other graduates, side by side on the riverbank. But now something special happened. The attendants called Vusi, and he sat down at my right side. This was the moment when a future sangoma was united with his or her *nyankwabi,* the child who carried the sangoma's medicine basket *(umtuntu)* and assisted with the rites. This was usually the sangoma's own child. I supposed that it was well known that Mahlalela had given his approval for the adoption, but now the community was for the first time acknowledging what they had come to accept: Vusi was my son. I was very moved and proud.

A sangoma brought a bowl of specially brewed beer, creamy brown in color, containing medicine and fresh chicken blood. She held the bowl to my lips and advised, "Drink well." I took some gulps, and she brought the bowl to Vusi's mouth. As my child and as someone who would share in the adventures ahead, he, too, had to be fortified. With the studious expression he wore whenever he encountered new experiences, Vusi drank. The brew remaining in the bowl was poured over our heads.

Vusi was dismissed. A middle-aged sangoma and her assistant appeared, and working with a razor she swiftly made incisions all over my body. The assistant quickly sealed each tiny wound with a powdery medicine intended to attract the Bandzawe spirits, who were important for the divination assistance they gave a sangoma. I had never been more thoroughly cut: around my skull, behind my ears, across my shoulders, chest, back, down my sides and spine, my arms, elbows, hands and legs, knees, feet and toes. Finally, my tongue: a quick prick, and a rub of powder, which was tasteless. The sangoma was so skillful I did not feel pain, only a sharp irritation quickly ended by the medicine's healing properties.

When we were finished, the cooking fires were burning along the riverbank, where the graduates' families and the people of Malibeni gathered for the big feast. Men and women sat in separate circles, with unmarried men forming a third circle. The children, who would be fed later, ran from the cooking pits with plates of roasted goat and chicken that the people ate with their fingers off beds of guava leaves. We graduates watched from afar; we'd already "used" these animals and were not permitted to eat them. Mzwane's family brought her some food from home, which she shared with us.

Pashamqomo called us to him one by one beneath a giant jacaranda tree. When I arrived, he prepared my graduation adornments from the moist black fur of my recently slaughtered goat. Slitting the hide with his knife, he made a vest and two bracelets which he put on me. The vest I could remove, but when dried on my wrists the bracelets would remain for years. A female assistant poured the yellow liquid from in the goat's gall bladder onto the tops of my hands and feet, and dripped the remaining gall onto my tongue. It tasted sweet. She inserted a reed into the bladder, blew, and made of it a small yellow balloon that Pashamqomo tied to the hair on the back of my head. When he dismissed me, the feast was concluding and a final rite remained.

The Bandzawe spirits had to bring us, the graduates, from their river home to the Indumba, where we would work together divining treatments for our patients. The journey began mid-afternoon.

The Bandzawe spirits could not walk, and thus we could not walk while in their control. Dozens of mats were lined up end to end upon which the spirits could propel themselves by leaping on their—our— hands and knees in a single file line. A convoy of attendants quickly gathered up the mats after the last spirit had passed over them, brought them forward, and laid them down again in front. Nqo(f)nqo(f) flailed at the three-drum setup and sangomas chanted, shook rattles, and moved alongside the spirits in possession of us. Our bodies were covered by white sheets, and our spirits mumbled and quaked and leapt forward on balled fists. I was in a trance and dimly saw the ground pass beyond the edge of the mats. For a quarter mile we moved under the Bandzawe's spell, following the mat path until we reached Gogo Simelane's homestead and entered her Indumba. The spirits greeted the assembly of sangomas that crowded the hut. Then they released us.

My full awareness returned, and with it exhaustion. I looked up to see Tablamanzi kneeling before me, her figure dark against a single shaft of sunlight that entered the wide circular hut. Her sangoma friend from the previous day's divination ritual was with her, and they both grabbed my hands with concern. Three knuckles were scraped raw and bleeding; the leaping lidloti had traveled on them. But I smiled. They smiled back. No problem.

Because it was over.

▲ ▲ ▲ ▲

Someone's spirit shouted. We rushed to change into our new ceremonial garments. The time had come for the final procession. By twos and threes, until the courtyard was full, the sangomas appeared. Many wore feathered headdresses, and as I danced with the others—partly in the throes of my lidlotis but still aware of what was going on around me—someone tied a headdress on me, a high affair of black feathers.

All weekend the drums had sounded quickly, but now they slowed to a somber beat. The senior sangoma, a short woman wearing long purple feathers in her hair, took her position at the head of a single file line followed by the other sangomas in order of seniority, the five graduates at the rear, and a new group of plainly dressed acolytes. The wooden dancing sticks I had held in my hands during kutfwasa had been replaced by a curving rubber *siwebhu* (ceremonial whip) and a *lishoba* brush of long, black ox tail.

Slowly and with great dignity, the procession began to make its way around the courtyard, past the seated visitors. My mind was alive with the thought, "I did it! I did it! I did it!" I felt—how? Like a person released from a long prison sentence. But also like a person who had swum an ocean and climbed a mountain peak. I felt good, happy, relieved, grateful, humble, triumphant.

The processional song was called *Siyenga*. The leader in front sang its haunting melody in full voice, and we joined in. There was no song of the sangomas more starkly beautiful than this one. But for a long time I was puzzled by the words, which translated as: *You, you are cheating me, Mdzimba/Traveling difficulties are refused, Mdzimba/Even now they are cheating me, Mdzimba."*

Mdzimba was the name of a mountain whose bladelike flank cast Prince Vovo's homestead into shadow on winter afternoons. Like his brothers and sisters, the kings and queens, the prince would be buried within its caves; the mountain was a royal graveyard. In the song, Mdzimba represented death, and if it claimed a person too soon, it was cheating him or her of life. The "traveling difficulties" were encountered on the journey from life to death, and the sangomas sang that they were rejecting these.

It was a lament, this song, and I came to see its point. As sangomas, we were in a sense being snatched away from life prematurely. It was our lidlotis who had brought us into the realm of the dead, even now cheating us of our mortal innocence. In place of this innocence came an awesome knowledge and responsibility. Some sangomas could not bear it and were crushed by it. And all of us felt its weight.

And so we sang with sadness, but also with a touch of defiant pride, our terrible lament.

> *You, you are cheating me.*
> *You, you are cheating me,*
> *Mountain of Death!*

I was filled with emotion as the procession slowly advanced at a stately pace, singing this dirge. For I knew I had cheated, too, and was changed because of it. I had confounded a fate that was to have been mine: a fate of never understanding the spiritual powers within and around all people, a fate of being glib and cynical because it was easier and more popular to sneer than to learn and appreciate.

But mostly I had cheated a fate in which I, as a white man and an American, was to die without ever having an inkling of the wonders of the realm that I had now entered.

Emotion blocked my throat, and I was no longer able to sing. My eyes were liquid pools, and my body shivered at that lovely, haunting melody, those words that were a cry from the heart of every sangoma. The song would be in my dreams until I died.

And after.

▲ ▲ ▲ ▲

It was evening and the visitors were leaving. The families of the other graduates piled into the flat beds of their trucks and drove off as we waved and shouted our good-byes. But others would remain through the night. The sangomas were still present, and there was a festive feeling to the evening. All five graduates had made it through kuphotfulwa. Now people lounged about, sharing tins of home-brewed beer. Fires blazed in courtyards around the homestead. I went from group to group, from person to person, exchanging greetings and news. Because of the rigorous rites of the past three days I hadn't been able to talk to the many people who had come.

But before another moment went by, I wanted to go out alone into the field. There was a group of special individuals I wanted to address and thank. I had never seen them, of course; I couldn't say what even one of them looked like. But they had brought me here, stood by me, and seen me through the graduation tests.

"Hey, Sibolomhlope!" I was leaving the cluster of huts, and I turned at the sound of my name. I saw Nqo(f)nqo(f), the skinny and unfailingly kind sangoma who was the magician on the drums. He'd been celebrating with home-brew this evening, I could see; his wispy goatee looked lopsided. I went and greeted him.

Nqo(f)nqo(f) reached up in the waning twilight and tenderly stroked the side of my head. Orange firelight touched his face, and I saw swimming in his eyes pride and affection. He smiled at me and said quietly, "Sangoma."

I nodded my head, and my throat was again thick with emotion. "Yes," I said to my friend. "Sangoma."

I finally made it to the field, and left the homestead's people and buildings behind. It was quiet where I now was. Scorpio, the winter constellation, snaked brightly overhead. The summer constellation, Orion, absent for months now, was appearing again two hours before dawn. Soon it would be high in the evening sky. I told the passage of time by the stars now. That endless passage. But for me time, too, was changing: I was older, and it was accelerating.

I was too elated to think of rest. But the ordeals of kuphotfulwa must have been catching up with me, because I felt drowsy. I could have sworn I had removed my ceremonial garments, but there I was, wearing them once more.

Ahead were bright lights from buildings at the edge of the field to the south. This was puzzling because there was no electricity here. There was power on the other side of the river at the border stations: the amber-colored arc lamps at the expensive red-tiled buildings on the South African side, and the duller white lamps beside the more modest structures on the Swazi side.

But these lights were from a different place. A very different place.

I approached until I saw clearly what they were illuminating and it could have been a ghost by the chill that passed through me.

It was the Princess Theatre, the movie theater my grandparents built back in 1915. I had seen her only in photographs, but there she now was: two stories high, with a luminous marquee in front. Sections of the neighboring buildings of downtown Republic, Pennsylvania, were dark on either side. "The Princess" glowed in neon along the marquee front.

I stood at the edge of a curtain of light that spilled out across the sidewalk and street from the illuminated underside of the marquee. There were no people about, no traffic on the street, though some 1930s cars were parked along the curb. The ticket booth was centered between the theater doors. I couldn't read the marquee clearly, though the name Shirley Temple stood out, my mother's favorite. As a teenage girl my mother had sold tickets in that booth out front.

I hadn't left Mahlalela's field; I'd only entered the House of Dreams. This had happened on other occasions since my return from the wilderness. It was perfectly natural, and I could not understand my apprehension. I knew I had to approach the theater, that something was waiting for me there, but I felt uneasy. I wondered which lidloti had brought the theater here tonight. My grandmother? Would I find her there?

I stepped from the street onto a cement sidewalk neither warm nor cold beneath my bare feet. A vivid, multicolored glow emanated from the rectangular, glass-fronted ticket booth. I moved toward it. A woman was inside. It was my mother! But she was not as she looked as a teenager in the forties. She was as she looked today. And the narrow interior of the ticket booth resembled a modern office, filled with gadgets that she as an executive would use.

I stood and gazed at her. Seated on the ticket seller's stool, my mother was attired in a smartly tailored cream-colored suit. She was speaking into a cellular phone. A fax machine whirring behind her spewed out a document. The screen of a personal computer was aglow with changing graphics of orange, yellow, purple, the source of the multicolored light I saw. Red lights blinked atop the telephone console, incoming calls awaiting my mother's attention. I shouldn't stare, I thought, because she was busy, and I felt like I was intruding. But it was so good to see her again

*after so long, I desperately wished to share the triumph of kuphotfulwa
with someone I loved, and it had been such a long time since I had seen a
truly chic woman. Yes, she was older. The flesh beneath her jaw was
looser. Yet all I could think of was how immaculate she looked.*

*She glanced at me, then down again as she abruptly ended her conver-
sation, "Ed, I'll have to call you back."*

Ed? My Uncle Ed, who died in '76?

*She put down the phone, looked me over, and said with disappoint-
ment, "So this is what you've been up to. Is that a dress?"*

*I sighed, "Oh, mother, this isn't a dress. It's a sangoma's ceremonial
dancing skirt. It's . . . I thought you'd be interested in this."*

*But, no, my mother, like most people, preferred her culture in a mu-
seum, preferably behind glass. I was now behind glass myself from her perspective inside the ticket booth. She shrugged, "Well, I don't know about
these things. It looks like a dress to me. These days, you never know."*

*"These days?" I grinned, looking about. "It must be 1935." I tried to
make out the year on a license plate on one of the bulky old cars parked
along the curb but could not. Faint music came from inside the theater. A
show was in progress.*

*My mother stated crisply, "It's 1990, as I think you know." Her ex-
pression changed as she looked at me, became sad, and I felt a tug of emotion. "When are you coming home?"*

"I don't know," I said haltingly.

*"Why? Just change out of those things and hop on a plane. Do you
still have a credit card?"*

*I looked down. "It's not that simple, really. You see, my lidlotis know
me in these clothes. If I were to suddenly stop wearing them, the spirits
might think I'm ashamed and was rejecting them. Then they might go
away."*

"But you can't go around looking like that. People will laugh."

"They do laugh," I reported somberly.

"Is that what you want?"

*"I can't stand it." I paused. "But it's a trade-off. I can do wonderful
things. And I've learned wonderful things."*

My mother sounded doubtful. "Such as what?"

*"Well . . ." Was this my valedictory? I said, "I've learned that we
really aren't alone in this life. And I've learned that many things are expected of us: that we make the right choices and that we really do look out
for our neighbors. But there are forces that can help us, and they want us
to succeed."*

I felt self-conscious talking this way, and I stopped. From behind me, a voice said, "That just about sums it up."

I knew that voice. I turned. He stood on the sidewalk. It was Harry. He was just a black silhouette. The theater lights, the glow from the marquee did not touch him. He was like a black hole. "Mind if I light up?"

"N-no," I said, surprised by his request. I supposed that smoking held no risk where he now was; it was a habit he kept for nostalgia's sake. But when Harry said he was lighting up, he meant it literally. I heard a metallic click of a cigarette lighter as the top flipped open. An orange flame revealed the front of an expensively tailored blue suit that seemed to date from the fifties, a narrow tie over a white shirt, and a sharp triangle of handkerchief above the jacket's breast pocket. The hand holding the gold lighter rose, and I saw him—I saw the face of a lidloti. Harry was a man in his fifties, tan, with silver hair combed back and parted. His eyes were closed and his brow was furrowed as he tilted his head down and lit the tip of a cigarette.

The lighter snapped shut, and he was all black again but for the dull glow of the cigarette tip, a red star that moved up and down in his hand, glowing bright when he inhaled but revealing nothing.

"You are eventually going back to the U.S.," Harry said. "I'm curious. What are your plans?"

"You don't know?" I asked in a bantering tone.

"I know everything. Tell my anyway."

"Well, I'll try to convince people I haven't lost my mind for starters."

His voice was mildly satirical. "I really ought to caution you, for your own sake, not to worry about what other people think. Your mother's right. Look at you. Who'd believe you? Better wise up. You're in a no-win situation."

It was a shock to hear this put so bluntly, and it hurt. "Then I've lost."

"Have you?" Harry's voice mellowed with good humor. "Ask."

He meant my mother in the ticket booth, and I turned quickly toward her. I had gained so much during this journey, but had I lost all that I once had? I saw at once from my mother's expression that I had not; her eyes burned with such intense love but also apprehension at what lay ahead for me that it was more than I could bear. I wanted to cry out, to break through the glass separating us, calm her fears with an embrace and say, "What's happened to me is not a terrible thing! It's a wonder, a glorious thing!"

I blinked, and the theater, everything, was gone.

I stood alone under the stars in the field.

thirteen

Sangoma

USI AND I walked together over a dusty footpath through the flat fields of the low veld country outside Malibeni. My son carried his things in a little bag that for him probably felt weighted with added significance. We had just left Mahlalela's homestead, the place he had lived most of his life but would now return only to visit. We were on our way to town, where Vusi would live with his new family: Evah, Nomoya, Sandile, and me. He was enrolled in a new and better school for the session that was to begin in a few days. We walked along under the hot sun, in no hurry; we'd be spending our nights at friends' homesteads along the way.

It was a new year now; late January, high summer in Swaziland. Overseas, my country was again at war, this time over oil. I had left during an economic boom but that was over now and the Bush recession was on. All that seemed impossibly distant as I went on with my new life amid spirits and ritual: participating in the king's harvest festival as a newly initiated member of the Inyatsi warrior regiment, drinking the seasonal maganu brew that had recently arrived with much ceremony, and driving two oxen up the road to Prince Vovo's homestead as kutfwasa payment to Gogo Ndwandwe, who was back from South Africa.

For two weeks following the kuphotfulwa graduation rites, I and the four other graduates were confined to the Indumba where we prepared our first medicines as sangomas. Whenever we ventured out, we had to wear cloths wrapped over our heads like veils. Until our confinement was over, we were not permitted to wear our lidloti charms and, unprotected, had to symbolically disguise ourselves from evil spirits. I endured it, though I kept breaking up while trying to establish the proper tone of parental authority with Vusi, impossible to do when you're a man wearing headgear like the Mother Superior's in *The Sound of Music*. Confinement ended with a private predawn ceremony, when we performed a final task. The five of us had to divine where our medicine necklaces were hidden. After we found them we put them on and dressed formally as new sangomas.

I then went to Manzini town, and was reunited with Evah and Nomoya. Evah was overjoyed by the news of the successful conclusion to my kuphotfulwa, and thus the end, at last, of my long kutfwasa. But I sensed something more in her embrace: relief. She admitted to having been much more afraid of the physically demanding tests than she had let on. "I thought you might get hurt!" She was relieved that I came out of it with only some scraped knuckles. Their first visit to Malibeni came a few weeks later. On the night of the full moon of a newborn child's third month, the baby by Swazi custom must be presented to her ancestors. The ritual was called *lalatela*. We arrived at Mahlalela's place by bus as the October moon grew full, and the people made a big fuss over Sibolomhlope's baby. Evah, like many Swazi town dwellers, was nostalgic for the sprawling country homesteads. She loved Malibeni—the river and fields, the newborn piglets squealing in their pen, even my rickety old hut.

It was a pastel springtime day, and at twilight the full moon lifted orange above the hills in a sky that was still deep blue. I waited until I felt the time was right, when the spirits would be out and active, and at nine o'clock I suggested to Evah that we go to the field. We wrapped Nomoya in a blanket and stepped out into the white light of a moon now high in the sky. We walked in silence over the furrowed earth, and at a spot that seemed right I cleared the ground of twigs and stones. We put down Nomoya and knelt beside her. The moon was like a beacon. I did not allow my shadow to fall upon my daughter. I wanted the spirits to see her clearly. As I gazed at her, I felt a rush of pride and gladness, and saw in Evah's eyes the same emotions. We clapped our hands simultaneously, and I addressed the ancestral spirits. I thanked them and introduced them to "a very special girl, our daughter." I asked the lidlotis to receive her, to be with her always, and to protect and guide her through her life ahead.

"*Siyabonga,*" Evah and I said together. "We thank you."

Although it was premature—Evah would not be formally presented to the spirits until the traditional Swazi wedding we were planning—I also introduced my bride to be. We would soon be wed by a judge at a civil ceremony in Manzini town. Such a marriage would not be recognized by either my church, where we'd also have a ceremony, or by traditional Swazi society, but I was eager to legalize our relationship.

Below us, Nomoya began to fuss and squirm. The full moon was too bright for her. I picked her up and looked into the sky. I wondered how many of those moons she would see during her lifetime. A thousand? In my thoughts I told her to cherish each one.

The little lalatela rite between family and spirits was over. As we returned to my hut, I was grateful that my new life was blessed by such moments.

Vusi doted on the baby that was now his little sister. Up to the end I was in suspense about the outcome of his adoption. Despite what Vusi and I meant to each other and how his life had changed, the bare facts on my adoption application looked dubious: I was young and unmarried with a child out of wedlock, an herbal healer who cured people with the aid of supernatural powers. But when we appeared at the Magistrates' Court in Manzini, Miss Vilane was on hand to testify that the Social Welfare Office was solidly behind the case. Mahlalela arrived with Vusi and me, and for the occasion he wore his traditional attire, including three red *ligwalagwala* feathers in his hair.

A hearing was held in the chambers of a thin, ill-tempered magistrate who was irritated because his staff had not told him about our appointment. For a moment I thought he'd throw us all out, but instead he had me stand, take an oath, and answer questions about my financial resources. There were too few chairs, so Vusi sat on my lap, providing graphic evidence of our closeness. The magistrate quizzed Mahlalela, who forthrightly declared his willingness to turn over the child to me.

The magistrate turned to me. "Having reviewed the evidence, and having reached my decision—"

I gulped uncontrollably, and the magistrate blinked and skipped a beat, his delivery thrown off by this reminder that his power to shape people's lives was such that even the white man quaked. "—that I find you, James Hall, a suitable parent, and I approve this adoption of the boy Vusi Malambe, who will henceforth be known as Vusi Malambe Hall. It is so ruled this sixth day of November, the year of our Lord Nineteen Hundred and Ninety."

"Thank God," I murmured. Vusi's head, close to mine, turned and he looked at me as if to say, "Is it over?" I nodded, and a smile lit up his face.

At the house I was renting in town, Evah and Sandile and Evah's mother, who would be spending half of each year with us, had welcomed Vusi into our midst with a big dinner that night. All of a sudden, it seemed, I had a very special little family, each of us aware of the unusual circumstances that had brought us together, and everyone grateful that fate, in the form of the lidlotis, had made this family possible. We loved and adored each other, and there wasn't a thing we wouldn't do for one another.

▲ ▲ ▲ ▲

I was thinking of my new family as Vusi and I put more distance between us and Malibeni, headed for our new life together in Manzini. A hot sun beat down as we strolled along the footpath leading through the low veld countryside. Small, distantly spaced homesteads and patches of forest alternated with stretches of flat plains, where umbrella trees cast small circles of shade. We passed an occasional cinderblock general store and stopped for a soda cooled in a gas-powered refrigerator. Like me, Vusi enjoyed walking. He was excited about living in town and what lay ahead.

For this child, the horizon was limitless. My heart was full with a father's pride for such a bright, engaging boy who was quick to win friends and eager to make the most of opportunities as only one could who had escaped a background of dire poverty. Of the seventy-six pupils in his first-grade class, including many who were also late starters, Vusi graduated in the first position. His was a voyage of discovery that seemed to parallel my own.

Where had mine brought me? I had come to realize that there was a spiritual realm beyond the material, worldly one I had once accepted as the only reality. I felt that the blinkers of so-called rationalism had been removed from my eyes, and my expanded vision was liberating. I felt free, as if I'd broken out of a box my society, culture, and time had made for me. As a Catholic, university-educated professional man from the American Midwest, my box did not contain a healer's grass spirit house in Africa. I continued to get letters from friends back home who still thought of me and wrote rather wistfully, now that economic hard times were showing the limits of material pursuits, how they'd like to break out of their own boxes and pursue their own adventures and dreams. And why not? If I could, anyone could. There was a world of possibilities for everybody. I wrote back that a person needn't go to the extremes I did, but the satisfactions of a personal journey awaited everyone.

I had no idea where mine would end; like the footpath Vusi and I now strolled it seemed to go on and on. I had no doubt that the days of the Indumba were numbered, at least the Indumba as it had been known for hundreds of years, and it seemed ironic that once I had attained entrance I could clearly see how endangered it was. The evidence was everywhere: the wilderness where we dug our roots was vanishing, powerful religious forces unable to attack each other found in sangomas easy targets whom they could condemn as satanic for communicating with the dead, and the hegemony of Western culture was expanding with its science, materialism, commerce, and industry that were all hostile to the anachronism of the tribal healer. Increasingly, our patients were showing up at night, in the dark, embarrassed to be seen consulting us.

Occasionally, I read some First World scientist's well-intended but condescending remark that tribal healers might possess some knowledge of herbal cures worth preserving. But this would only be to provide giant pharmaceutical companies with raw materials. And I wondered about myself. Why was someone like me brought into the picture now? If the lidlotis intended to enlist white allies to rescue the Indumba from its doom, weren't they just a trifle tardy? Despite the satisfaction I found as a healer, I increasingly wondered if my role was to bear witness and leave a record. Or, worse, a eulogy. Such a notion seemed a tragedy, for in the Indumba I had found something I hadn't known existed: magic on earth. There were powers here, spiritual forces. What would happen to mankind when the connection with these forces was severed? I'd feel adrift and orphaned, groping blindly like I used to through a world of scientific facts and consumer goods but devoid of wisdom, a world of light without illumination, of heat without warmth.

I thought about all the people who would never know the magic of the Indumba, denying with hostility disguised as skepticism that there could be magic anywhere. I decided to make up a little story about this to amuse Vusi while we walked beneath the sky's azure dome. I asked him, "Do you know there are some people who can't see colors?"

He smiled at me and shook his head. "It's true!" I asserted. "I once met a man who was color-blind. Not only that, he refused to believe there were colors. He said I couldn't prove to him that colors existed, so they didn't. What I called green and red and blue were to him just different shades of gray. I told him there are scientific instruments that can record the different wavelengths of colors. But he just said they recorded wavelengths of different shades of gray. He said my belief in color was a fantasy. It was psychological, which meant it was only in my head."

Vusi laughed again, and then was quiet. I knew he was thinking of a person who couldn't see the green of a leaf, the bright red of a ligwalagwala bird or the bronze of the sun, and how sad that person was even if he didn't know it. But I saw a flaw in my analogy: it was about someone whose condition was physiological. The blindness I confronted against the Indumba was willed. It made me sad thinking about it, sad for them, and sad for me, who could see but not convince others.

Vusi stopped walking so suddenly and with such a look of surprise that I tensed, turning.

Above us on a bluff was a lone zebra standing against trees and sky. It saw us, too, but did not appear concerned.

"Where does it come from, baba?" Vusi asked in a low voice, as if afraid to frighten it away.

"Hlane," I replied, naming the wild game reserve that was nearest to this place. Animals did wander away, like that rhinoceros I encountered during the bus trip.

But this zebra was different. There was something unusual about it. Why was it alone, when these animals rarely left the herd? It was real, I knew. Vusi saw it.

But Vusi sensed something, too. His voice still low, he asked, "Why has it come?"

Then I knew. This zebra had been sent by the lidlotis. And for the first time, a realization took hold: I was going away. Like Vusi, I was leaving Malibeni behind, the Indumba where I did kutfwasa, and that extraordinary episode in my life. After all the adventure, the good times and bad, I was leaving. Emotion caught in my throat, and I could barely answer. "He's come to say good-bye."

The zebra seemed to be staring at me. Vusi was looking at me also. He saw the tears in my eyes, and this disturbed him. "Why do you cry, my father?"

I shook my head, took his hand, and squeezed it. How could I answer? Did I cry because of the difficulties we both faced ahead? Did I cry because I had been given an unimaginable gift even though I was unworthy? But, no, there was another reason. And so I told my son, "I guess . . . because it's over."

Vusi looked at me seriously. "What are you going to do, my father?"

He seemed afraid for me, and I couldn't let him be. I dropped to one knee before him so we were at eye level, and I smiled. "I can't say. But I'm not afraid."

"Because you're an *umbutfo!*" he declared, giving the term for a member of the king's warrior regiments, which I had recently joined. I smiled; warriors were afraid of nothing. I reminded him, "And because we have our lidlotis."

Vusi nodded. I looked at him and sang a line from the *kuphotfulwa* song:

> *Khambo lekwaliwa*
> *Khambo lekwaliwe, Mdzimba!*

> Traveling difficulties are rejected
> Traveling difficulties are refused, Mdzimba!

Vusi looked at me, smiled, and we sang the chorus together:

Wena, uyangiyena
Wena, uyangiyeng'Mdzimba!

You, you are cheating me
You, you are cheating me, Mountain of Death!

But as Vusi knew, it was we who were cheating those who wished to stop us. This was not an ending for us but a beginning.

I stood and looked down at my son. "I love you, Vusi."

"I love you, baba."

The zebra turned and disappeared into the bush. Vusi waved and shouted, "Good-bye, zebra! Good-bye!"

Yes, I thought, until we meet again.

I took Vusi's hand. We headed toward the place where the morning sun had risen. This small, winding path led eventually to the border, meeting a road that cut across Mozambique. A vast expanse of ocean lay beyond, and then a golden coast I used to know.

But this road never really ended. Not in this life, and not in the next. I walked along with my son. A lone bird sang from a treetop. All else was silence but for a distant, deep beating of drums that I now could hear but never could before.

Epilogue

FOUR YEARS HAD PASSED from the time I left America to undergo kutfwasa, and my return for a brief visit in the fall of 1992. I found it difficult to discuss with family and friends what it is I do in Africa, and my attempts to recount how I became a sangoma were met with stares of amazement that left me too flustered to continue. In Swaziland, sangomas do not speak of their work, which is understood by the people to be the inviolate spiritual province of the lidlotis. Such deference would not do for Americans, who view all secrecy with suspicion. Perhaps, I thought, I could induce onto the written page those words I could not speak. And then I could go back to the Indumba.

For I still have much to learn; the wonder is continuous and has lost none of its luster. At night, the shayelwa drums bring forth new discoveries. The knowledge of herbal medicines will take a lifetime to master. I'm settled with Evah, Nomoya, and Vusi in a congenial little house in Manzini town, and spend my days shuttling around the countryside treating patients, digging roots, and, always, learning.

I am sometimes troubled by the irreconcilability of my old and new lives, by my conflicting roles as a modern American and as a diviner and healer of timeless provenance. I am *ngcondvombili,* "He of two minds," as the Swazis refer to a child of mixed parentage.

Yet, the bones continue to reveal their messages, the drums sound, and the cyclical seasons are echoed in births and deaths within the Indumba. My own spirit house has found a building site. The king has granted me, through his chief in rural Enyangeni, a piece of land for my homestead and farm, and my Indumba. The gift is in recognition of my service in his royal regiments, where for several weeks each year I and a thousand other warriors do His Majesty's bidding, marching in columns bearing fighting sticks and cowhide shields to work in his fields, slaughtering beasts for the feasts at the iNcwala harvest festival, and performing the sacred ceremonies through which the nation's ancestral spirits are petitioned.

Among my closest friends and most faithful patients are the men of my regiment, proud and rugged in their warrior gear. I am in their debt for seeing me through a recent spiritual crisis when I again doubted my future and that of all sangomas, only to have my brooding cut short by an onslaught of Swazi warriors who came to me for treatments, potions, and advice about their ancestors. We were on a royal hunt in the wilderness of a game park, and it felt good to be needed and useful, and the spirits themselves seemed exhilarated through vicarious witness as we ran half-naked through tall grass and cool streams, chasing impala buck with our spears flashing in the sunlight, a herd of giraffe rising against the sky ahead . . .

But that is another story.

James Hall
Manzini, Swaziland
Africa
May 1994